Systems Modelling

Systems Modelling

Theory and Practice

Edited by

Michael Pidd

Department of Management Science
The Management School
Lancaster University

John Wiley & Sons, Ltd

Other Wiley Editorial Offices

John Wiley & Sons Inc., 111 River Street, Hoboken, NJ 07030, USA

Jossey-Bass, 989 Market Street, San Francisco, CA 94103-1741, USA

Wiley-VCH Verlag GmbH, Boschstr. 12, D-69469 Weinheim, Germany

John Wiley & Sons Australia Ltd, 33 Park Road, Milton, Queensland 4064, Australia

John Wiley & Sons (Asia) Pte Ltd, 2 Clementi Loop #02-01, Jin Xing Distripark, Singapore 129809

John Wiley & Sons Canada Ltd, 22 Worcester Road, Etobicoke, Ontario, Canada M9W 1L1

Wiley also publishes its books in a variety of electronic formats. Some content that appears
in print may not be available in electronic books.

Library of Congress Cataloging-in-Publication Data

Pidd, Michael.
  Systems modelling : theory and practice / editor Michael Pidd.
    p. cm.
  Includes bibliographical references and index.
  ISBN 0-470-86731-0 (pbk: alk. paper)
  1. Decision making – Simulation methods.   2. Management – Simulation methods.
  I. Pidd, Michael.
  HD30.23 .S94 2004
  658′.001′1 – dc22   2003025149

British Library Cataloguing in Publication Data

A catalogue record for this book is available from the British Library

ISBN 0-470-86731-0

Project management by Originator, Gt Yarmouth, Norfolk (typeset in 10/12pt Baskerville)
Printed and bound in Great Britain by TJ International Ltd, Padstow, Cornwall
This book is printed on acid-free paper responsibly manufactured from sustainable forestry
in which at least two trees are planted for each one used for paper production.

Contents

Contributors

Fran Ackermann
Department of Management Science, University of Strathclyde

Joyce Brown
The Inland Revenue

Peter Checkland
The Management School, Lancaster University

Ceri Cooper
The Inland Revenue

Colin Eden
Graduate School of Business, University of Strathclyde

Roger Forder
Defence Science and Technology Laboratory

Sue Holwell
Technology Faculty, The Open University

Ruth Kowalczyk
The Management School, Lancaster University

Michael Lyons
ST*R, BT Exact Technologies

John Morecroft
London Business School

George Paterson
Visiting Professor, Department of Management Science, University of Strathclyde, formerly of Shell International

George Pickburn
Information Management Department, Defence Science and Technology Laboratory

Michael Pidd
The Management School, Lancaster University

Sean Price
Department of Informatics and Simulation, Cranfield University (RMCS)

Alan Robinson
Policy and Capability Studies Department, Defence Science and Technology Laboratory

Preface

In our complex world it is all too easy to make changes to the way that things are done and, later – often too late, find that unintended consequences follow. We need ways that will help us to plan and design improvements and we need new systems that operate as intended. One way to do this is to model the systems and changes before they are implemented. Doing so sounds simple enough, but it turns out to be very difficult in complex systems that involve people.

This book brings together some ideas, hence its title, about how systems modelling can be improved. The ideas are works in progress and stem from the work of the INCISM network funded by the UK's Engineering and Physical Sciences Research Council (EPSRC). INCISM is an abbreviation of Interdisciplinary Research Network on Complementarity in Systems Modelling. It was established as a response to a call from EPSRC for "networks of researchers from different disciplines to develop a potential agenda for future research into systems theory." Most of the authors of this book's chapters were active participants in the work of INCISM.

The original core members of INCISM came from three academic departments and from three organizations that are major users of systems modelling. These are:

- Lancaster University Department of Management Science;
- University of Strathclyde Department of Management Science;
- Cranfield University/Royal Military College of Science;
- Shell International Ltd;
- BT Exact Technologies;
- Dstl Analysis.

This mix of academics and practitioners was to ensure that the meetings addressed issues that are of practical importance and of theoretical significance. This is based on a belief that many interesting things take place on the interface of theory and practice.

Likewise, the chapters of this book address practical and theoretical issues. The practitioners all have long experience in reflective practice. The experience on which they draw is not just based on a few short-term interventions, but on the day-to-day need to bring about improvement in organizations through systems modelling. The academics involved are all involved in operational research and systems modelling with external clients, as well as in teaching and research. Some of their work, most notably that of Checkland and Eden and Ackermann, is based on action research in which the research ideas develop as the real-life needs of clients are addressed. Bringing the two groups together produced the insights found in this book. Both parties believe that progress is made by linking theory and practice, which is why they participated in the work of INCISM. They wished to avoid sterile debate in which theory and practice exist in different worlds.

The main interest of the INCISM network was the combined use of what have become known as "hard" and "soft" approaches in systems modelling. This complementary use is not always straightforward, but as illustrated here is certainly possible and can bring great benefits.

Any book needs some organization if the reader is to find her way around it. To some extent, the early chapters explore more general issues, starting with an introductory chapter to discuss the type of systems modelling that interests the authors. The chapters by practitioners and academics are interwoven, which illustrates that theory and practice are relevant to both parties. You will not find a single, monolithic view about how both hard and soft approaches can improve systems modelling. Instead, the chapters contain insights and ideas that, we hope, will stimulate you to develop your own ideas and will lead to improved systems modelling.

Though I am the editor of this book, it should be clear that it is the result of the insights and efforts of all contributors. Since I am editor, though, I have tried to ensure a reasonably consistent style throughout. Hence, if there are mistakes and unclear sections, I am the person who should be blamed.

Acknowledgements

This book stems from the INCISM network, funded by EPSRC. Chapters 6 and 11 are Crown Copyright.

1 Complementarity in systems modelling

Michael Pidd
Lancaster University

1.1 Systems modelling

The aim of Operational Research and Management Science (OR/MS) is to improve the way that organizations operate, which is usually done by building and using systems models. Sometimes, systems models are intended to represent the main features of an existing set of operations, or of some new ones. In such cases, the idea is to use the model as a vehicle for experimentation in the belief that the insights gained can be transferred to the operations being modelled. The model becomes, in effect, a surrogate that can be manipulated much more cheaply, safely and conveniently than that which is being modelled. This, however, is not the only way in which models are used in OR/MS, for a model may also represent people's beliefs or opinions, rather than some relatively objective reality. These models, though not objective creations, enable people to explore one another's ideas in a way that is impossible if those concepts remain as mental models. In both cases, models serve to make things explicit in such a way that understanding and change can occur.

Ackoff (1987), Pidd (2003), Powell and Baker (2003) and Rivett (1994), among others, discuss some principles for the building and use of systems models. With the exception of Ackoff, however, they assume that mathematics and statistics lie at the core of such modelling. This impression is confirmed by examining the OR/MS journals, such as *Management Science, Operations Research*, the *Journal of the Operational Research Society* and the *European Journal of Operational Research*. The papers that they contain are mainly discussions of mathematical and statistical approaches, and it would be easy, though wrong, to assume that little else of use can be said about systems modelling. There is much more to OR/MS than this, and highly skilled practitioners have a broad set of competences that enable them to operate successfully.

Most textbooks on OR/MS include chapters that introduce the techniques and approaches regarded as core material. These usually include the use of mathematical programming methods for optimization, decision trees for making decisions under uncertainty, queuing models for waiting lines and simulation techniques to understand the dynamic performance of a system. In

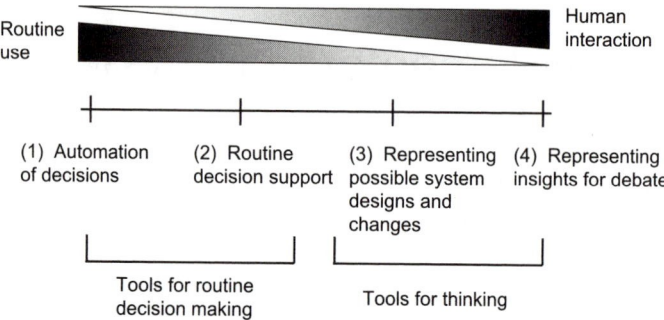

Figure 1.1—A spectrum of systems modelling approaches.

a mathematical programming approach, the modeller must decide which are the decision variables and devise an objective function that relates them to the performance measure that is being optimized. Also, she must develop a set of constraints that define the boundaries within which this optimization must be conducted. To build a discrete simulation model, she must understand how the objects of the system being simulated, known as entities, interact and change state to produce the behaviour of the system being simulated. Each such technique has a defined structure that provides a framework within which a model can be constructed. The structure, or frame, is constant across all applications, whether, for instance, a simulation is of a hospital emergency department or a manufacturing plant. In one case, the entities may be doctors, nurses and patients; in the other, they may be machines and jobs being processed (i.e., there is an underlying logic that is independent of the particular situation). A skilled modeller becomes adept at taking this common structure and using it to represent the important features of the situation being analysed and learns how far this can go before the model becomes too distorted to be of real use.

However, there are other ways in which models can be built and used for situations in which the irregularities and novelty dominate. To explore these different ways, consider the spectrum of approaches in Figure 1.1. At one extreme, models are used to support routine decision making, including what will shortly be defined as the automation of decision making, and for routine decision support. At the other extreme, models are used to support people who are thinking through difficult issues either by representing possible system designs and changes, or by representing insights that are debated.

1.1.1 Models that automate routine decision making

Figure 1.1 shows, at one extreme, that models are used to replace human decision making and action. As an example, consider the fly-by-wire systems and autopilots used on modern jetliners. These rely on duplicated control systems that can fly the plane without human intervention and may include such capabilities as fully automatic landings. These automatic systems rely on sensors that detect the current position of the aircraft's flying surfaces and its speed, altitude, attitude and other data. These data are transmitted to on-board computers that use models to decide how the plane should be flown and that send instructions to actuators that operate the aircraft's controls, changing or maintaining the way it actually is flown This is only possible because the behaviour of the aircraft is well understood, through established theory that has been captured in computer models. These well-validated models dictate how the aircraft should be flown under known conditions. They form the basis of the decisions taken by the computers, allowing the plane to be flown safely and economically with little or no human intervention. They are an extreme case of the way in which models, often unknown to us, replace human decision making in important areas of life.

Also at the left of Figure 1.1 are systems that replace humans in other types of routine decision making, such as the revenue management systems used by budget airlines on their websites. Anyone who has booked seats on these sites knows that the price offered for tickets on a particular flight will vary during the booking period up to the departure date of the aircraft. Known as dynamic pricing, this relies on a number of models, including some that predict the revenue and others that forecast booking rates at different prices. If the actual booking rate is lower than expected, prices will be automatically reduced; but if they are higher, prices will be raised. In both circumstances, the idea is to shift the actual bookings closer to the planned booking profile. The aim is to squeeze the maximum revenue out of the flight, supported by appropriate marketing campaigns and incentives. These systems, used also by hotels and holiday companies, run on a day-to-day basis without human intervention, though people are monitoring how well these systems are performing through time and may tweak the models' parameters as appropriate.

To build a model that will be used as the basis for the automation of routine decisions, the idea is to capture the regularities inherent in a particular recurring situation and to use these to improve on human decision making in later, similar situations. The fly-by-wire and autopilot systems in an aircraft can simultaneously monitor all the control surfaces and, using models to integrate that information and to compute what action if any should be taken, can adjust the operation of the aircraft. As long as the behaviour of the aircraft is within the performance envelope for which the models were constructed, the plane can be safely flown by the fly-by-wire autopilot. If, however, the plane is beyond that envelope, then disasters can occur, as has been claimed in the occasional crashes of highly automated aircraft.

The same is true of the dynamic pricing systems discussed above, which may also need to be modified if the external environment of the airlines or hotels changes markedly. As I am writing this paragraph, a US-led coalition has invaded Iraq to remove Saddam Hussein from power, and coincidentally a dangerous form of pneumonia (SARS) has broken out in South-East Asia. The war and SARS have had a major effect on the bookings for long-haul flights and for hotel rooms. Judging by the special offers and reduced fares currently available, the dynamic pricing models have been adjusted in the hope of gaining at least some revenue, though flights have also been cancelled and removed from the schedules.

Essentially, this use of modelling to automate decision making relies on regularity and reproducibility, a point discussed in a different context by Checkland and Holwell in Chapter 3. Attempting to use such models in situations that are not similar enough to the regularity that allowed their construction is a recipe for disaster. Human intervention is needed if this happens, though it should be noted that when such systems are routinely used humans may, through lack of practice, be unable to intervene and take control should that be needed.

1.1.2   Models as tools for thinking

At the opposite end of Figure 1.1 are approaches in which models become "tools for thinking" as in Figure 1.2 (taken from Pidd, 2003). These models are used as part of an intervention aimed at the improvement of an existing system or the design of a new one. Used in this way, these models do not replace human action, but support it. The simplest such support is offered by tools that use computer power to perform calculations more accurately and much faster than most humans. For example, a structural engineer may be asked to design a bridge for a particular purpose and might use a decision support system (DSS) to help in this task. Such a DSS might include possible generic bridge designs that can be parameterized to fit particular loads and spans. Using such a tool, the engineer can quickly compare options to develop a number of feasible outline designs, though she must still come to her own conclusions about the most appropriate design. She uses the DSS as a tool to support her thinking, not to replace it. As is also the case with the modelling approaches on

Figure 1.2—Models as tools for thinking.

the left-hand end of Figure 1.1, the person who uses the model to support their thinking is probably not the person who developed it.

As another example of models used as tools for thinking, consider the scheduling of aircrew for an airline. Whereas the above bridge designer used a decision support model to aid in a physical design, scheduling of aircrew is a non-physical domain – though it obviously has material consequences. An OR/MS study of this scheduling might, after much creative work, lead to the development of an optimization model with which the airline can schedule its crew each month to meet objectives, such as low cost and fairness. Whenever a new schedule is required, the optimization routines suggest what it should be, and in many circumstances this schedule may be directly implemented. In other circumstances, though, the model can only suggest the core of the schedule, which is then modified to accommodate factors that could not be built in to the model. As well as using the model to develop the schedule, it can also be used to consider changes that are needed in response to particular events (e.g., severe weather that leaves crew stranded in the wrong place). The model can be used as a "what-if" device to enable people to devise effective strategies in novel situations. The models do the hard work, freeing the human to think through the proposals that emerge from their use.

However, there are other ways in which models can be used as tools for thinking, especially when people need to plan changes in existing systems or wish to design new ones. In these circumstances, special purpose models are built to support the work being done. These models are not intended for later reuse or continued use, as in the case of the bridge designer or crew scheduler above, but are tools that support the thinking that goes on during the intervention. Once the work is complete, the models may be discarded or forgotten, as they have served their purpose. These are single-use models.

Some single-use models are would-be representations of the real world as discussed in Pidd (2003). For example, computer simulation models are often used in the design of new logistics, health and manufacturing systems. In these cases, the modeller develops computer programs that represent important aspects of the ways in which the system is intended to operate. Because these models are dynamic, they can be used to develop high-quality designs. As an example, see Park and Getz (1992) who provide a detailed account of the use of simulation models in the design of facilities for pharmaceutical manufacturing. Models as would-be representations of the real world are not limited to simulations and other approaches, such as decision analysis (Watson and Buede, 1987) and optimization (Williams, 1999), can be used in the same way. Whatever the type of model, it is used to help people think and debate about feasible and desirable action, not as the sole basis for that action. Used in this way, models may evolve as the project proceeds, being modified to allow new issues to be addressed. Once the project is complete, the models have served their purpose and are not expected to continue in use – though the experience gained in building and using them may well be reused. As discussed in Pidd

(2003), these models should be developed parsimoniously, starting with a model that is simple and adding refinements as needed.

Models, when used as tools for thinking, need not be limited to would-be representations of the real world of the type discussed above. Instead, as suggested by Checkland (1995) they can be devices to support debate by providing external representations of people's insights and beliefs. When facing novel or difficult situations, most of us begin with beliefs and expectations that stem from our education and experience. These form mental models that we use to process new information that may, over time, lead to their revision. Since many difficult problems are tackled by teams of people, it is sensible to provide ways in which people's mental models can be made more explicit, thus opening them to debate and discussion with other people. This process of explication may also be a help to individuals themselves since it allows them to reflect on their own views.

The usual problem with people's insights and opinions in complex situations is that they are not easily accessible to others, which can lead to debates characterized by misunderstanding and confusion. If people can understand their own views in the light of those held by others, then there is the chance that debate and discussion will progress rather than sink into the all too familiar swamp of fruitless argument and misunderstanding. A model of people's insights and opinions is a form of external representation – not of some tangible real world system, but of human insights and opinions that are then accessible to others for debate. Used in this way, a soft model is a tool that can support the thinking of groups and individuals as they try to make progress in difficult and complex situations.

Chapter 6 describes the way in which SSM (Soft Systems Methodology; Checkland, 1981) was used in a review of operation of the UK's personal tax system. The project included a series of workshops in which the views of a range of stakeholders were captured and expressed using root definitions. In like vein, Eden and Ackermann (1998) demonstrate how cognitive-mapping approaches may be used to support people as they think through strategic issues individually or in teams. Conklin (2001) describes the use of Dialog Mapping, an approach based on IBIS (Conklin, 1996) in which the deliberations of a group are captured in a model that is used to record decisions and to support future deliberations. Models used in this way are not intended as representations of real world systems, but instead capture the insights of people and make them accessible to others. They differ from those used to support routine decision making. They are not would-be representations of the real world, and they usually focus on the irregularities and novelty of a situation, rather than its regularities.

1.2   Messes and wicked problems

The standard techniques of OR/MS are very effective and valuable in those circumstances in which there is a common situational logic. However, they are less useful in those situations that Ackoff (1974) termed "messes". Building on Ackoff, Pidd (2003) discusses the ways in which people use the term "problem" and provides a spectrum containing three points as examples:

- **Puzzles**: situations in which it is clear what needs to be done and, in broad terms, how it should be done. Finding a solution is a process of applying known methods (e.g., a particular mathematical method) to come up with the solution to the puzzle.
- **Problems**: situations in which it is clear what needs to be done, but not at all obvious how to do it. Thus, the problem is well defined or well structured, but considerable ingenuity and expertise may be needed to find an acceptable, let alone optimal solution.
- **Messes**: situations in which there is considerable disagreement about what needs to be done and why; therefore, it is impossible to say how it should be done. Thus, the mess is unstructured and must be structured and shaped before any solution, should such exist, can be found.

Working in physical planning, Rittel and Webber came up with the term "wicked problems" to describe the same idea. Churchman (1967) seems to have been the first to cite the term, basing this on their work. Somewhat later, Rittel and Weber (1973) discussed the idea at length. Messes and wicked problems are impossible to solve, in the sense of a complete and closed approach that sorts out any difficulties once and for all. Instead, people work with them, much as a sculptor would, shaping and moulding until some satisfactory outcome is reached. Wicked problems and messes are novel and, in many of their aspects, non-recurring since they are not situations in which identical decisions must be made on a routine basis. Figure 1.3 is another version of Figure 1.1 in which puzzles, problems and messes/wicked problems have been located on the spectrum of modelling approaches.

What then is the role of modelling in working with wicked problems? Can modelling approaches make any contribution to situations of great novelty in which there is little regularity on which to base a model? Are such situations simply the wrong place to use rational approaches? To answer these questions, it is helpful to distinguish between two extreme types of rationality, following Simon (1954). The first type, which is what most people assume when they talk of rational analysis, is known as *substantive rationality* and is described by Simon as follows.

The most advanced theories, both verbal and mathematical, of rational behaviour are those that employ as their central concepts the notions of:

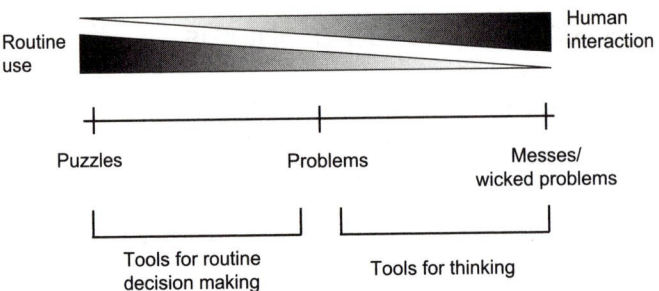

Figure 1.3—Modelling approaches, puzzles, problems and messes.

1. *a set of alternative courses of action presented to the individual's choice;*
2. *knowledge and information that permit the individual to predict the consequences of choosing any alternative; and*
3. *a criterion for determining which set of consequences he prefers.*

In these theories rationality consists in selecting that course of action that leads to the set of consequences most preferred (Simon, 1954).

It was earlier mentioned that many mathematical and statistical models assume regularity and that such models can be used to help manage situations that recur. In such situations it may indeed be possible to meet the requirements specified above by Simon. However, when a situation is novel and includes many irregularities, this type of rational modelling may be impossible because the full set of alternatives is not known, we cannot predict the consequences of choosing any alternative and there is no agreed criterion for choice.

Hence, Simon (1954) suggested a second type of rationality, *procedural rationality*, which can be applied in situations that are novel and include much irregularity (i.e., wicked problems or messes). Procedural rationality stresses the design of processes to support decision making based on human deliberation when substantive rationality is impossible or inappropriate. Procedurally rational approaches should support the following:

- The discovery of alternatives: this is needed because, in such situations, it is not a question of comparing options that are known. The discovery of options is time-consuming, expensive and may be a political process as people discuss what they regard as feasible.
- The development of acceptable solutions when there is conflict over ends as well as means. These may only emerge as people discuss what is feasible and reach acceptable agreement over what is desirable. This is common in wicked problems or messes.
- The systematic gathering and analysis of information, recognizing that doing so incurs costs and takes time and that perfect information is never available when tackling wicked problems and messes. Thus it would be a

mistake to assume that procedural rationality encourages irrationality. Information and its analysis is still regarded as crucial, but is placed within cognitive and economic limitations.

- The use of bounded rationality that recognizes people's cognitive limitations. Whether we like it or not, people's preferences may be inconsistent and may change over time as new options, information and opinion emerge. Within such preferences they do not expect to optimize in any global sense, but rather to satisfice across the acceptable solutions known to them.

In a way, Simon's procedural rationality is an admission of defeat. It recognizes that substantive rationality, for all its appeal, rests on behavioural and other assumptions that are faulty. Using procedural rationality, humans can find their way to improvement and, as far as this book is concerned, the question is "how can systems modelling help?" Possible answers to this question are explored below and start from a recognition that people should be supported in ways that do not add further bounds to the inherent problem with bounded rationality.

1.3 Hard and soft approaches

Most textbooks on OR/MS devote virtually all of their space to the description of mathematical and statistical methods that have been found useful in tackling a range of fairly well-defined problems. Correctly or not, these methods are often described as hard OR/MS approaches. Other books (e.g., Rosenhead and Mingers, 2001) are devoted to the discussion of what have become known as soft approaches. In many ways, these soft approaches embody the requirements for procedural rationality as discussed above. There are many ways in which hard and soft approaches may be distinguished. In Chapter 3, for example, Checkland and Holwell discuss the philosophical differences in terms of epistemologies and ontologies.

This book stems from the work of INCISM (Interdisciplinary Research Network on Complementarity in Systems Modelling) which was briefly described in the Preface. The network brought together academics and practitioners, all interested in how hard and soft approaches may be used in a complementary manner. As well as the philosophical view of the terms hard and soft OR referred to above, the INCISM meetings also explored some practical and pragmatic implications of the terms as they are used in everyday OR practice. Table 1.1 captures some of these practical and pragmatic aspects, which represent the ways in which active theorists and practitioners view the differences. The discussion of these aspects given here is based in part on Brown et al. (2004), and it is important to realize that some of these aspects

Table 1.1—Practical aspects of hard and soft OR.

	Hard OR	Soft OR
Methodology used	Based on common sense, taken-for-granted views of analysis and intervention	Based on rigorous epistemology
Models	Shared representation of the real world	Representation of concepts relevant to the real world
Validity	Repeatable with comparable with the real world in some sense	Defensibly coherent, logically consistent, plausible
Data	From a source that is defensibly there in the world, with an agreed or shared meaning, observer-independent	Based on judgement, opinion, some ambiguity, observer-dependent
Values and outcome of the study	Quantification assumed to be possible and desirable. From option comparison based on rational choice	Agreement (on action?), shared perceptions. Informing action and learning
Purpose of the study	For the study: taken as a given at the start For the model: understanding or changing the world, linked to the purpose	For the study: remains problematical For the model: a means to support learning

overlap with one another. It is also important to realize that "pure" hard and soft approaches are extreme points on a spectrum and that points in between do exist – thus, some of the aspects discussed are stereotypical at times.

1.3.1 Methodology

The first row of Table 1.1 refers to the role of methodology in OR/MS, of which two aspects are of interest. First, a methodology embodies a set of principles and often unspoken assumptions that underpin what we do. Second, methodology may come to describe the methods and procedures that we choose to use – based on those prior methodological principles. INCISM participants agreed that hard and soft approaches embody different methodologies. As can be seen from Table 1.1, the methodology of hard OR is typically based on taken-for-granted views of analysis and rationality (i.e., few people engaged in hard OR make much effort to select a methodological stance and may be unaware that the methods they used are based on principles that can be understood, described and discussed). The methodology in use, if considered at all, is based on a common sense understanding of rational enquiry in which a model is built as a would-be representation, albeit a partial one, of some aspect of the real world and is then used to explore aspects of that world. The core of the approach is an assumption that the model will shed useful light on changes that should be made to the real world. As Checkland (1981) points out, this implies a positivist ontology in which the world, or at least the objects of interest, are taken to be "out there" and can be identically known by different observers acting objectively.

By contrast, in soft OR, methodology needs to be based on careful considera-tion and reflection because the approaches are usually based on an ontology that allows observation to be much more personal (i.e., it accepts that different people may legitimately experience and interpret the same things quite differ-ently). This does not of course imply that all interpretations are legitimate; it is still possible to be wrong. There is a much greater stress on self-awareness in soft OR, for the consultant needs to think very carefully about her role, so as to be aware of what she is doing in the particular social context of the study. It is usually assumed, in hard OR, that there is no real need to justify the methods and approaches in use, since they are taken to rely on unproblematic assump-tions about external reality based on objective rationality. By contrast, there is a danger that soft OR could drift off into sloppy and purely relativistic thinking, were it not to be grounded in a careful consideration of methodology. It is precisely this rigorous concern for methodology that made SSM attractive for the tax policy study discussed in Chapter 6. The Inland Revenue study team was determined to use an approach that could be audited and that was defendable.

1.3.2 Models and modelling

The second row of Table 1.1 refers to the use of models in both hard and soft OR/MS. This has already been touched on earlier, but bears repetition here. Figure 1.4 is an attempt to capture the important differences between hard and soft modelling. Underlying truly hard OR is a view that a model is a would-be representation of some aspect of the real world that should be validated before being used. This does not mean that a hard OR analyst assumes that her model is complete or fully detailed, for many writers argue that simplification is inevitable in modelling and some argue that it is desirable (e.g., Powell, 1995 and Willemain, 1994). Modelling, in these terms, is an activity in which technical methods and insight are used to develop an external representation that is intended to provide useful insights into that which is being modelled. The tax policy study described in Chapter 6 includes both hard OR/MS (rigorous data mining) and a soft approach (Checkland's

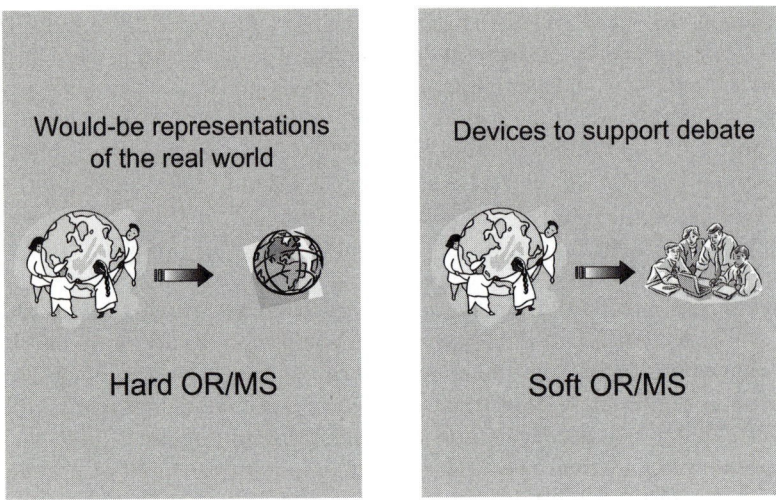

Figure 1.4—Hard and soft modelling.

SSM), and the study would have been much weaker had only one approach been used.

Figure 1.4 highlights the major differences between hard and soft modelling, and its second aspect relates to what is included and excluded. Both hard and soft approaches are shown as a globe surrounded by people with an arrow to indicate the modelling process. In hard OR/MS the model is shown as the globe, but minus the people. This relates back to the earlier notion that such models capture the regularities in the situation, and if human action is included at all it is as the behaviour of representative groups. Thus, in the data mining discussed in Chapter 6, the investigations uncovered different taxpayer groups, such as company directors, young people and so on. Though no pair of company directors will be identical, they are similar enough to be treated as members of the same class in the cluster map, and it is this group behaviour that is being modelled (i.e., the model is based on regularities even when human behaviour is involved).

As a contrast, the right-hand side of Figure 1.4 relates to soft modelling, which is depicted as consisting only of people – the regularities of the globe have disappeared. This is rather a caricature, but does represent the idea that the prime concern in soft modelling is to understand the worlds and world views of the people participating in the study. Again, as stated earlier, the idea is to support debate by explicating the ideas, insights and worldviews of the people involved. In soft OR/MS, a model is taken to be a representation of concepts relevant to understanding and working in the real world. These can include concepts that occur to the analyst as well as those produced by other participants in the study. This modelling is a process of learning and shaping, leading to an understanding of the interpretations of those involved. In the tax study of Chapter 6, the models developed were abstract representations of the features held to be desirable and necessary in a future tax system.

1.3.3 Model validity and validation

The third row of Table 1.1 refers to model validity, a topic briefly introduced earlier. If a model is intended, as in hard OR, as a representation of the real world, then it must be possible to compare it in some way or other with that real world. Without such a comparison, which can amount to a Turing test, what faith can there be that the model is valid and can be trusted? Of course, even in hard OR this argument is on very shaky ground if the models are of possible future systems as they might be, not as they are. In these cases there is no referent system against which the model is to be compared. As discussed in Pidd (2003), full model validation is best regarded as an ideal to which the modeller must aspire, rather than as a state that can actually be reached.

For this reason the computer simulation community increasingly refers to model credibility assessment (Balci, 1987), realizing that the important issue is whether people have enough confidence in the model to act on the insights that it produces. This credibility comes from the way it was built, from the way that the people who built it seem to act and on the basis of the insights that it produces. This same issue of credibility can be seen in the tax study of Chapter 6, in which tax policy experts agreed that the models resulting from data mining had face validity (i.e., they were in accord with their experience). It is important to realize that this credibility was established over a period of time, as the results of a sequence of data-mining results was discussed with tax experts. In this way, their confidence grew in the models, the methods used and in the people who carried out the work. Even in hard OR/MS, validation is sometimes problematic and is based on a process that aims to establish credibility.

In soft OR it is better to ask whether a model is defensibly coherent, logically consistent and plausible. For example, in SSM (the soft approach used in the tax study) conceptual models are usually expected to comply with known theory about the behaviour of physical systems. Thus, they must be self-maintaining through control mechanisms and their performance must be measurable, conceptually at least. In addition, the models developed were expected to be plausible in the context of operational policy for taxation (i.e., they had to embody principles that could be logically defended in the arena of tax policy). In addition, of course, the models need to have face validity (i.e., any immediately apparent oddities should be deliberate and not a result of sloppy work). In cognitive mapping the credibility comes from the way in which the maps are built by the analyst and the clarity with which participants can see that their opinions are represented.

1.3.4 Data and their use

The fourth aspect of Table 1.1 is the role of data in the work being done. Since in hard OR a model is intended as a representation of some aspect of the real world, the role of data is crucial. Data are used in building a model (e.g., an exploratory data analysis may provide clues as to what variables should be included in a model). Data are also used in establishing the parameters of a model whose structure and general features are already determined. Thus, a simulation of an emergency room may include a triage nurse whose main task is to see patients on arrival and decide whether they are emergencies, whether they need treatment or whether they should be sent to a non-urgent clinic of some kind. To simulate her actions, the modeller will need to know how long she takes to examine patients and to determine their triage status. This will not be a fixed time, but will vary stochastically and could be determined from records, if accurate ones exist, or from a special data collection exercise. Most hard OR/MS modellers will not necessarily take data at face value – since the reason for their original collection may not fit well with the model being built. Nevertheless, the data are used to ensure that the model is a good representation of some aspect of the real world. Thus, underpinning much hard OR/MS is a view that data come from a source that is defensibly there in the world (it is not just arbitrary), that they have an agreed or shared meaning (possibly based on known theory; e.g., in statistical method) and as far as possible are independent of observer bias. Such assumptions need not be limited to purely quantitative data, but could also apply to qualitative data (e.g., the rules to be applied when collecting taxes).

By contrast, things are not so simple in soft OR, for which data are always regarded as based on judgement and opinion. Thus, the conceptual activity models of SSM represent an idealization of the factors captured in a root definition, which itself only make sense in the light of the world view or Weltanschauung. Similarly, the links established between concepts on a cognitive map are intended to show the relationships as articulated by the person or group whose map is being constructed. The mapper may choose to intervene, to question whether that is really what was intended, but the map itself rests on data that are subjective. In the tax study described in Chapter 6, the data used in the hard OR came from the Inland Revenue's records of UK taxpayers; the data for the soft study were collected in workshops and interviews with stakeholders.

1.3.5 The value or outcome of the study

What of the value and outcome of the study or intervention, shown as the fifth element of Table 1.1? It is often assumed that any OR/MS study, whether hard or soft, is intended to produce tangible and measurable benefits in terms of cost savings, extra income, better customer service or some such performance measure. This benefit may be achieved through implementing recommendations (e.g., a new way of routing trucks that travel between customers), or it may come from a newly designed and implemented system as in an embedded scheduling system for aircrew. Is there any difference between soft and hard OR/MS in this regard?

It is usually the case that hard OR analysts, in public at least, claim to produce a tangible product in the form or recommendations, system design or change in the everyday real world. Many OR consultants sell their services on just this basis, and some charge for their time as a percentage of audited savings that result from their work. This is then a very appealing view that can easily be justified, or not, by a comparison of costs and benefits. In the tax study, the outcome of the hard OR was a set of models that represented archetypical taxpayer groups and the ways in which they interact with the tax system. In soft OR, things are not so simple, since the stress is on helping people to agree in situations where there may be disagreement and conflict about objectives as well as about what should be done. It may be that, once this agreement has been reached, it is possible to engage in some hard OR to decide exactly what should be done. In the tax study the soft OR resulted in agreed recommendations of the ways in which the operation of the UK's personal tax system might be changed.

It is fair to say, though, that even very hard OR projects may result in learning and may be used as a device to help people think through their objectives, and even soft OR can result in very tangible recommendations. Effective learning is more difficult if the OR/MS work has been done as an "expert-mode" consulting assignment on a "hit and run" basis (i.e., if the consultant is brought in purely for expertise and then uses this to make recommendations based on analysis conducted away from the organization, there will be limited learning). This danger is absent in soft OR/MS studies, for close interaction between the consultant and client is fundamental in this work.

1.3.6 The intended purpose of the intervention

Finally, Table 1.1 shows that the intended purpose of soft and hard OR studies may differ. Perhaps this should have been discussed before the other aspects, but it is simpler to understand at this stage. In a hard OR study, the terms of reference for the study are agreed as quickly as possible at the start of the work, and the aim is to meet those terms of reference. This assumes that the people drawing up those terms are clear about what needs to be done and why it needs to be done, but they wish to find the best way to do it. This is appealing, but is sadly often wrong. Very often people do not know what they want, they look for help because they know something is wrong or may need doing, but they are not quite sure what this might be. Usually, the very first task is to work with the client to decide what needs to be done – often known as problem structuring. Similarly, the purpose of the modelling is to achieve as good a fit as is possible between the real world and the model, to enable the model to be used as a vehicle to see what would happen in the real world if particular actions were taken.

In soft OR, things are very different, for the model is used as a vehicle to support the learning of the participants in the study. Further, the purpose of the study itself is something that is open to question throughout the engagement. Of course, this cannot go on for ever, life is too short and people do need to agree what should be done. Nevertheless, it is axiomatic in soft OR/MS that terms of reference for a study are a starting point and not an intended destination and that some aspects of problem structuring continue throughout an engagement. This is why some writers (see, e.g., the full title of Rosenhead and Mingers, 2001) regard soft OR/MS methods as problem-structuring approaches, and some people use the abbreviation PSA to refer to this.

1.4 What do we mean by complementarity?

The INCISM network that led to this book had, as its theme, "complementarity in systems modelling". So far, this chapter has explored what we mean by systems modelling and it is now time to explore the theme of complementarity. Though complementarity is not a common term, it is used in several domains, including the algebraic modelling of some dynamic systems in terms of differential equations (e.g., see Ferris et al., 1999). In OR/MS the term was popularized by Flood and Jackson (1991), who examined six different systems approaches and suggested how they might be unified under a single approach – Total Systems Intervention (or TSI). In TSI, complementarity involves the combined use of the six approaches across six archetypal problem contexts.

- Systems dynamics: introduced by Forrester (1961), continued by his colleagues at MIT and elsewhere and popularized in Senge (1990). System dynamics uses difference equations, a simplified form of differential equation, to model structures that lead to organizational dynamics.
- Viable system diagnosis: developed by Beer (1985), based on his own viable systems model (Beer, 1979, 1981) which draws analogies between the cybernetic principles embedded in organisms and their parallels in organizational systems.
- Strategic assumption surfacing and testing: developed by Mason and Mitroff (1981) and intended for use in working with wicked problems (Rittel and Webber, 1973) by helping participants to co-operate.
- Interactive planning: developed by Ackoff (1974) with the intention of

helping organizations and groups to envisage and create desirable futures using systems ideas.

- Soft systems methodology: developed by Peter Checkland (1981) and developed further by colleagues at Lancaster and elsewhere (see Chapter 3) to help individuals and groups tackle wicked problems.
- Critical systems heuristics: developed by Ulrich (1983) as an approach that recognizes that power and coercion are exercised in most wicked problems.

The idea of TSI is that by examining aspects of the problem context, it is possible to develop contingent approaches that fit particular circumstances. This is far from simple when different systems methodologies make different assumptions, an issue discussed in Brockelsby (1993), Mingers (2001) and Mingers and Gill (1997).

Why should it be difficult to combine methodologies? Ormerod (2001) provides evidence that, whatever the theoretical problems, people do attempt to combine the different approaches in practice and that their efforts lead to successful OR/MS. Does it matter that there are theoretical problems if smart people are able to get by in *ad hoc* ways? To answer that question, we need to stand back a little and consider what have come to be known as paradigms. It should be noted that this debate is not unique to OR/MS, but crops up in many areas, such as organization theory (e.g., see Scherer, 1998).

1.4.1 Paradigms

The term "paradigm" entered common use through the work of Thomas Kuhn (1970), who was trying to understand how scientific work developed and was concerned as much with the social processes involved as with the logic of scientific discovery. He was puzzled by the way that dominant ideas and theories remain so, even when there is increasing evidence that this dominance is unjustified. To describe the processes involved he used the term "paradigm" to depict a conceptual framework within which scientific theories are constructed for a particular field of scientific endeavour. At its simplest, an idea or theory retains its power because of its role within a paradigm, rather than just because it satisfactorily explains observable phenomena. A paradigm, then, is a network of assumptions, ideas and theories that are mutually reinforcing. In Kuhn's terms, normal science is that which operates within an established paradigm and which serves to explore the intellectual space defined by its paradigm. Revolutionary science is that which challenges the orthodoxy of the day with new findings and observations and new theories that cannot be explained within the existing, dominant paradigm.

Whether or not all OR/MS is scientific, the idea of a paradigm is useful when thinking about the complementary ways that hard and soft methods and approaches may be used. Do hard and soft OR constitute different paradigms or are they just variations on a theme? For Kuhn (1970) different paradigms were incommensurable, by this meaning two things. First, that different paradigms apply their own standards to the puzzles and problems on which they work. Second, that though two paradigms may seem to apply the same concepts, they mean quite different things by them. Both imply that people who work within different paradigms see the world and any problems that they face quite differently. The problems with this view for OR/MS is that, as Ormerod (2001) points out, some people do manage to work with both soft and hard approaches. This suggests either that Kuhn is wrong about incommensurability, or that soft and hard OR do not in fact sit within different paradigms.

Brockelsby (1993) discusses these issues in addressing what he terms "Enhanced OR" (EOR), this being an OR in which different methodologies are in use and are accepted as legitimate. "If we think of methodology choice as cultural activity, then OR analysts are best conceptualised as contextually and historically situated actors. As members of particular groups, they have been acculturated into viewing the world in distinctive ways and these meanings have a huge bearing on the doing of OR research. In the complementarist conception of EOR, the research act is viewed as a rational act involving real choice, but it is questionable whether this theory of research is compatible with the multi-cultural reality of OR today. ... Much of the 'doing' of the research is less a matter of choice and free will, it emerges out of the framework of the culture, or subculture, to which the scientist belongs" (Brockelsby, 1993, p. 153). That is, in most cases we do not choose a particular methodology by a conscious selection process, but our background and unconsidered assumptions lead us to it, unawares.

1.4.2 You choose

Figure 1.5 shows three different ways in which soft and hard OR/MS approaches can relate to one another. In the left-hand part of the figure, the soft and hard approaches are completely distinct and should be regarded, in

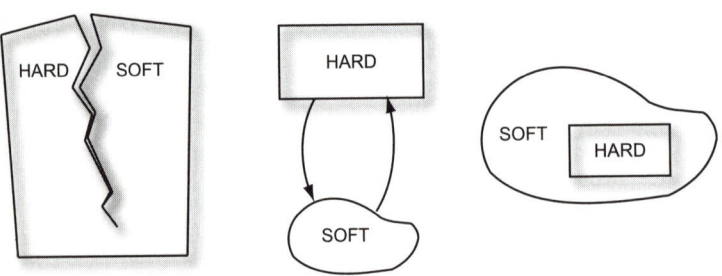

Figure 1.5—Relationships between hard and soft.

Kuhn's terms, as incommensurable. In the middle part of the figure, the two are seen feeding off one another in an eclectic and pragmatic way. In the right-hand part of Figure 1.5, soft OR/MS methods are seen as containing the classical hard approaches, in the sense that the understanding of meanings gained in soft OR/MS enables a sensible attempt at hard OR/MS. Rather than suggest which of these is closest to the truth, this chapter ends by suggesting that you read the contributions to this book and start to make up your own mind. Sometimes, the journey is more important than the destination.

References

Ackoff R.L. (1974) *Redesigning the Future: A Systems Approach to Societal Planning.* John Wiley & Sons, New York.

Ackoff R.L. (1987) *The Art of Problem Solving.* John Wiley & Sons, New York.

Balci O. (1987) Credibility assessment of simulation results: The state of the art. In *Proceedings of the Conference on Methodology and Validation, Orlando, FL*, pp. 19–25.

Beer S. (1979) *The Heart of the Enterprise.* John Wiley & Sons, Chichester, UK.

Beer S. (1981) *Brain of the Firm,* 2nd edn. John Wiley & Sons, Chichester, UK.

Beer S. (1985) *Diagnosing the System for Organization.* John Wiley & Sons, Chichester, UK.

Brockelsby J. (1993) Methodological complementarism or separate paradigm development – Examining the options for enhanced operational research. *Australian Journal of Management*, 133–57.

Brown J., Cooper C. and Pidd M. (2004) A taxing problem: The complementary use of hard and soft OR in public policy. Submitted to *European Journal of Operational Research*.

Checkland, P.B. (1981) *Systems Thinking, Systems Practice.* John Wiley & Sons, Chichester, UK.

Checkland P.B. (1995) Model validation in soft systems practice. *Systems Research*, **12**(1), 47–54.

Churchman C. (1967) Wicked problems. *Management Science*, **4**(14), B141–2.

Conklin J. (1996) The IBIS manual: A short course in IBIS methodology, available at http://www.gdss.com/wp/IBIS.htm

Conklin J. (2001) The Dialog Mapping experience – A story. Working paper, available at http://cognexus.org/dmepaper.htm

Eden C.L. and Ackermann F. (1998) *Strategy Making: The Journey of Strategic Management.* Sage Publications, London.

Ferris M.C., Fourer R. and Gay D.M. (1999) Expressing complementarity problems in an algebraic modeling language and communicating them to solvers. *SIAM Journal on Optimization*, **9**(4), 991–1009.

Flood R.L. and Jackson M.C. (1991) *Creative Problem Solving: Total Systems Intervention.* John Wiley & Sons, Chichester, UK.

Forrester J.W. (1961) *Industrial Dynamics.* MIT Press, Cambridge, MA.

Kuhn T.S. (1970) *The Structure of Scientific Revolutions,* 2nd edn. University of Chicago Press, Chicago.

Mason R.O. and Mitroff I.I. (1981) *Challenging Strategic Planning Assumptions*. John Wiley & Sons, New York.

Mingers J. (2001) Multimethodology – Mixing and matching methods. In J.V. Rosenhead and J. Mingers (eds) *Rational Analysis for a Problematic World Revisited*. John Wiley & Sons, Chichester, UK.

Mingers J. and Gill A. (1997) *Multimethodology: Theory and Practice of Combining Management Science Methodologies*. John Wiley & Sons, Chichester, UK.

Ormerod R. (2001) Mixing methods in practice. In J.V. Rosenhead and J. Mingers (eds) *Rational Analysis for a Problematic World Revisited*. John Wiley & Sons, Chichester, UK.

Park C.A. and Getz T. (1992) The approach to developing a future pharmaceuticals manufacturing facility (using SIMAN and AutoMod). Presented at *Proceedings of the 1992 Winter Simulation Conference, Arlington, VA, December 1992*.

Pidd, M. (2003) *Tools for Thinking*. John Wiley & Sons, Chichester, UK.

Powell S.G. (1995) The teacher's forum: Six key modeling heuristics. *Interfaces*, **25**(4), 114–25.

Powell S.G and Baker K.R. (2003) *The Art of Modeling with Spreadsheets*. John Wiley & Sons, New York.

Rittel H.W.J. and Webber M.M. (1973) Dilemmas in a general theory of planning. *Policy Sciences*, **4**, 155–69.

Rivett B.H.P. (1994) *The Craft of Decision Modelling*. John Wiley & Sons, Chichester, UK.

Rosenhead J.V. and Mingers J. (2001) *Rational Analysis for a Problematic World Revisited: Problem Structuring Methods for Complexity, Uncertainty and Conflict*, 2nd edn. John Wiley & Sons, Chichester, UK.

Scherer A.G. (1998) Thematic issue on pluralism and incommensurability in strategic management and organization theory. Consequences for theory and practice. *Organization*, **5**, 2.

Senge P. (1990) *The Fifth Discipline: The Art and Practice of the Learning Organization*. Currency/Doubleday, New York.

Simon H.A. (1954) Some strategic considerations in the construction of social science models. In H.A. Simon (ed.) *Models of Bounded Rationality: Behavioural Economics and Business Organization*. MIT Press, Cambridge, MA.

Ulrich, W. (1983) *Critical Heuristics of Social Planning*. Haupt, Bern, Switzerland.

Ulrich W. (1994) *Critical Heuristics of Social Planning: A New Approach to Practical Philosophy*. John Wiley & Sons, Chichester, UK.

Watson S.R. and Buede D.M. (1987) *Decision Synthesis: The Principles and Practice of Decision Analysis*. Cambridge University Press, Cambridge, UK.

Willemain T.R. (1994) Insights on modelling from a dozen experts. *Operations Research*, **42**(2), 213–22.

Williams H.P. (1999) *Model Building in Mathematical Programming*, 4th edn. John Wiley & Sons, Chichester, UK.

2 Insights from complexity: organizational change and systems modelling

Michael Lyons
BT Exact

2.1 Introduction

This chapter looks at how the development of complexity theory sheds light on the complementarity between hard and soft approaches. The chapter starts with an introduction to complex adaptive systems (CASs), a notion derived from studies of non-equilibrium physical, chemical and biological systems. Properties of such systems as self-organization, emergence and evolution have been investigated using a variety of experimental methods and "hard" quantitative models.

Many human and social systems can be likened to CASs, and much of complexity theory is concerned with applying the concepts derived from the study of CASs to social systems, such as economies, companies and other organizations. Thus complexity theory has implications for management theory. The second section of this chapter, therefore, looks at the way concepts derived from the study of well-defined physical and chemical systems (essentially, a hard approach) can be applied by analogy to management (soft issues).

The third section looks at the role of models in the management of organizations and how simulation approaches developed for CASs can be applied to managerial issues. Earlier work by the author (Lyons, 1999, 2002) has emphasized the need to take into account the wider political context in which a model is developed and used. Here, drawing on analogies between evolution and organizational learning, the emphasis is on the need for a diversity of models to explore options and support strategic decision making.

Complexity demonstrates complementarity between hard and soft in two distinct ways. First, hard models of physical systems have been used to identify key concepts that by way of analogy can be applied to softer, social systems. In turn, ideas from complexity, particularly those relating to evolution, provide insights into the role of multiple quantitative models in exploring different strategic options.

2.2   Complex adaptive systems and complexity

Although complexity science is derived from classical science, there are some significant differences between the two approaches. Classical science is based on a reductionist view of the world, in which entities are generally treated as independent and systems are taken to be close to equilibrium. Largely as a result of computational limitations, dynamics are assumed to be linear (itself a reasonable assumption close to equilibrium) and the test of understanding is prediction. Models (theories) are validated if they accurately predict experimental results.

Complexity science recognizes that entities (or agents) are interdependent. Furthermore, many of the systems studied are far from equilibrium and give rise to dynamics that are non-linear. Complex systems frequently show structure (self-organization) and emergent properties that could not be predicted from the properties of the individual entities. Thus, complexity science is holistic in nature and understanding is no longer demonstrated by prediction (since it is no longer possible to predict in advance the behaviour of a complex system), but characterized by an awareness of the limits of predictability.

Complex systems are often described as being on the "edge of chaos", displaying self-organized order. These systems are continuously changing, but preserve some degree of structure at all times. Such change is varyingly described as learning, evolution or adaptation, depending on context. From the modelling viewpoint we are dealing with systems that are dynamic in nature and for which static models, based on equilibrium or stasis, are inappropriate. One result of this emphasis on dynamic systems is that we can no longer expect models to predict. Because the systems are continually changing, outcomes of changes are path-dependent and may be multi-valued. The object of a model is no longer to predict but to understand. Some authors question the extent to which a model can aid understanding, as similar results or outcomes can be the result of a number of different dynamical processes – the fact that a model can reproduce observed behaviour does not guarantee that the underlying assumptions are correct. "Computational models are particularly good at developing theory [and] suggesting the logical consequences of a set of assumptions ... [But] ... computational models do not prove these theories they help develop ... Expectations that computational models can demonstrate or prove anything beyond theory building is asking too much of them and will lead to disappointment" (Krackhardt, 2001, p. 243). This is consistent with Schrage's view that "... models are most useful when they are used to challenge existing formulations rather than to validate or verify them" (Schrage, 2000).

There is a deeper link between models and complex systems highlighted by Holland (1995), who suggests that complex adaptive systems anticipate the future by means of various internal models that are simplified representations of the environment. Holland distinguishes between a tacit internal model that prescribes current action under an implicit prediction of future state and an overt internal model that provides a basis for explicit (internal) exploration of alternatives. This distinction provides an admirable means of describing the use of models in strategic decision making. A successful modelling approach involves taking tacit internal models (held by individuals) and turning them into overt internal models that can be debated, criticized and simulated. This is discussed in more detail below (see Section 2.5).

2.2.1 Specifiable and non-specifiable complex systems

Figure 2.1 shows some of the different types of models developed within a telecommunications company. They include detailed models of networks as part of the design and build process, models of various processes within the organization as well as models to support business decisions and strategic analysis.

It is useful to think in terms of specifiable and non-specifiable systems. In the former, it is possible in principle to specify fully the entities forming the system and the interactions between them. Thus, telecommunications networks are in this sense specifiable. This means that the network could be modelled and its behaviour fully understood. Models and simulations are seen as a means of engineering systems to meet specific performance characteristics.

Non-specifiable systems are much more common and include industries, societies, consumers and markets. In the field of management, the concept of complexity is becoming increasingly popular and is clearly being applied to non-specifiable systems, involving people and human institutions. Some authors, notably Stacey (2001), object to the notion of a "system" involving humans, largely on the grounds that it is too mechanistic a description. While recognizing this danger, it can be argued that social entities, such as economies, societies and organizations, do consist of many actors and many interactions between these actors – the key features of a complex system. The concept of a human system seems to the author to be a useful one, providing

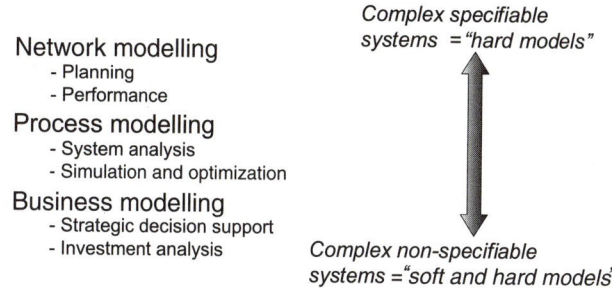

Figure 2.1—Types of model.

one keeps in mind that it is simply one possible description. In non-specifiable systems it is often difficult to identify all the possible types of entity (e.g., we do not have a full description of all possible roles and players in the information industry). Furthermore, to identify all the possible interactions is impossible. Yet, strategic decision making will involve anticipating the behaviour of other players in a market (customers, competitors, etc.), frequently in a situation of incomplete information. A mixture of hard and soft approaches is needed. Decision making is best seen as a process of negotiation, as discussed by Eden and Ackermann in Chapters 8 and 9, and modelling is only one part of this. Models allow users to investigate alternative strategies and understand implications of specific courses of action. A key role in this area therefore is "hypothesis testing".

Process modelling lies between these extremes: there is not only a mechanical aspect (data flow, sequencing, etc.) that can be modelled and engineered much like the specifiable systems but also a human aspect in that such systems interact with and are influenced by human beings.

A number of different types of complex system have been modelled, including avalanches in sand piles, weather systems, stock markets, fisheries, ant colonies and flocks of birds. The results of these models give rise to some general messages about the characteristics of complex systems. First, the impact of any change to the systems is unpredictable beyond certain (imprecise) limits. Such limits may be in terms of time: thus, the UK weather can be predicted reasonably accurately one or two days in advance, but not three months in advance. Or the limit of predictability may be in terms of scope: in certain parts of the world, earthquakes are relatively frequent, but the size of the next quake cannot be predicted. Second, models of complex systems frequently show characteristic dynamic behaviours. Thus, although weather may be unpredictable, we can describe typical weather systems: anti-cyclones, depressions. Similarly, models of stock markets show that booms and busts are typical behaviour of such institutions.

2.3 Complexity and management

The terms "hard" and "soft" have arisen in the context of systems thinking in OR (Operational Research). How closely linked are OR and complexity and is the latter just the latest variant of "soft" systems thinking? I would suggest that the scope of complexity thinking or complexity management is very much greater. OR interventions are primarily aimed at decision support. In contrast, the development of complexity management has arisen in part as a response to the increasingly uncertain and dynamic commercial environment facing most companies. Complexity looks not only at the making of specific decisions but also at the way the company is structured and managed.

2.3.1 Decision making and strategy

Complexity has implications, for example, for the way companies develop strategies. Eden and van der Heijden (1995) and van der Heijden (1996) identify three approaches to strategic planning:

- *rationalists*, who aim to plan an optimum strategy in a forecast environment;
- *evolutionists*, who emphasize the complexity and uncertainty of the world and the way companies' strategies emerge through political processes (and may deny any value to analytical approaches); and
- *processualists*, who not only recognize the uncertainty of the future but also hold that it is not entirely unpredictable. The processualist will not only recognize the political processes at work in the formation of strategy but also accepts the value of analytical and rational techniques (e.g., simulations and scenarios planning) in helping to structure the political debate.

Complexity theorists will follow Mintzberg (1994) in rejecting the rationalist approach: in an unpredictable world it is not possible to forecast and optimize with any accuracy. Rosenhead (1998), in a critical review of complexity and management, highlights the tendency of some writers to reject a role for analytic methods in management, emphasizing instead the importance of political processes in determining strategy. This same emphasis is evident in the Journey Making approach of Eden and Ackermann (1997). However, the evolutionist approach seems unnecessarily extreme: complex systems may well be unpredictable in the long term, but over short timescales their behaviour is predictable. Furthermore, analytical approaches (simulations) can give warning of possible future behaviours. The processualist approach is adopted in this paper. Models are developed to improve strategy development, but it follows from the above that model building should not be seen as an end in itself, Rather, it is part of a wider decision-making process which is essentially social in nature, involving negotiation and debate – as assumed in soft OR approaches, such as strategic options development and analysis (SODA), soft systems methodology (SSM) and the Strategic Choice Approach (SCA).

Complexity management looks beyond the individual decision to the process by which an organization adapts and responds to changes in its environment. For simplicity, we usually assume managers have just one problem to look at, and the decision-making process is one of seeking options (alternative solutions) and by some cognitive process choosing the "best" solution (Figure 2.2). This is a rational choice model.

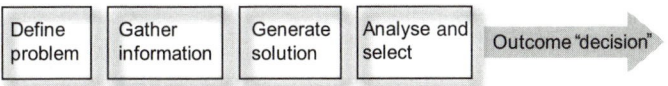

Figure 2.2—A rational model of decision making.

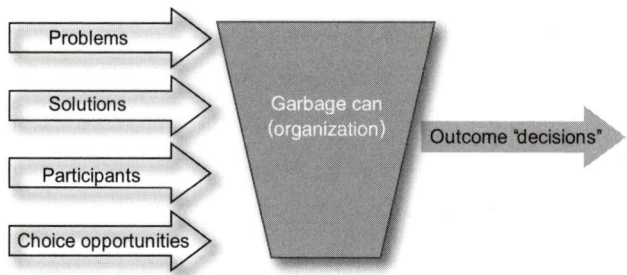

Figure 2.3—"Garbage can" model of decisions (plural) making process
in organizations.

However, in messy reality managers are faced with a constant stream of
problems and alternative courses of action (Figure 2.3). We can no longer
think of a "problem" in isolation, but have to consider the many competing
demands for managers' attention (Cohen et al., 1972).

2.3.2   Management approach

Complexity management typically emphasizes the following:

- In an unpredictable and changing environment, a fixed plan for change is no
  longer possible.
- The ideal organizational form is adaptive, decentralized and self-organizing.
  Examples of effective adaptive systems include Linux, the Internet, the
  human immune system and markets.
- Organizational policies and goals are emergent and indeterminate.

Given this emphasis, it is not surprising that many theorists are evolutionists,
who see no role for analytical processes. Drawing largely on evolutionary
systems, the complexity approach emphasizes the importance of encouraging
a diversity of ideas and approaches, more interactions between more people
(so ideas can spread and be discussed more quickly) and autonomous decision
making. The complexity approach is presented as a way of dealing with the
following problems:

- responsiveness/change;
- performance and search;
- intractable (wicked) problems, as described by Churchman (1967) and
  Rittel and Webber (1973).

In this chapter the focus is on the last of these (wicked problems), since this is the
area that is closest to OR concerns.

2.3.3 At the edge of chaos?

How can an organization be structured so that it can respond quickly and flexibly to a changing environment? The ideal is for the organization to be at the "edge of chaos" (see e.g., Brown and Eisenhardt, 1998; Pascale et al., 2000). Like so much in complexity, the concept is based on models of physical systems, particularly the NK models of Stuart Kauffman (Kaufmann, 1995, chap. 4). Kauffman modelled Boolean networks in which N nodes were connected together, each node having K inputs. The value of a given node (0 or 1) depended on the values of the K input nodes. Kauffman found that by varying the values of N and K, a wide range of dynamic behaviour could be observed. If $K = 1$, then the network soon settled down to a single static state. For large K's the network was continually changing in a pattern that was unpredictable and chaotic. However, for $K = 2$ the patterns of dynamic change were cyclic. The system showed "order" at the boundary between chaotic and static behaviour – hence "edge of chaos".

Further work by Kauffman (1995, chap. 10) suggested that there is a tendency for complex adaptive systems to evolve to a state at the edge of chaos. Evolution among a group of species can show two characteristic types of behaviour. One is a stable situation where species have evolutionarily stable strategies (Maynard Smith, 1982). The populations do not evolve, as any new strategy will be less successful than current strategies. This is analogous to a Nash equilibrium in game theory, which occurs when no player can benefit by changing his strategy if the other players keep their strategies unchanged. The other extreme situation is known as the Red Queen effect, in which evolution in one species (e.g., more effective defence against a prey species) triggers an evolutionary change in another (e.g., better hunting capabilities in a predator) which in turn triggers further evolution in the first species. In this situation, there is never any stability. Building on his NK models, Kauffman showed that for co-evolving populations there was a range of behaviours between these two extremes: fitness of populations was highest in the intermediate ("edge-of-chaos") state and ecosystems frequently evolved to this intermediate state.

Evolution to the "edge of chaos" has also been seen in much simpler systems (i.e., sand piles). Per Bak et al. (1988) modelled the behaviour of a sand pile that is being replenished by a constant flow of sand. They found that sand piles adopt a constant shape (slope angle). At this angle, avalanches occur to maintain the overall shape of the pile. These avalanches occur at random intervals and their sizes follow a power law distribution in which there are very many small avalanches, fewer medium-size avalanches and at rare intervals an occasional large avalanche. Similar distributions are found for a number of natural phenomena (e.g., for earthquakes). Bak et al, (1988) described this behaviour as self-organized criticality. Kauffman (1995) draws attention to the similarity between this behaviour and "edge of chaos" phenomena.

The origin of the term "edge of chaos" may be in hard modelling, but the application of the concept to organizations is by way of metaphor. Organizations need to be both dynamic and ordered: too much rigidity and the organization is unable to respond to events quickly enough (and may indeed be unable to respond at all). But if there is no structure or common objective among the people, the organization will fall into anarchy and again be unable to produce a coherent response to change. For this to work, it must be possible for people to be able to hold and express alternative views of the future and how the company should respond.

Intuitively, the concept is attractive. But it is difficult to decide when an organization is at the "edge of chaos" and the term is falling out of favour. Some of the models above suggest that if a system (organization in this case) is pushed out of equilibrium, then it will eventually restructure toward "the edge of chaos". Most large companies are assumed to be too rigid (Lewin and Regine, 1999; Pascale et al., 2000), suggesting there is not enough interaction between people in different units. The NK models imply that greater responsiveness can be attained by increasing the connectivity (interactions) across an organization (so ideas and problems are shared) and by increasing the diversity within the organization. Increased connectivity is often coupled with the need for an organization to be pushed "out of equilibrium" in order for existing links to be weakened and new structures to emerge. In practice, this can be achieved by management imposing a constant pressure for change (as in the example of BP exploration, Section 2.4.4), having "flatter" organizational structures, smaller business units (~ 200 max.), flexible teams (so greater mixing of workers over time) and distributed power. Interestingly, many literature examples are small, professional services organizations.

For example, St Luke's Communications is a highly successful advertising agency founded by Andy Law and David Abraham (Lewin and Regine, 1999). Law and Abraham took over the London branch of a large traditional advertising agency – Chiat/Day – with the aim of creating a company based on shared values of honesty and ethics. The agency is a co-operative: everyone working at St Luke's has an equal share of the company. Starting with 35 people, the co-operative developed the notion of a company with "virtually no hierarchy, no bureaucracy, where everyone could say what they wanted, wear what they wanted, and come in when they wanted" (Lewin and Regine, 1999, p. 97). There are no offices or personal desks, thus encouraging random, casual interactions between people. Furthermore, the more usual linear processing of clients by different departments (the brief is passed from accounts to planning to the creative department and back to accounts again) has been replaced by a "brand room" in which everyone involved in a particular account (including the client) gathers together. The result is a more dynamic environment in which creativity is speeded up. Lewin and Regine describe this as a non-linear process.

This way of working requires everyone to know and trust each other.

As St Luke's grew, this became more problematic; the solution was the "magic number" rule: if a team grows to more than 35 people, it splits. Even with this rule, Lewin and Regine's interviewees noted that unlike the early days it is no longer the case that everyone knows each other. It seems that as organizations get larger the lessons of complexity become more difficult to apply.

2.3.4 Performance and search

In a dynamic and competitive environment, innovation is crucial to maintaining competitiveness. Innovation can cover both the redesign of processes (to improve performance) and the development of new products and services. Traditional approaches to new products and services assume a well-ordered gatekeeper approach (shown in Figure 2.4) in which ideas are assessed at various points and a decision made to continue or abandon that project. The problem with this approach is that it is rarely possible to tell which ideas will truly be successful, since this depends on a context that is changing with time. A number of innovative companies have institutional arrangements that adopt a more flexible, evolutionary approach. Pascale et al. (2000) describe Intel's R&D as a "mad scientists' lab" in which the work organization is messy, overlapping, webbed, redundant. The key challenge was to invent breakthrough chips and halve cycle time. But Intel's R&D community crossed technology, manufacturing and sales – all of whom drive discovery. Instead of the planning cycle typical of many research programmes, individuals take collective and independent action, resulting in activity that is chaotic, uncoordinated and duplicated. On the face of it, this is not an efficient operation. Output was characterized as including half-finished prospects, serendipitous connections, false starts and occasional breakthroughs: Intel's discovery process generated 10 dead ends for every breakthrough. Significantly, there was no orderly funnel to screen ideas, and it was observed that proposals that looked weak at the beginning finished strong and vice versa – a reflection of the difficulty of anticipating success in advance.

A more formal approach that still drew on evolutionary models was that of Capital One (Anderson, 1999). This company targets direct market credit

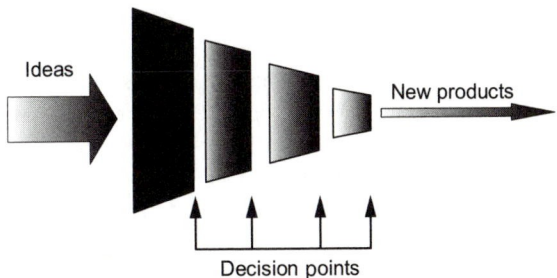

Figure 2.4—Gatekeeper approach to innovation management.

card offers to customers with the aim that 80% of these offers should have been invented in the previous two years. Output has included new lines of business, such as direct marketing of cellular phone services. There was constant testing of offers to identify which were succeeding or failing (99% of tests failed). Thus, the process involved constant generation of new ideas and a selection environment to kill unsuccessful offers. A key metric was the expected or realized lifetime Net Present Value (NPV) of the customer, but the selection environment recognized a trade-off between goals. Selection systems included algorithms to predict returns (particularly, lifetime NPV per $ invested) and the need for "ideas stewards", who had to win support from colleagues. Here we begin to see a mixture of "hard" and "soft" approaches within the complexity framework. The selection environment clearly reflects an evolutionary model for innovation, but the selection process itself is based on both hard (predictive algorithms) methods and more human-centred approaches ("ideas stewards").

2.3.5 Intractable (wicked) problems

Wicked problems are typically those where the problem description is incomplete, ill-defined and ill-structured. Often such problems are systemic in nature, so that no one in the organization has a complete view of the issues. A typical response is to attempt to redesign the system. However, unless a full view of that system has been obtained, the redesign is unlikely to be successful. For this reason the complexity approach is to encourage and enable a solution to emerge from all those involved.

A characteristic feature of a systemic problem (and a working definition) is that everyone knows there is a problem, but no single person or unit can solve it. Formally, a systemic problem is one where the formal processes within an organization, the roles and responsibilities of units, and the incentives and expectations of individuals all interact within a single system to give rise to undesired outcomes. Systems theory suggests that specific events or outcomes are the result of the underlying behaviours of people and processes, which are themselves the product of the way in which the system is structured (see Figure 2.5).

But changing a system structure is both difficult and time-consuming. Often, the problem is one of co-ordinating changes across the system (Jaikumar, 1986; Parthasarthy and Sethi, 1993; Senge, 1990; Wolstenholme, 2002). The structure of the system has built up over many years, reflecting the history of the organization. During its development the system will have gained a set of characteristics that tend to reinforce each other. Feedback loops and other characteristics of the system will mean that the effect of a change in behaviour (or even a change in part of the structure) may be neutralized. The unaltered parts of the system will simply adjust to accommodate the changes, and the

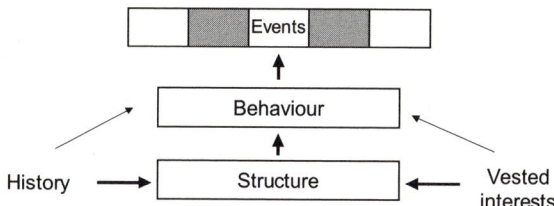

Figure 2.5—Specific events are the results of system behaviour, which in turn reflects the system structure.

overall behaviour is unchanged. In a human system, as Machiavelli pointed out, change is likely to be opposed by those who benefit from current arrangements, while support from potential gainers is rarely more than lukewarm.

Managers tend to focus on parts of a system, because this is all they have a view of and because of a prevailing reductionist viewpoint that assumes a complex system can be broken down into a number of smaller units which can be managed independently. Implicit in this is the assumption that by maximizing local performance, a global optimum in performance can be obtained. In fact, such an assumption is only true if the component units are independent entities. But if performance of one unit is determined in part by what other units do, then the assumption breaks down. An improvement in one area may be achieved at the expense of another area (e.g., by "shifting the burden"). For example, hospitals may seek to reduce costs by closing geriatric wards. But this means more people are having to be cared for in the community (shifting the problem to social services): the overall cost to the public purse may not be decreased. If social services do not have enough capacity, then elderly people may still have to occupy hospital beds. In complex systems, local optimization does not necessarily lead to global optimization. (For similar examples see, e.g., Wolstenholme, 1990.)

Recent government proposals to solve this problem by allowing hospitals to charge social services for occupied beds are a classic example of trying to solve a systemic problem by focusing on events. In fact, the situation is very complex and involves factors outside the control of either social services or the health authorities. For example, Wolstenholme (2002) gives a good description of the systemic factors affecting patient waiting times and the failure of various well-intentioned initiatives to solve the problem.

The conclusion, then, is that the solution to a systemic problem must involve looking at the impact of changes on as much of the system as possible. Partial solutions are likely to be ineffective and may even make things worse. Furthermore, changes throughout the system must be co-ordinated – it is not sufficient for individual units to change without understanding the impact such changes will make on other parts of the system.

2.4　Working with systemic problems

2.4.1　So why can't I solve a systemic problem?

With this introduction to complex systems and systemic problems we can begin to look at the barriers to solving systemic problems.

Lack of incentives. There is no point in trying to change a system unless there is some benefit to me. Incentives may be formal or informal. Formal incentives are often based on individual targets and encourage some local optimum outcome. However, as we have seen above, local optimization will not necessarily lead to the optimum global outcome. If the best overall outcome requires me to miss my local target, then there is a strong incentive for me to resist change. There can also be a lack of informal incentives; these are closely related to expectations of both individuals and those around them.

Limited resources. As will become apparent, solving systemic problems requires patience, persistence and a lot of effort. But managers are very busy dealing with urgent operational matters – it is difficult for them to give time and attention to longer term strategic issues, especially if the payback is uncertain and sometime in the future. Furthermore, getting to a solution may require financial investment, people and knowledge the manager does not possess (certainly, knowledge of other parts of the system).

Limited levers to change. Regardless of their position in the organization, all managers in practice have only a limited number of levers they can change. A CEO will set overall strategic direction and can influence divisional targets, but will have little direct control over day-to-day operations. An operational manager may have the ability to improve the local efficiency of his own area of responsibility, but have little say in how his targets are set, or how internal management systems are designed. Because systemic problems involve many parts of the organization, and at many different levels, there is no one who can single-handedly change it.

Limited power/authority. This is a consequence of the two factors above. The most senior managers in the organization may in principle have the authority to force through a systemic change, but they will have neither the time nor the detailed knowledge necessary to ensure such change is effective. In contrast, managers at lower levels in the organization may collectively have the necessary knowledge, but will not have the authority to impose changes in other units or at higher levels.

Uncertain outcomes. This is where we started: I may try to improve things locally, but because I cannot alter other parts of the system I cannot be sure that my changes will lead to the desired outcome. They may even have a negative effect on either my own performance or that of others.

2.4.2 Why can't others solve a systemic problem?

If I can't change things, then it is natural to assume someone else must be able to. But, in practice, others are faced with the same limitations as myself. No one "owns" the system. In fact, most organizational systems have emerged over many years. Thus, there is no proper plan or map, but the system will have developed a number of features that are self-supporting. This has the virtue of not only making the organizational "system" resilient to internal and external shocks but also makes it very resistant to change. As we have seen above, the levers of control that can be exercised by any individual manager are severely limited, and for the most senior managers the levers may well be limited to creating appropriate incentives (setting targets).

2.4.3 So what can we do?

Clearly, change is difficult. It requires understanding and agreement from a large number of different people; it may require investment in new processes and systems and may also need changes in attitudes and relationships between individuals. Such change will only occur slowly and if there is constant pressure for change. In complexity terms this is equivalent to pushing the system "out of equilibrium". There are two approaches to system change. One is a well-defined, planned approach. This involves analysis of the current system, identification of problem areas and design of a new system. Such an approach is well suited to and probably essential for the change of technical systems and processes (IT, computing, manufacturing, financial, etc.).

However, such systems are part of a wider system involving people. Changing a system involving people is more difficult, since it has to take into account the aspirations, expectations and incentives of individuals and to be effective requires their commitment. For human systems the planned approach is much more problematical, often appearing as a heavy-handed imposition "from on high" and can often seem to take little account of workplace realities. In this case an emergent approach may be better, in which senior managers (and/or external factors) impose a steady pressure for change, but let the new system "emerge" through the interactions of individuals.

So how does this work in practice? The first thing to note is that, as discussed above, it is essential for all to recognize that there is a problem and that it is a joint problem, which must be solved jointly. It cannot be solved by an individual, nor can it be solved by individuals working independently. Above all else, finding a solution will require constant discussion. People's attitudes are crucial. At the very least, they need to identify common objectives or a common vision of what is to be achieved. They may also need to agree on the exact nature of the problem, for initially each will only have a partial view. As is recognized in compendia such as Rosenhead and Mingers (2001), soft OR methods used for problem structuring can help to support this negotiation.

All involved need to be committed to change. This should follow on from the development of a common view of the problem. However, as well as recognizing a need for change in general, there must also be a willingness on the part of individuals to change attitudes and the way they work.

All involved need to have the authority to act and the appropriate levers. This is likely to mean that change starts at the top, since so much of the behaviour of the company is driven by its organizational structure and the incentives placed on the heads of the major divisions. These are things that can only be changed by senior managers. A change from individual targets to a joint target related to the key performance indicators (KPIs) of the company as a whole will immediately force divisional managers to look at how they work together. Similarly, an organizational structure that minimizes the interactions between different divisions (perhaps based on a Viable Systems approach) will make individual targets more meaningful.

There is a tendency for such work to be delegated, because it is time-consuming, and there are always more urgent operational tasks demanding attention. However, there is no point in delegating responsibility for ideas, unless the authority or power to implement them is also delegated. At the most senior level, managers need to develop a vision of what they want to achieve and develop a set of incentives, which is consistent with the desired behaviour and which encourages managers lower in the organization to introduce further appropriate change.

2.4.4 The example of BP exploration: a complexity approach?

The complexity literature contains a number of examples of successful companies that have introduced change in accordance with complexity principles. An excellent example is the turnaround of BP Exploration (BPX) by John Browne (Pascale et al., 2000, chap. 6). This is discussed in detail, since it describes a successful approach to a "wicked problem". The analysis draws on both systems and complexity theory. The discussion illustrates how complexity concepts can be used to describe strategic change. But it is recognized that this is only one way of interpreting events.

BPX was in trouble: business was declining and the market becoming more competitive. Part of the solution was to downsize – a normal management decision. However, the most important task was "to inject new energy into the lacklustre BPX team and motivate rival geographic regions to co-operate. This could not be accomplished by edict" (Pascale et al., 2000).

The kick-off event   At a kick-off event for BPX's top 100 managers, the strategic position of BPX was reviewed and the downsizing of 1,400 professionals (10%) announced. However, Browne then spoke, highlighting the need for the organization to change and become much more nimble. This was essential, but something he could not achieve without the help of all in the room: "I need your help. We've got to figure out how to do this together."

Participants were then divided into teams to carry out an organizational audit using a standard framework – Seven S (these are the key levers that make an organization tick: hard – Strategy, Structure, Systems; soft – Style, Staff, Shared values and Skills). Each team was given one S and had to describe how it was manifested formally and informally in BPX. A second stage looked at how this picture of BPX mapped on to what was required for success in the future. It became apparent that more time was required, and the end of meeting was postponed in order to complete the discussions. This both signalled the importance placed on this work and reflected the fact that solving difficult problems cannot always be achieved according to a fixed timetable. When teams reported at the end of the evening, it was clear that organizational habits and protocol were preventing change: "The way this place works makes it impossible to succeed. Short of a thoroughgoing reinvention of ourselves, we're stuck."

The second workshop – six weeks later   To maintain momentum, Browne and his top eight managers identified "Nine Big Problems" and within six weeks announced that 120 managers would meet to develop a "journey map for addressing these problems". Suggestions that a small "task force" could do the job were rejected by Browne: "This work *is* the essential work of the business." By the time of the meeting, the 120 had been divided into teams, chosen to reflect political and substantive hurdles to be overcome, each looking at each one of the "Nine Big Problems". The meeting took three days: "by the second day, deep-seated philosophical differences and mistrust between co-workers could no longer be politely sidestepped." On the third day, teams started to converge on a plan.

The green papers – 90 days later   Each team was then charged with developing the plans and producing a "green paper", summarizing findings and recommendations. When managers complained they did not have time to do their jobs, Browne responded "perhaps solving these kinds of problems *is* the job of senior managers. Maybe we should be delegating more of the routine stuff to develop the ranks below." Managers lower in the organization found their input was being sought more, and more was being delegated to them.

The Phoenix meeting – six weeks later   The final event (at Phoenix) gave each team a four-hour slot, of which only 15 minutes was for presentation of findings and recommendations; the remainder was for discussion. The event was intense and lasted several days, with sessions going on to 10 p.m. "Browne and his top team stayed up to 1 or 2 a.m. deliberating on what had been proposed, reaching resolution, and committing resources" (Pascale et al., 2000). The approach generated fresh solutions and commitment to execute them. The momentum was sufficient to reverse BPX's fortunes in oil exploration.

There are a number of lessons to be learned from this story, but it does illustrate some of the points made above:

- First, it required recognition by Browne that the problems faced by BPX could not be solved by management edict.
- Second, it required consistent pressure from Browne and his top team to maintain momentum. Targets and deadlines were set, but these focused on the activities of senior managers rather than on the more usual measures of output. In effect, the deadlines created the incentives for senior managers to work together and to commit the time necessary to do the job.
- Third, it took time to develop an effective plan. Despite the pressure and intensity of the project, it took six months from the kick-off meeting to the final planning event in Phoenix.
- Fourth, the solution required the active involvement of the most senior managers; they were unable to delegate this work to a task force, forcing them to consult their reports and delegate more routine work.
- Finally, finding solutions required senior managers from different parts of the company to work together, both to identify the key issues and develop plans for change.

This example illustrates one approach to dealing with a wicked problem. Much of the discussion above draws on traditional systems theory. Complexity theory draws attention to the way Browne's pressure for change shifted the company out of an equilibrium state, toward a more chaotic state where new modes of working could be adopted. Complexity would also emphasize how the setting up of small, cross-divisional teams to work on specific issues, coupled with frequent workshops, helped to generate new connections or relationships between people in the organization. The series of workshops bringing together all the top managers (i.e., all those with major influence on the issues) is reminiscent of the "non-linear" style of working in the brand rooms of St Luke's, described in Section 2.3.3. Thus, the experience of BPX can be described in complexity terms, but the same events can be described in other ways.

2.5 The simulation of complexity

Although the above discussion on "wicked problems" concentrated on interactions between managers, the approach also reflected one model for these problems (based on systems theory). Implicit in the BP example was a high level of analysis underpinning the discussions. In this section the role of models (both quantitative and qualitative) is considered and, in particular, the use of models derived from complexity studies.

The classical view of management sees the manager as a "controller" and management as an act of rational control. In line with a scientific approach that distinguishes clearly between the observer and the observed, the manager is seen as separate from the processes managed. The emphasis is very much on rational decision making and is consistent with a "hard" approach to modelling. This approach has been heavily criticized in recent years (see, e.g., Mintzberg, 1994; Stacey, 2001), reflecting in part the fact that in human interactions it is impossible to be an impartial observer.

The view of the manager from a complexity viewpoint draws more heavily on the human relations school. The manager is seen as a coach or steward with a role as a market maker, rather than a controller. As discussed above, the objective is to keep the firm in the "sweet spot" between chaos and rigidity – a zone of creative adaptability. Two important mechanisms for doing this are:

- to encourage diversity of thought (so the firm has a wider range of ideas and views to consider);
- to facilitate the creation of more connections between people (so that ideas can be promulgated, discussed, combined and criticized).

This has implications for the way organizational knowledge and learning are handled. Whereas approaches based on division of labour often result in the deskilling of people, with key knowledge embedded in the process, the need for constant innovation requires exploitation of the knowledge and skills of all workers. Much of this is tacit – embodied in flows and interactions. Thus, a manager needs to make (or facilitate the making of) this tacit knowledge explicit. Once made explicit (and therefore explicable to others) it is possible to aggregate and recombine explicit knowledge into emergent models. Here we begin to see one of the roles of models – both qualitative and quantitative – as a means of making certain forms of tacit knowledge explicit. Thus model building and organizational learning are closely linked (Senge, 1990). In this context the development and use of multiple models is a useful means of creating diversity and conveying ideas.

Although many models adopt a relatively static view of the world (consistent with a determinist, positivist view of the world), complex systems models highlight the dynamics of change. It is assumed that organizations and industries are complex systems characterized (typically) by high numbers of component entities and a high degree of interconnection (and, hence, interaction). In this context, the outcome of any change to the system (such as an investment decision or policy change) cannot always be predicted. To some extent this reflects the cognitive limits of human beings; humans find it difficult to understand the behaviour arising from mutually interacting entities. As de Guess (1988) notes, "most people can deal with only three or four variables at a time, and do so through only one or two time iterations". Similarly, Larichev and Moskovitch (1985) suggest that "decision makers completely apprehend only those decision problems in which a maximum 5–8 structural units interact in the knowledge representation."

Holland (1995) characterizes complex adaptive systems as a network of agents in which control is highly dispersed; there is both competition and co-operation between agents. There are many levels of organization: the system constantly revises and rearranges building blocks with experience. Agents anticipate the future using various internal models. And, typically, there are many niches within the system, each of which can be exploited by an agent. These characteristics can also be applied to the commercial environment. Intuitively, therefore, the study of complex adaptive systems and the concept of complexity are readily applicable to strategic decision making within companies. If the economy is a complex adaptive system (Anderson et al., 1987) a proper understanding of complexity theory should provide a better basis on which to build strategic models. To some extent this is true, in that models built to study complex systems often require fewer abstractions. However, the advantage of a model is that it is a simplification of reality that enables people to understand key aspects of a situation. There is a danger that a more realistic model is, in fact, too complex, so that it is no longer possible to understand the output or to decide how to act. Simple models, based on an equilibrium system, may be preferred because of the illusion of prediction and certainty they give the user.

The focus on individual agents immediately suggests agent-based modelling as an appropriate method to study complex systems (see, e.g., Epstein and Axtell, 1996; Holland, 1998). This technique involves creating a population of discrete entities, or "agents", each representing an individual member of a population (e.g., of consumers, traders, companies, etc.). Each of the agents can interact with other agents or the environment in which the population exists, according to rules that embody a set of goals, beliefs and actions. Agent-based modelling enables the problem to be addressed using a bottom-up approach. The goals, beliefs, actions and interactions (rules) are microscopic attributes of the agents. The overall, macroscopic, behaviour of the system appears as a result of the combined effect of all the microscopic attributes and the complex interactions between them.

Clearly, the outcome of the model depends crucially on the "rules' followed by individual agents and the way these agents interact. Thus, recent work on product diffusion (Collings, 2001; Collings et al., 2000) involved adopting a specific learning model (Rogers, 1995) for agents and a model of the social interactions between agents (Watts and Strogatz, 1998). As Lyons et al. (2002) point out, the identification of appropriate cognitive and learning models is a key part of the modelling process; the choice of learning model

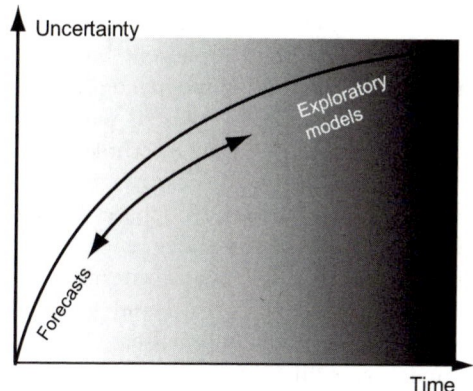

Figure 2.6—Forecasting models versus exploratory models.

could radically alter the results of the model. Rather than a predictive tool, the models can be seen as a means of testing alternative hypotheses.

There is still the question of what information can be derived from a model or simulation. As we saw above, one school of thought is essentially negative – models are confined to the role of theory development or for challenging existing formulations. A more positive view is that "Models allow us to broaden our viewpoint beyond our fixed notions, based on current reality, of what can transpire. These scenarios help expand our linear expectations to include all the possible futures we may encounter" (Farrell, 1998, p. 85). Both viewpoints reflect the idea that, except over the very short term, models allow one to explore the outcomes of alternative strategic choices, rather than providing a forecast of a predetermined future (Figure 2.6).

Thus, the type of knowledge coming out of complex systems models is itself "complex" (or at least complicated!) – not single-valued answers (this is what you should do), but rather a statement of options that place limits on the extent to which control can be exercised. This pushes much of the decision making back to higher cognitive levels (Humphreys, 1986; Lyons, 1999), where objectives and values dominate. In reality, of course, decisions have always been made on the basis of the decision makers' values. Schrage (2000) points out that the types of models produced by an organization reflect the values and perceptions within the organization.

In general terms, models (Schrage, 2000):

- act as tools for negotiation;
- create/unearth choice;
- define a context for trade-offs.

In this list we see a clear departure from the idea of a single objective model that predicts an optimal strategy. This reflects a general characteristic of social systems. Such systems are undoubtedly complex and adaptive, but unlike the physical sciences there is no complex, coherent body of theory to describe them. Instead, a number of different and independent theories coexist. Models of social systems – often conceptual – represent tentative theories providing one view of an issue. Such models are rarely interlinked and are not necessarily mutually incompatible. For example, consider the different schools of thought in politics, sociology, psychology as well as debates between neoclassical and other types of economists. As discussed above, even complexity theory when applied to management is just one way of interpreting events. For social systems, the postmodernist view that truth and knowledge are subjective, social constructs seems to make much more sense.

Thus, different models give different views of a problem and reflect choices made earlier in a decision process. There is no single model that will incorporate all aspects of a strategic problem. This implies that there could be advantages in developing multiple models of a particular decision to reflect different viewpoints. This is Schrage's (2000) view: "... the companies that want to see the most models in the least time are the most design-sensitive; the companies that want ... one perfect model are the least design-sensitive." In fact, in a population, different agents will have different models (rule sets) to guide them. This in itself can give rise to interesting interactions. Some work (e.g., Arthur, 1994) has shown how a near-optimal solution is obtained by the interplay of different (evolving) decision-making models within a population. Arthur envisaged a population of 100 agents who wish to attend a bar with a capacity of 60. If more than 60 agents turned up on any night, the place became too crowded and agents would not enjoy the experience. Individual agents were given rules to decide whether or not to go to the bar on a particular night, chosen at random. If the rule did not work (i.e., did not predict an uncrowded bar), then it could be changed for another rule. Surprisingly, numbers attending the bar each night quickly settled to the ideal of ~ 60. But, in this context no single rule (model) can be considered right or wrong; the outcome is an emergent property of the population.

2.6 Conclusion: complementarity intrinsic to complexity?

Looking at the way ideas about complex adaptive systems have developed has provided an insight into the relationship between "hard" models and "softer" approaches. The study of non-equilibrium physical and chemical systems led to the development of the concept of CASs. These systems are characterized by high numbers of component entities and a high degree of interconnection (and, hence, interaction). This means that the outcome of any change to the system cannot be readily predicted.

Techniques to model CASs grew out of a "hard", positivist view of the world, but the concepts have been extended to include social systems, such as economies and organizations. In the process the notion of "complexity" has developed. Complexity is in part a reflection of cognitive limitations on the part of human beings. When applied to social systems the discussion often takes the form of metaphor and analogy. "Complexity" thus encompasses both "hard" and "soft" views.

Complexity theory provides a useful way of interpreting and guiding management, particularly the management of change in a dynamic environment. However, complexity is just one management model; other descriptions can also be used. Thus, although both the setting up and structuring of St Luke's (see Section 2.3.3) was interpreted in terms of complexity concepts by Lewin and Regine (1999), for the founders Aristotelian ethics was the dominant model.

In practice, complexity management is often driven by an individual, frequently the CEO, who rejects command and control and uses complexity science as both a description and a justification of their management approach. Complexity thus provides a vocabulary, often derived from "hard" physical sciences. We have seen that complexity has implications for:

- organizational structure;
- decision making;
- management approach.

Often, as seen with St Luke's, complexity management is coupled to ethics or values – the need to encourage a diversity and autonomous action implies a respect for other people (and their ideas) and a high level of trust. There is strong emphasis on relationships, with co-ordination in a company being driven by a common vision rather than common procedures.

There are a number of issues relating to complexity as a management concept. As a discipline, complexity is very wide-ranging and ill-defined. To claim that complementarity between "hard" and "soft" approaches is intrinsic to complexity would involve imposing a definition that not all could agree to. Indeed, the role of quantitative models (if any) is still a debatable point in the complexity community. In many contexts, complexity appears to be more akin to a philosophical approach, providing underlying principles for managing uncertainty. But is it distinctive? The practice of complexity management seems to resemble much from the human relations school of management. Yet, by also drawing on models derived from physical sciences, it could claim to be a synthesis of human relations and scientific management. The relationship between scientific understanding of complex adaptive systems and the application of this understanding to humans, institutions, management and policy is still being worked out.

The interplay between "hard" and "soft" models and complexity is not straightforward. Many of the ideas underpinning the complexity metaphor are derived from "hard" models of physical systems. But complexity also has implications for the way models are used to support strategy and decision making. The emphasis on unpredictability and the limited control possible in complex systems means that there is an intrinsic recognition that, except in limited circumstances, the predictive capability of any model whether "hard" or "soft" is limited. Models are better seen as tools for uncovering assumptions and exploring the implications of alternative actions.

References

Anderson P. (1999) Seven levers for guiding the evolving enterprise. In J.H. Clippinger III (ed.) *The Biology of Business*, pp. 145–52. Jossey-Bass, San Francisco.

Anderson P.W., Arrow K.J. and Pines D. (1987) *The Economy as an Evolving Complex System*, Santa Fe Institute Studies in the Sciences of Complexity Vol. 5. Addison-Wesley, Reading, MA.

Arthur W.B. (1994) Inductive reasoning and bounded rationality (the El Farol problem). *American Economic Review* (Papers and Proceedings), **84**, 406, available at http://www.santafe.edu/arthur/Papers/Pdf.files/ElFarol.pdf

Bak P., Tang C. and Wiesenfeld K. (1988) Self-organized criticality. *Physics Review A*, **38**(1), 364–74.

Brown S.L. and Eisenhardt K.M. (1998) *Competing on the Edge*. Harvard Business School, Boston.

Churchman C. (1967) Wicked problems. *Management Science*, **4**(14), B141–2.

Cohen M.D., March J.G. and Olsen J.P. (1972) A garbage can model of organizational choice. *Administrative Science Quarterly*, **17**(1), 1–25.

Collings D. (2001) Individual based customer modelling. Presented at *International Conference on Forecasting in Communications (ICFC2001)*.

Collings D., Reeder A.A., Adjali M.I., Crocker P. and Lyons M.H. (2000) Agent based customer modelling: Individuals who learn from their environment. Presented at *Proceedings of Congress on Evolutionary Computation 2000 (CEC2000, San Diego, CA, July 2000)*, pp. 1492–7, ISBN 0-7803-6375-2.

de Guess A. (1988) Planning as learning. *Harvard Business Review*, March–April, 74.

Eden C.L. and Ackermann F. (1998) *Strategy Making: The Journey of Strategic Management*. Sage Publications, London.

Eden C. and van der Heijden K. (1995) Detecting emergent strategy. In H. Thomas, D. O'Neal and J. Kelly (eds) *Strategic Renaissance and Business Transformation*. John Wiley & Sons, New York.

Epstein J.M. and Axtell R. (1996) *Growing Artificial Societies*. Brookings Institution Press, Washington, DC.

Farrell W. (1998) *How Hits Happen*, p. 85. Harper Business, London.

Holland J.H. (1995) *Hidden Order: How Adaptation Builds Complexity*. Addison-Wesley, Reading, MA.

Holland J.H. (1998) *Emergence: From Chaos to Order*. Oxford University Press, Oxford, UK.

Humphreys P.C. (1986) Intelligence in decision support. In B. Brehmer, H. Jungermann, P. Lourens and G. Sevón (eds) *New Directions in Research on Decision Making*. North Holland, Amsterdam.

Jaikumar R. (1986) Postindustrial manufacturing. *Harvard Business Review*, 69–76.

Kauffman S. (1995) *At Home in the Universe*. Oxford University Press, New York.

Krackhardt D. (2001) Viscosity models and the diffusion of controversial innovation. In A. Lomi and E.R. Larsen (eds) *Dynamics of Organizations*. MIT Press, Cambridge, MA.

Larichev O.I. and Moskovitch H. (1985) *Limits to Human Decision Makers' Effectiveness*, Preprint. VNIISI, Moscow. Quoted in P.C. Humphreys (1986) Intelligence in decision support. In B. Brehmer, H. Jungermann, P. Lourens and G. Sevón (eds) *New Directions in Research on Decision Making*. North Holland, Amsterdam.

Lewin R. and Regine B. (1999) *The Soul at Work: Unleashing the Power of Complexity Theory for Business Success*. Texere, London.

Lyons M.H. (1999) Computer models in a complex commercial environment. Presented at *EIASM 2nd Workshop on Complexity, 25–26 June 1999, Brussels*.

Lyons M.H. (2001) Knowledge and the modelling of complex systems. Presented at *NexSus Workshop 'Living with the Limits to Knowledge', 22–23 June 2002*.

Lyons M.H., Adjali M.I., Collings D. and Jensen K. (2002) Complex systems models for strategic decision-making. In G. Frizelle and H. Richards (eds) *Tackling Industrial Complexity; The Ideas that Make a Difference*, Proceedings of 2002 Conference of Manufacturing Complexity Network, pp. 1–25. Institute of Manufacturing, Cambridge, UK.

Maynard Smith J. (1982) *Evolution and the Theory of Games*. Cambridge University Press, Cambridge, UK.

Mintzberg H. (1994) *The Rise and Fall of Strategic Planning*. The Free Press, New York.

Parthasarthy R. and Sethi S.P. (1993) Relating strategy and structure to flexible automation: A test of fit and performance implications. *Strategic Management Journal*, **14**, 529–49.

Pascale R.T., Millemann M. and Gioja L. (2000) *Surfing on the Edge of Chaos*. Texere, London.

Rittel H.W.J. and Webber M.M. (1973) Dilemmas in a general theory of planning. *Policy Science*, **4**, 155–69.

Rogers E.M. (1995) *Diffusion of Innovations*. The Free Press, New York.

Rosenhead J. (1998) Complexity theory and management practice, available at http://www.human-nature.com/science-as-culture/rosenhead.html

Rosenhead J.V. and Mingers J. (2001) *Rational Analysis for a Problematic World Revisited: Problem Structuring Methods for Complexity, Uncertainty and Conflict*, 2nd edn. John Wiley & Sons, Chichester, UK.

Schrage, M. (2000) *Serious Play*. Harvard Business School Press, Boston.

Senge P. (1990) *The Fifth Discipline: The Art and Practice of the Learning Organization*. Currency/Doubleday, New York.

Stacey R.D. (2001) *Complex Responsive Processes in Organizations: Learning and Knowledge Creation (complexity and emergence in organizations)*. Routledge, London.

Watts D.J. and Strogatz S.H. (1998) Collective dynamics of "small-world" networks. *Nature*, **393**, 440–2.

Wolstenholme E.F. (1990) *Systems Enquiry: A System Dynamics Approach*. John Wiley & Sons, Chichester, UK.

Wolstenholme E.F. (2002) *Patient Flow, Waiting and Managerial Learning – A Systems Thinking Mapping Approach*, Working paper. Cognitus, Harrogate, UK, available at http://www.cognitus.co.uk/healthcare.html

Van der Heijden K. (1996) *The Art of Strategic Conversation*. John Wiley & Sons, Chichester, UK.

3 "Classic" OR and "soft" OR – an asymmetric complementarity

Peter Checkland* and Sue Holwell†
* Lancaster University and † The Open University

3.1 Introduction

About 30 years ago the inside front cover of each issue of the *Journal of the Operational Research Society (JORS)* carried a definition of OR (Operational Research). Its focus was on the use of "the methods of science" to deal with "the direction and management" of "large systems" of "men [*sic*], machines, materials and money". Its distinctive approach lay in developing "a scientific model of the system" in order to "help management determine its policy and actions". This definition was wisely abandoned after a few years, but it provides a useful summary of what would now be thought of as the "hard" systems thinking of the 1960s: the assumption that there are "systems" out there in the world which the logic-based methods of science can "engineer" to achieve their defined objectives. The word "science" is used in each of the three sentences in the *JORS* definition, and the definition itself would apply equally well to other approaches developed in parallel with classic OR: Bell Telephone's "Systems Engineering" (Hall, 1962) and RAND Corporation "Systems Analysis" (Hitch, 1955).

Had this narrow definition of OR not been dropped, it would certainly be necessary to drop it now, when the phrase "soft OR" – as something complementary to the "hard" thinking of classic OR – is now in good currency, especially in Europe. (In America the hold on academe of the philosophical and sociological assumptions taken as given in the narrow definition is much stronger, and soft OR is emerging more slowly there.)

However, the fact that "soft OR" has become a meaningful phrase does not mean that there is agreement on exactly what it means, even though there is now broad agreement that such approaches as Soft Systems Methodology (SSM) and Strategic Options Development and Analysis (SODA) (both described by their originators in Rosenhead and Mingers, 2001) are examples of soft OR. The difference between "hard" and "soft" (systems) thinking is frequently dealt with in the following way: it is stated that the "hard" variety, as in classic OR, Systems Engineering and RAND Systems Analysis, is appropriate in well-defined problem situations in which well-defined objectives are accepted, and the live issues concern how best to engineer a system to meet them – such as: How can we maximize the output from this ammonia plant? On the other hand, "soft" approaches are said to be appropriate in messy problem situations, characterized by obscure objectives and multiple clashing viewpoints. This is not untrue, but its outline of the application area of hard and soft approaches tells us nothing about the difference between them and how they relate to each other. To spell that out is the purpose here; the intention is to define the hard/soft distinction precisely and to indicate the inevitable relation between the two kinds of thinking which follows from their definition. In order to achieve that, the origination of the methodology of classic OR will be considered, then the emergence of the "soft" outlook in the development of SSM which was its source; the final sections will cover the distinction between the two very different but related ways of thinking and the relationship between them.

3.2   Classic OR methodology

During the First World War scientific thinking seems to have had little or no impact on the military mind. At the Battle of the Somme which opened on 1 July 1916, the British offensive was preceded by what was then the biggest bombardment in the history of warfare. The German defences were pounded for a week before the battle started, and in the last hour before the British troops went forward a quarter of a million shells were fired – the guns being heard in London (Gilbert, 1994, p. 258). The British High Command simply made the assumption that the bombardment would leave no one alive in the enemy trenches. Now, any vestige of thinking scientifically would lead to an obligation to check that the assumption was correct before sending the foot soldiers forward. To be fair to General Douglas Haig, commanding the British troops, with whom historians have dealt harshly, he had made tentative suggestions that patrols should be sent out first to check the success of the bombardment, but he was overruled by his superiors. The troops were told to walk slowly across no-man's-land, something in which they had no choice, since they were each carrying 66 pounds of equipment (Liddell Hart, 1934, 1997, pp. 239, 240). The Germans emerged from their deep dugouts, manned their machine guns and fired into the close-packed waves of men approaching them. The British lost more than 20,000 men on the first day of the battle, the highest loss in a single day during the Great War.

Over 20 years later in the Second World War, scientific thinking had become an important part of the armoury of war. Indeed, a good case can be made that the war was won by the Allies as a result of their superior science (see, e.g., Buderi, 1998; Checkland and Holwell, 1998a; Hinsley and Stripp, 1993; Jones, 1978, ch. 5). During the early 1940s it became the norm for scientists to be attached to military operational groups, bringing a scientific perspective to the planning and analysis of military operations. The phrase "operational research" emerged.

In 1943 the physicist P.M.S. Blackett, one of the scientists from whose wartime work the new discipline of OR emerged, wrote a report (included in Blackett, 1962, pp. 176–98) which describes experiences in the Royal Air Force: "A Note on Certain Aspects of the Methodology of Operational Research." In it is a revealing passage that constitutes the single most important early statement about the core ideas at the centre of OR:

> *Predictions about the future are of course always subject to much uncertainty, but experience has shown that many more useful quantitative predictions can be made than is often thought possible. This arises to a considerable extent from the relative stability over quite long periods of time of many factors involved in operations. This stability appears rather unexpected in view of the large number of chance events and individual personalities and abilities that are involved in even a small operation. But these differences in general average out for a large number of operations, and the aggregate results are often found to remain comparatively constant* (Blackett, 1962, p. 178).

Worth noting here is Blackett's surprise that although any one instance of an operation may be dominated – since human beings are involved – by "chance events" and "individual personalities and abilities", nevertheless, if an operation is carried out repeatedly, then the results of analysis remain "comparatively constant". Fundamentally, Blackett is recognizing with surprise that the logic of a situation which is repeated time and again survives the individual quirks of its execution from instance to instance. Hence, such a situation can be analysed scientifically and will yield results that can be expressed statistically. This discovery of the logic of situations which recur is the crucial step in the creation of OR.

In the military context in which it was developed there were many examples of operational "situations which recur" and hence were susceptible to scientific analysis – for example: Coastal Command aircraft searched daily in the North Atlantic for German U-boats, which had to spend four hours out of every twenty-four on the surface recharging their batteries; during the Battle of Britain there was a continual need for the data from radar screens to be transformed into information about the height, direction and speed of incoming enemy bombers so that the necessary flight paths of defending fighter planes could be worked out. This feature of OR's original context was extremely influential when effort was made to transfer what had been learnt in wartime to post-war work in civilian organizations. "Problem situations which recur" were duly recognized in industrial companies and other organizations; thus we find Wild (1972, p. 65) suggesting that ". . . although problems tend to differ in practice this difference often derives from their content details rather than from their form."

He goes on to say that there is general recognition of the following problem forms:

- allocation problems;
- inventory problems;
- replacement problems;
- queuing (or waiting line) problems;
- sequencing and routing problems;
- search problems (concerned with location);
- competitive or bidding problems.

Ignoring for the moment the fact that most managers would argue that most of their time and energy is focused on the "content details" that make their current problem situation unique, rather than the form that may make it general, it is clear that the management scientist, the operational researcher, will be very interested in the logic of the form of the situation, since this logic will enable algorithms for a given problem form to be developed. This is what has happened, and it leads to the myriad OR textbooks that devote successive chapters to the applied maths of queueing theory, depot location, equipment replacement, etc. Classic OR is the useful fruit of Blackett's recognition that there is situational logic even in situations that contain motley collections of human beings.

Two further characteristics of classic OR are relevant to the present discussion. The first is revealed both in the OR Society's now-abandoned definition of the subject and in the first-ever textbook of OR, written by Churchman, Ackoff and Arnoff, published in 1957. The definition assumed that OR would be applied to "large systems" and that the distinctive approach was to develop "a scientific model of the system". The textbook declares that:

> *The comprehensiveness of OR's aim is an example of a "systems" approach, since "system" implies an interconnected complex of functionally related components* (p. 7) *and OR is concerned with as much of the whole system as it can encompass.* ... (p. 8).

Later, Churchman et al. state that: "Management, men, machines and materials constitute a system ... by virtue of organization" (p. 110) and their text may well be the source of the now-unfortunate "4m's" phrase used in the Society's definition. Whether or not that is so, these uses of the word "system" are of prime importance both in understanding the hard/soft distinction in systems thinking and in understanding how difficult it is for many people to get beyond the linguistic habit illustrated in these quotations. This issue will be returned to later in this chapter.

The final characteristic of classic OR which is relevant here is, more accurately, a characteristic of its literature: that it has concentrated mainly on substantive material to do with the algorithms, modelling techniques and the like and has markedly neglected the process of intervening in real situations using OR. The huge literature on OR techniques is hardly balanced by the handful of lonely volumes that focus on process: the short book by Boothroyd (1978) and the collections edited by Tomlinson and Kiss (1984) and Keys (1995). It is important to note this, since the process thinking within the "soft" perspective complements the focus on technique in the "hard" tradition, as will be shown here.

3.3 Soft systems methodology

In the late 1960s the statistician Professor Gwilym Jenkins was invited to establish a postgraduate Department of Systems Engineering at the then new university at Lancaster. Although the initial appointments in the Department brought in chemical engineering and control engineering expertise, Jenkins' vision for the Department was always a broad one. He interpreted the word "engineering" in the broad sense that you can engineer a meeting with someone, or engineer the release of hostages. In line with this thinking Checkland was recruited from industry to initiate research that addressed the question: "Can the approach of Systems Engineering, recently established and demonstrably successful in technically defined problems, be applied also to management problems, broadly defined?" It seemed obvious that truly to understand such problems it would be necessary not simply to study them from the outside; rather, coping with them needed to be experienced alongside the managers who were trying to do just that. Hence an "action research" approach was adopted (Checkland and Holwell, 1998b).

This entailed entering problem situations in organizations outside the University, taking part in the would-be problem solving, rather than simply observing it, and using that experience to address the research question. In 1972 a consultancy company wholly owned by the University was set up in order to facilitate access to serious real world problem situations. The objective was not to do consultancy for its own sake; the consultancy was simply the means of getting access to and involvement in the kind of messy situations that managers of all kinds and at many levels deal with in their professional lives.

The action research programme ran for 30 years and SSM is its outcome. The approach began to emerge in early experiences, as Systems Engineering was found not to be transferable to management situations, and it was developed, refined, tested and redeveloped in continuous cycles of learning from experience.

SSM's development and use is described in detail in several books (Checkland, 1981, 1999, 2001; Checkland and Holwell, 1998a; Checkland and Scholes, 1990) as well as in many papers. No detailed account of the methodology will be repeated here. What follows will instead indicate the reasons why 1960s' "hard" Systems Engineering was not rich enough to cope with the complexity of managerial (as opposed to technical) problem situations, and will describe how a complementary alternative to 1960s' systems thinking emerged.

In starting a Systems Engineering study the first questions addressed are: "What is the System of concern?" and "What are its objectives?" These are taken to be unproblematical, and they provide the basis for creating a system to meet the declared objectives using an array of techniques, such as, these days, sophisticated computer-based modelling, cost-benefit analysis of alternatives, risk assessments and, during implementation, use of project management techniques. If, for example, the system of concern is taken to be a new telecommunication system, then once the objectives of the system are carefully defined all subsequent activity flows from that definition. That subsequent activity may include revisiting the objectives as learning occurs, but the systems engineering team is not expected to explore the whole context of the telecommunication system, including its social and cultural features. Their professionalism is in creating a telecommunication system that meets the technical objectives in an efficacious, efficient and effective way. History provides a hideous example of this key aspect of systems engineering which makes this point. During the Second World War the company Topf and Sons engineered the ovens for incinerating corpses in the concentration camp at Auschwitz-Birkenau, designing for a required capacity of 576 corpses per day (van Pelt and Dwork, 1996, p. 321). There are records of discussions between Topf and the SS concerning increasing oven efficiency, which are described in van Pelt and Dwork's book; but the methodology of Systems Engineering, as such, does not raise broader questions of the reasons for creating the system of concern, in this case a system to turn mass murder into an industrial process.

When, in the action research programme at Lancaster, attempts were made to use Systems Engineering in management problem situations, that approach's initial questions were quickly found to be too narrowly framed, too reductionist. Suppose, for example, you were asked by the International Olympic Committee (IOC) to conduct a broad systems study of the future of the Olympic Games and you thought to use Systems Engineering. It would be quickly apparent that there is no single account of the Games as the "system of concern" which would be generally acceptable: that "system" would be very differently described (and hence so would system objectives) by the IOC itself, by the host city, by would-be host cities, by athletes, by athletes' coaches, by officials, by spectators, by hot dog sellers, by sponsors, by television companies, by television viewers who have no interest in athletics and resent their domination of the schedules every four years or by a terrorist group who see world interest in the games providing an opportunity to gain publicity for their cause. This list could go on and on, and this is what happens as soon as you move outside technically defined problem situations and into human problem situations. In a real world example in the early stages of the action research programme, Checkland and mature Masters student Dave Thomas worked in the British Aircraft Corporation on the Concorde project to create the world's first supersonic passenger-carrying aircraft. They could not begin to engage with the real issues in the situation until they abandoned their initial naive statement of objectives which saw Concorde simply as a complex engineering project. Concorde was that, but it was simultaneously much more besides – that "more" deriving from the fact that it was the Anglo-French Concorde project, set up by a treaty, no less, between Britain and France at a time when President de Gaulle was vetoing British entry into the European Common Market. The French President made it clear that he regarded the project as a touchstone of Britain's sincerity in applying for membership (Wilson, 1973, pp. 31–2).

These examples illustrate that multiple conflicting objectives from multiple stakeholders are the norm in human situations. Rational intervention in such situations requires that to be accepted.

Reflection on early experiences in the action research programme led to useful learning, aspects of which can with hindsight be seen to be important in shaping the future of the research. It was recognized that most of the thinking in systems engineering is only systematic (ordered, logical) rather than systemic (pertaining to the whole), once the system of concern and its objectives have been defined; but it was also realized that all of the problem situations entered did at least have one thing in common: they contained people trying to act purposefully in a way meaningful to them. It was therefore decided to take human activity as a systems concept and see where that led. Ways of making systemic models of purposeful activity were developed. They were structured sets of activities constituting a purposeful transformation (input into output) process, together with activities monitoring performance against defined criteria so that control action could be taken if necessary. (This reflects the core systems concept, namely the notion of an adaptive whole that can in principle survive through time in a changing environment.)

This became a usable practical concept when two features of such models were accepted. First, it is important to emphasize that each purposeful activity model is an account of a *concept* of purposeful activity, not a would-be description of real world action, which is always complex, messy and changing. Second, each stark model has to be built according to a particular declared worldview (Weltanschauung). Thus in the notional study of the Olympic Games mentioned earlier a dozen different roles relevant to the Games were listed. These represent a dozen different worldviews; each could lead to an activity model based on a particular perspective on the Games. None of them would describe the buzzing confusion that is the real world of the Olympics. They are purely devices, intellectual devices, enabling us through their use calmly and in an ordered way to explore issues related to the Games with people who care about their future.

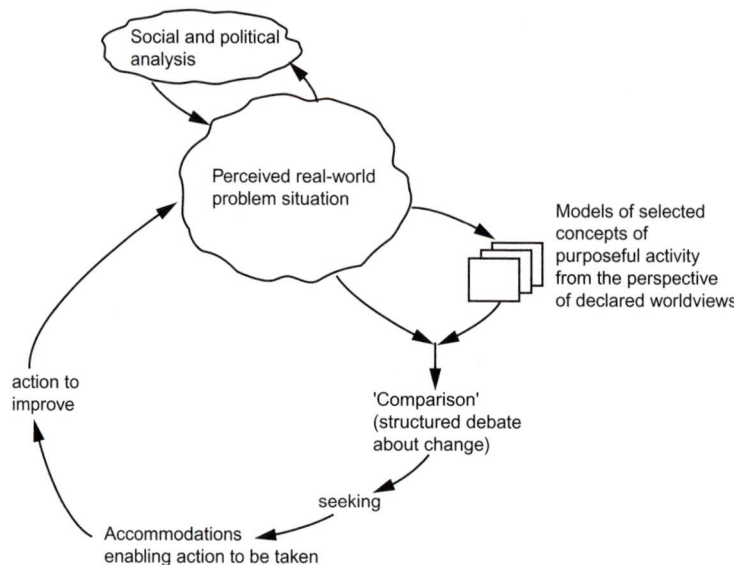

Figure 3.1—The learning cycle of SSM (soft systems methodology).

From this thinking, cursorily summarized here, SSM emerged as a consciously constructed learning system to explore the complexity of real world action. The learning system takes the form shown in Figure 3.1. The cycle does not start from a defined problem; it starts from a perceived situation in human affairs which some people regard as problematical, as worthy of serious attention aimed at "improvement". Initial exploration of the situation includes mapping the interactions that lead to its complexity and carrying out (or rather making initial forays at) analyses of the intervention itself, the social character of the perceived situation and its politics (its dispositions of power). From this exploration some hopefully relevant purposeful activity models are built. These devices are then used to structure participative debate about possible change which could count as "improvement" of the situation. The debate may occasionally reveal (or create) a consensus about "change to bring about improvement". However, in our experience this is a very rare occurrence. The norm is that what is sought in debate is accommodation between people who have different, conflicting world views, different values, different criteria for judging good/bad, acceptable/unacceptable. An accommodation is a readiness to accept a version of the situation which people having different worldviews can accept, can at least live with. It is finding accommodations that enables social life in groups to roll onward through time. Organizations (and, for that matter, families) that survive through time as coherent entities do so because they have found such accommodations.

It is obvious that Figure 3.1 represents an action-oriented approach. Its aim is "action to improve", based on change that may be structural, procedural or attitudinal and will usually entail a mix of all three. It is also obvious that implementing change, being itself a purposeful act (and rarely an easy one to achieve), can itself be explored using the same learning system, which is in principle a never-ending process. Starting and stopping studies and interventions using SSM is a somewhat arbitrary act.

In the pliable amalgam of processes captured in Figure 3.1 we have come a long way from the logic-based procedures of the 1960s. Classic OR, Systems Engineering and RAND Systems Analysis all aspire to stay as close as possible to the paradigm of natural science. Their aspiration is to apply scientific thinking, as far as it is possible, to human affairs. The action research showed that Systems Engineering was not rich enough intellectually to be applied unchanged in management situations. The changes that had to be made to make it truly relevant in that sphere were in fact so drastic that it had to acquire a new name, and became SSM. This represents more than a linguistic change. The exigencies of the situations in which the action research experience was acquired required a wholly different way of using systems concepts. That in turn required words to mark the difference between the systems thinking of the 1960s and that developed later: "hard" and "soft" emerged and became accepted as making a sharp distinction. The nature of that difference is the subject of the next section.

3.4 "Hard" and "soft" perspectives

The point has been made above that the impulse behind both classic OR and the several forms of systems thinking which emerged in the 1960s was to bring a scientific approach to problems and issues arising in management situations. In seeking to do this, these approaches were inevitably taking as given the fundamental assumptions of the natural science paradigm. These assume an external world that may be objectively investigated empirically, by disinterested observers, to create true knowledge based on the empirical data from repeatable experiments. This is the core of "positivist philosophy" (of which Kolakowski, 1972 provides a clear, short survey), and it provides the philosophical underpinning of classic OR. Clearly, the transfer of this set of assumptions from natural science, where they are astonishingly successful, to the study of social phenomena that play a role in management situations is not a little problematical. But it is achieved most closely in the sociological tradition associated with Emile Durkheim (1858–1917). He sought a "social science" that would make an objective study of social facts, these being manifestations of a society as a whole – for example, the suicide rate in a particular society is a social fact about that society, one that transcends the individuals who constitute it. Durkheim himself made a famous study of the phenomenon of the suicide rate in different societies, and his celebrated methodological rule is: "consider social facts as things".

This way of thinking about social phenomena generates one of the major traditions in sociology, that of "structural functionalism", or now more usually "functionalism". In his book *The Rules of Sociological Method* (1895) Durkheim sees a "social organism" as a set of relations persisting through time as the result of functional subsystems that contribute to the equilibrium-maintaining processes of the social system as a whole. Sociological analysis then proceeds by asking: "What is the function of this subsystem in maintaining the whole?" For example, a Western functionalist sociologist, observing a rain dance by villagers on a South Sea island and knowing that dancing can't actually affect precipitation from rain clouds, would argue that the function of the rain dance is to increase social cohesion among the village community.

This is the kind of sociology that – normally unacknowledged – underpins the "hard" approaches: classic OR, Systems Engineering and RAND Systems Analysis. That is why in the first OR textbook Churchman et al. (1957) view an organization as a structured set of subsystems and write of OR as concerned with "as much of the whole system" as possible.

In the development of SSM out of the failure of the "hard" approach, the failure was not at the level of technique, it was more fundamental than that. The simple questions, "What is the system of concern?" and "What are its objectives?", which could have come straight from Durkheim, resting as they do on positivist philosophy and functionalist sociology, were simply not rich enough to encompass the multifarious flowering confusion that characterized the management situations addressed in the action research programme. In developing an alternative approach that could begin to cope with the richness encountered, it was not a question of adjusting techniques, it required a shift to a different philosophical and sociological perspective, a different worldview. In fact, it is because "hard" and "soft" indicate fundamentally different taken-as-given assumptions about the nature of social reality that it is possible to define sharply the difference between the "hard" approaches from the 1960s and the more recent "soft" approaches.

The crucial characteristic that makes SSM different from classic OR and other "hard" approaches is its acceptance that in any social situation different individuals will in general perceive the situation differently. Thus, anyone familiar with life in organizations knows that when managers come away from a meeting each of them will in a real sense have attended a different meeting. They will have noticed different things as significant and will have evaluated what happened differently, using criteria of good/bad, acceptable/unaccept-able which others may not share. In a phrase, the individuals have "different worldviews", different ways of perceiving the world which in turn stem from the differences of genetic inheritance and experience of the world from one individual to another. It is the introduction of the concept of "worldview" which leads to SSM having the form of an organized system of inquiry, one which tries to learn its way to accommodations, enabling "action to improve" to be taken. This shape for SSM emerged as action research experiences accumulated; subsequently, since this outcome was so far away from the "hard" thinking at the start of the research it was felt necessary to address the question: "What tacit assumptions, philosophically and sociologically, are being made when SSM is used?" This issue is tackled in chap. 8 of *Systems Thinking Systems Practice* (Checkland, 1981). The conclusion reached is that SSM is based neither on positivism, philosophically, nor on functionalism, sociologically.

It was impossible to make sense of the experiences in real situations, in organizations of many kinds, on the basis of the model that sees organizations as reified systems of linked functions which seek to achieve defined objectives. Rather, what was experienced in large corporations and small firms, in private organizations and in the NHS and other public bodies, was a never-simple continuous process in which groups of people tried to create versions of perceived reality which enabled (or prevented) action. It was a process in which meaning was created by the people who took part in it. Sociologically, this sits not with Durkheim but in the other major tradition within sociology: that stemming from the work of Max Weber (to whose work Shils and Finch, 1949 edit a useful introduction). Weber (1864–1920) was a contemporary of Durkheim, but his voluminous writings do not mention the latter's functionalist approach. For Weber, human interactions were affected by something missing from the non-human world (namely, attribution of meaning that leads to intentional action). The sociological task was to find the patterns and structures in actions which were subjectively meaningful to the people involved. This was interpretive rather than functionalist sociology; it helped to make sense of the development of SSM, and this sense-making extended to the philosophical stance that underpins both interpretive sociology and therefore SSM.

For Weber, the ability of human beings to attribute meaning to perception of the world they perceive makes the "social sciences" fundamentally different from natural science in which disinterested observers produce tested knowledge about an independent external reality. This links Weber's outlook to the philosophical school of thought that is counter to that of positivism (namely, phenomenology). This tradition arose from German philosophical work on intentionality, its most important founding figure being Edmund Husserl (1859–1938). This tradition does not reify external reality, rather it accepts that between us and the world outside ourselves lie the mental processes through which we engage with the perceived world: all our knowledge of external reality is mediated by and through those mental processes. Therefore, in perceiving the world it is the perceiving that is prime, not the external world. Hence, Husserl develops a philosophical method that thinks its way beyond the "natural attitude" in day-to-day life, in which we make "common sense" judgements about the reality of the world and its events, and that makes a resolute attempt to suspend our usual naive beliefs

Table 3.1—Hard and soft systems thinking compared.

Hard systems thinking	Soft systems thinking
• Oriented to goal seeking	• Oriented to learning
• Assumes the world contains systems that can be "engineered"	• Assumes that the world is problematical but can be explored using systems models of concepts of purposeful activity to define "action to improve"
• Assumes systems models to be models of (part of) the world (*ontologies*)	• Assumes systems models to be devices: intellectual constructs to help debate (*epistemologies*)
• Talks the language of "problems" and "solutions"	• Talks the language of "issues" and "accommodations"
• Philosophically: positivistic	• Philosophically: phenomenological
• Sociologically: functionalist	• Sociologically: interpretive
• Systemicity: lies in the world	• Systemicity: lies in the process of inquiry into the world

After Checkland (1985).

and to focus sharply on the data of pure consciousness. (Luckmann, 1978 edits a useful collection of papers concerning phenomenology and its implications for sociology.) Out of this tradition comes a constructivist view of social reality, in which it is seen not as a "thing" but as a process in which social reality is continuously created and recreated in human discourse and action. This clearly maps our experience with SSM. In 1981 the answer to the question: "What is the nature of social reality implied by SSM?" was:

> ... *social reality is the ever-changing outcome of the social process in which human beings, the product of their genetic inheritance and previous experiences, continually negotiate and re-negotiate with others their perceptions and interpretations of the world outside ourselves* (Checkland, 1981, p. 284).

More than 20 years of further experience in using SSM have not given cause to change that statement.

This discussion leads to the distinctions between "hard" and "soft" thinking collected in Table 3.1.

From this, the sharpest possible expression of the difference between the "hard" systems thinking of classic OR/Systems Engineering/RAND Systems Analysis and the "soft" systems thinking of SSM is as follows: that where the "hard" approaches assume the world to be a complex of interacting systems, SSM assumes that the process of inquiring into the world can be organized as a (learning) system.

Note from this that SSM is systemic in two senses: as a whole it is an organized learning system and within that learning system it happens to use systems models (of concepts of purposeful activity) as intellectual devices to structure debate about change. Note also that the SSM process can make use of other kinds of models, not simply activity models (Winter, 2002).

Here, then, expressed in Table 3.1 are two different ways of thinking about the perceived world and about intervening to improve it. It remains finally to relate these two ways of using systems ideas to each other, asking: "What is the relationship between them?"

3.5 The relation between "hard" and "soft" perspectives: an asymmetric complementarity

Given that the "hard" and "soft" perspectives rest on two very different (and mutually incompatible) ways of capturing and construing the perceived world outside ourselves, it is unlikely that the relationship between them will be simple. But since both yield approaches having practical value in intervening to improve problem situations, the relation between them ought not to be arcane. In order to explore it, consider the situation in Figure 3.2. Here a thinker T, though part of the real world, has performed the familiar mental act of thinking about: "How can we think about the perceived world?" Two positions are identified. Observer O surveys the world, takes it as given and boldly produces ontological statements having the form: "The world is ...".

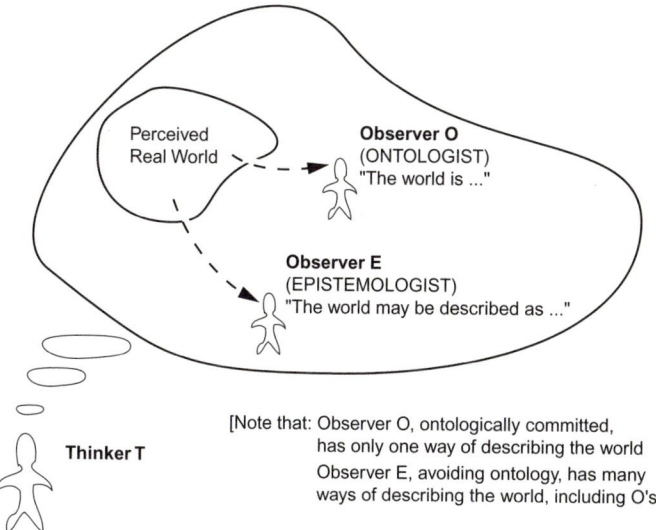

Figure 3.2—The thinker and the two observers.

Observer E, more circumspect, makes epistemological statements having the form: "The world may be described as ...". We have met these observers before; they are, respectively, in the management science field, the hard systems thinker (O) and the soft systems thinker (E).

Observer O – positivist, functionalist, working at the level of ontology – sees systems in the perceived world: some of which can be made to work better; or new systems can be designed and implemented; or the systems may be part of the regularities of the universe (frogs, foxgloves, chemical reactions); or they may have an existence deriving from the (human) logic of situations (manufacturing operations, fishing, refuse collection) (Checkland, 1983). Observer E – phenomenologist, social constructivist, avoiding ontological commitment – sees the perceived (social) world as: culturally extremely complex; capable of being described in many different ways; and sees "system" as one useful concept in ensuring good-quality debate about intentional action. The two observers both agree that the notion "system" can be useful, O seeing it simply as a name for (parts of) the real world, E seeing it as a useful intellectual device to help structure discussion, debate and argument about the real world.

In seeking to take practical action observer O, given his or her commitment to a systems ontology ("There are systems out there") has one strategy available: make models of (parts of) the real world, show that they are valid models, and manipulate them to find improvements that might be implementable in the real world system – the approach of classic OR. For observer E, however, the position is different. Because E's stance is not ontological, but rather epistemological ("Systems models can be useful intellectual devices to help thinking about the world"), a wide range of models can be constructed to help debate. That wide choice of possibly relevant models could of course in principle include, if it appeared to make sense in a particular case, consciously adopting the "hard" stance, choosing for specific reasons to see part of the real world as a system to be "engineered". An epistemology will always be able to subsume ontologies. Such a choice would be made by observer E without ontological commitment, but the work done would be exactly that to be found within a "hard" study. Thus the relation between "soft" and "hard" is that the former is the always-relevant general case, with the latter as a sometimes appropriate special case (Checkland, 1985, pp. 764–6).

A real world example: in a study to rethink information systems in the Engineering Division of British Airways, then recently formed by merging previously separate European and "overseas" (long-haul) operations, the information needs analysis was based on a model of an organized function to take aircraft out of service, maintain them so that they are safe to fly and return them to the Operations Divisions. The specific reasons for working with this model of part of the real world was that in an airline there will be no hint of dissent that to be viable there has to be such a system in place which is efficacious, efficient and effective! This was the "hard" core of a study that was not short of complex cultural issues arising from the merger.

Thus we see that "hard" and "soft" approaches are complementary to each other, but their complementarity is asymmetric. Any problem situation in human affairs will always at some level entail differences of worldviews, judgements, interpretations; the "soft" position enables that to be explored, but within that exploration any or all of the "hard" framework and techniques can be adopted as a conscious strategy. The reverse strategy (moving from "hard" to "soft") is, paradoxically, not available, for making it entails abandoning the ontological stance, and doing that puts the user into the soft paradigm! Hence we have the benign asymmetry of the "hard"–"soft" relationship.

3.6 Conclusion

It was mentioned earlier in this chapter that the literature of OR reveals a surprising lack of interest in its process. This exploration of the relation between classic OR and one of the main versions of "soft OR" shows a benign complementarity between "hard" and "soft" which draws attention to the process of intervening in real situations to bring about improvement. Since even the most austere mathematical model will be put to use within a social situation which "soft" methods can encompass, there is a pointer here to addressing the process lacuna. Further discussion here would be outside the scope of this book, but this is an item that ought to be on the agenda of the management science community.

References

Blackett P.M.S. (1962) *Studies of War*. Oliver & Boyd, Edinburgh.

Boothroyd H. (1978) *Articulate Intervention*. Taylor & Francis, London.

Buderi R. (1998) *The Invention that Changed the World: The Story of Radar from War to Peace*. Abacus, London.

Checkland P. (1981) *Systems Thinking Systems Practice*. John Wiley & Sons, Chichester, UK.

Checkland P. (1983) OR and the systems movement: Mappings and conflicts. *Journal of the Operational Research Society*, **34**(8), 661–75.

Checkland P. (1985) From optimizing to learning: A development of systems thinking for the 1990s. *Journal of the Operational Research Society*, **36**(9), 757–67.

Checkland P. (1999) *SSM: A 30-year Retrospective*. John Wiley & Sons, Chichester, UK.

Checkland P. (2001) Soft Systems Methodology (chap. 4) and Soft Systems Methodology in action: Participative creation of an information strategy in an acute hospital (chap. 5). In J. Rosenhead and J. Mingers (eds) *Rational Analysis for a Problematic World Revisited*. John Wiley & Sons, Chichester, UK.

Checkland P. and Holwell S. (1998a) *Information, Systems and Information Systems*. John Wiley & Sons, Chichester, UK.

Checkland P. and Holwell S. (1998b) Action research: Its nature and validity. *Systemic Practice and Action Research*, **11**(1), 9–21.

Checkland P.B. and Scholes J. (1990) *Soft Systems Methodology in Action*. John Wiley & Sons, Chichester, UK.

Churchman C.W., Ackoff R.L. and Arnoff E.L. (1957) *Introduction to Operations Research*. John Wiley & Sons, New York.

Durkheim E. (1895) *The Rules of Sociological Method*, translated by Solovay and Mueller, edited by G. Catlin. The Free Press, New York (1964).

Eden C. and Ackermann F. (2001) SODA – The principles. In J. Rosenhead and J.F. Mingers (eds) *Rational Analysis for a Problematic World Revisited*. John Wiley & Sons, Chichester, UK.

Gilbert M. (1994) *First World War*. Weidenfeld & Nicolson, London.

Hall A.D. (1962) *A Methodology for Systems Engineering*. Van Nostrand, Princeton, NJ.

Hinsley F.H. and Stripp A. (1993) *Codebreakers*. Oxford University Press, Oxford, UK.

Hitch C.J. (1955) An appreciation of systems analysis. In S.L. Optner (ed.) *Systems Analysis for Business Management*. Penguin, Harmondsworth, UK.

Jones R.V. (1978) *Most Secret War*. Hamish Hamilton, London.

Keys P. (ed.) (1995) *Understanding the Process of Operational Research*. John Wiley & Sons, Chichester, UK.

Kolakowski L. (1972) *Positivist Philosophy*. Penguin, Harmondsworth, UK.

Liddell Hart B.H. (1934, 1997) *History of the First World War*. Macmillan, London.

Luckmann T. (ed.) (1978) *Phenomenology and Sociology*. Penguin, Harmondsworth, UK.

Optner S.L. (ed.) *Systems Analysis for Business Management*. Penguin, Harmondsworth, UK.

Rosenhead J. and Mingers J. (eds) (2001) *Rational Analysis for a Problematic World Revisited*. John Wiley & Sons, Chichester, UK.

Shils E.A. and Finch H.A. (1949) *Max Weber's Methodology of the Social Sciences*. The Free Press, New York.

Tomlinson R. and Kiss I. (eds) (1984) *Rethinking the Process of Operational Research and Systems Analysis*. Pergamon Press, Oxford, UK.

van Pelt R. and Dwork D. (1996) *Auschwitz*. Yale University Press, New Haven, CT.

Wild R. (1972) *Management and Production*. Penguin, Harmondsworth, UK.

Wilson A. (1973) *The Concorde Fiasco*. Penguin, Harmondsworth, UK.

Winter M.C. (2002) Management, managing and managing projects: Towards an extended Soft Systems Methodology. PhD thesis, Lancaster University.

4 The effectiveness of high-dependency care

Ruth Kowalczyk
Lancaster University

4.1 Introduction

What contribution can OR/MS (Operational Research/Management Science) approaches make to tricky issues in social policy? In the UK's National Health Service (NHS), hospitals provide two broad categories of inpatient care. Those who are ill enough to need normal hospital care are accommodated on conventional medical, surgical and similar wards. Others, whose needs are much more severe but who are likely to recover with major intervention, will spend some time on intensive care units (ICUs) or on high-dependency units (HDUs). ICUs and HDUs are expensive to provide and they require highly trained staff. This chapter describes a study of ICUs and HDUs, examining their performance and investigating their effectiveness using both quantitative and qualitative approaches.

4.2 The issues

4.2.1 Intensive care

An ICU provides "a service for patients with potentially recoverable diseases who can benefit from more detailed observation and treatment than is generally available in the standard wards and departments" (King's Fund Panel, 1989, p. 428). Patients may require intensive care after critical surgery or, for example, after a major road or aviation accident. Moving patients a long distance for intensive care is undesirable, since the transit may worsen their condition and the resulting travelling distance makes it hard for their loved ones to keep in close contact. It is not surprising, therefore, that most significant population centres require an ICU, but this relies on highly trained staff who are provided in greater numbers than on conventional wards and who are familiar with increasingly sophisticated medical technologies. Thus, providing care on an ICU is much more expensive than providing care in a conventional hospital ward.

4.2.2 High-dependency care

Many hospitals also offer high-dependency care, which is "a standard of care intermediate between the general ward and full intensive care" (ICS, 1990, p. 3). HDUs have appeared following problems with ICUs and their transfer and discharge policies. ICU beds are, sadly, in great demand and staff are under enormous pressure to discharge patients into normal care as soon as possible. However, early discharge can be disastrous for the patient and may lead to death or readmission. Patient transfers, premature discharges, re-admissions and the care of high-dependency patients on the ward are all associated with higher mortality rates.

High-dependency beds can be part of an ICU, may adjoin it or be wholly separate. A mixed or adjoining facility enables easy transfer of patients between intensive care and high-dependency care, but patients may receive a standard of care that exceeds their needs. While a completely separate facility will prevent patients receiving excessive care, limited access to intensive care may cause the level of care to be inadequate. The responsibility for managing high-dependency care may be with surgeons, physicians or intensivists. The latter are specialists in such care and their background may be as anaesthetists, surgeons or physicians. Anaesthetists are most used to caring for acutely ill patients requiring intensive care, whereas surgeons and physicians are more used to caring for patients who are recovering.

4.3 Effective high-dependency care provision

The key aim in providing high-dependency care beds is to improve patient care by providing a level of care that matches patients' needs. The study described here aims to understand how high-dependency care is provided and so help improve the effectiveness of that care.

4.3.1 Links to ICUs and conventional wards

It is important to realize that providing high-dependency care can have unintended consequences. For example, providing an HDU may improve the integration of ICUs and the rest of a hospital by providing a link between the ICU and the conventional ward. This may, in turn, have an effect on the performance of the ICU and the care of its patients. On the other hand, high-dependency provision may deskill the nurses on conventional wards since they may lose contact with any patients requiring more complex treatments (i.e., an HDU may lead to a conventional ward becoming less effective).

4.3.2 Type of care provided

High-dependency care can act as a step-up facility, receiving patients only from the ward, or as a step-down facility, receiving patients only from intensive care, or as both. Providing only a step-down facility means that patients will receive care that matches or exceeds their need and some will continue to receive unneeded intensive care, which has cost implications. However, if only step-up care is available and there are no strong links to intensive care, patients may receive care that is inadequate for their needs.

4.3.3 Collaborative work

Professional pride is high among doctors, and close collaboration between different specialties can be hard to achieve. However, in an HDU such collaboration between anaesthetists and others might be the most effective way to provide high-dependency care.

Nursing resources can be organized in several ways for an HDU. Staff may be based only on the HDU, may rotate between high dependency and intensive care, or may rotate between high-dependency care and the wards. If nurses are based only on an HDU or rotated between the HDU and the ward, it is possible that they may not have the skills required to care for patients at the higher levels of dependency. Similarly, nurses who only work on an ICU and an HDU may not have the skills required to care for patients at the lower levels of dependency.

4.3.4 Supply and demand

It should be obvious that high-dependency care is only worthwhile if a hospital has enough HDU beds to meet the demand for this care. If provision is inadequate, introducing high-dependency care can have only a limited impact on care provided in intensive care and on the wards.

4.4 Methods and methodology

4.4.1 Using quantitative and qualitative approaches

Fulop et al. (2002, p. 9) comment that "a key challenge for research in health service delivery and organisation is that the phenomena under study ... are complex and difficult to define", and intensive care is very complex. It is complex because there are so many different factors that affect the outcomes from it, both internally from within the ICU and externally from elsewhere in the hospital or the NHS. There are also many different outcomes that can be seen as measures of success, including patients' survival, cost-effectiveness and the provision of quality care to both patients and relatives.

A study of an organization can focus on different levels. A macro-level study might provide a national overview of the intensive care service, while a micro-level study might look at the day-to-day workings of an ICU. In this study quantitative methods are used to investigate macro-aspects while qualitative methods are used to explore micro-aspects. Such a division is not universal in evaluation research, and other studies may use different means to achieve the same ends. Both types of method are useful, because the management of the intensive care service within the context of the hospital and the NHS is at an organizational level between the macro and micro-levels.

Quantitative and qualitative methods provide answers to different types of questions. In general, quantitative methods can shed light on the detail of the service that is being provided (e.g., the ratio of staff to patients in each unit, and what the outcomes are of that service). Whereas qualitative methods can provide insight into how the service is being provided and why the provision of this service produces the outcomes that it does. As Berk and Rossi (1990, p. 8) comment "different methods have different strengths and weaknesses, and . . . the particular questions being asked should be coupled with the most effective research methods." The use of a single method to study a complex area like intensive care might lead to important relationships being missed, so a combination of quantitative and qualitative methods is used to provide a thorough understanding of the service.

4.4.2 Methodology – why bother?

Often the combined use of quantitative and qualitative methods is criticized, particularly by academics, for being too pragmatic, only concerned with what seems to work with no concern for whether the methods fit together. One way to address this concern is to use a framework that supports the use of multiple methods and that represents the overall approach being taken. For example, one framework often used by management scientists when studying a particular problem is action research. This allows the researcher to provide feedback to the organization on how a problem should be tackled and then to evaluate the success of the suggested ways of tackling the problem as they are implemented.

However, there is a deeper level to this criticism that arises from the possibility that the person using multiple methods may have a view of the world and what exists within it (ontology) that does not fit with his view on how he can learn about that world (epistemology). For example, quantitative methods focus on measurement and are usually linked to a positivist ontology, because positivism limits study of the world to the bit that can be observed. Qualitative methods, which often reveal people's opinions and feelings, are often linked to a social constructionist ontology, within which the social world

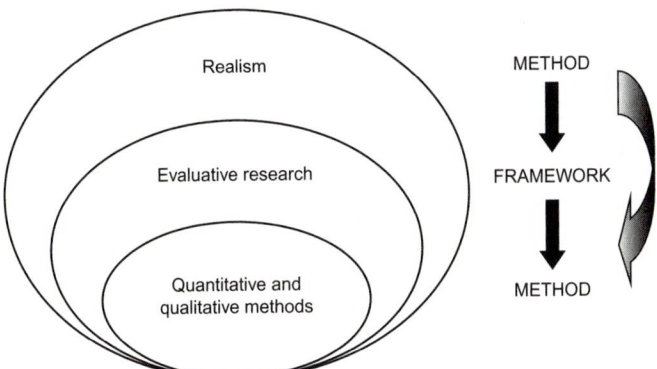

Figure 4.1—Ontology, framework and method.

is seen as being made up of people's perceptions or social constructs. Thus there can be a clash of ontologies and epistemologies unless great care is taken.

To counter this criticism the researcher needs to understand the framework used to support the study and the overriding ontology used to underpin it. In this study of intensive care, an evaluative research framework and a realist ontology are used, and these are briefly introduced in the next section. Figure 4.1 depicts the relationship between ontology, framework and methods in the context of this study. It shows that the choice of ontology has implications for the choice of framework and methods, while the choice of framework has implications for the choice of methods.

4.4.3 Evaluative research

Everybody evaluates. Each time a decision is made we look at different options and choose between them. Many scientific studies include evaluation, but as Chelimsky (1997, p. 106) puts it "evaluation is a secondary preoccupation in most research disciplines, so that many strong researchers . . . actually conduct evaluations without realising it." An evaluation attempts to judge the quality and impact of what is being provided and is used to investigate real, rather than theoretical, problems or issues. Because an evaluation focuses on the practical world of decisions and action, the researcher should think about the effect his presence may have on the subject being studied and the effect of the changing context in which the study is situated.

One distinct difference between everyday use of evaluation and its use within evaluative research is that evaluative research is a highly political activity, situated at the junction between policy and practice. Berk and Rossi (1990, p. 12) comment that "evaluations are almost entirely confined to issues that are contained in the current 'policy space'" (i.e., issues that are of current interest and public concern). Therefore, evaluative research studies may have a major impact on the lives of those studied (e.g., there may be job losses if a study suggests that a public service is not operating efficiently). Because results may be controversial the audience may try to discredit them, so it is especially important to take an ethical approach and be rigorous during the design and the process of the study. It is important to represent all the stakeholders' views, but this may prove difficult because of the differences in power between the client, who has commissioned and paid for the evaluation, and many of the other stakeholders. The audience for evaluative research includes practitioners, commissioners, politicians and the general public, and there is a need to communicate results clearly to all audiences.

Evaluative research has been used as a framework for studies that use quantitative and qualitative methods and that are underpinned by a realist ontology. Therefore, it is compatible with the methods and ontology used in this study.

4.4.4 Realism

An individual's view of the world and what exists within it (ontology) determines how he can learn about that world. Within a social constructionist ontology the social world is seen as being made up of people's perceptions or social constructs. While realists would agree that the social world is mainly made up of people's perceptions or social constructs, they would say that there are also underlying structures that exist independently of our knowledge of them. These two positions could lead to different interpretations of the same event.

Suppose, for example, that a new policy on how patients should be transferred between ICUs is introduced to the intensive care service. A social constructionist explanation of how this policy is operationalized would focus on the individuals involved in applying this policy, how they interpret it and their relative power in this situation (i.e., a social constructionist explanation would focus on the agency within the situation, the role of the individual). A realist explanation would consider all these things, but would also look at understanding why and how this policy came into being and would look for social structures that supported the policy. One example of a health-related social structure that will have affected the introduction of a patient transfer policy is the medical profession. It is a social structure because although it is made up of individual doctors it has effects that could not be caused by any individual doctor. The medical profession will have strongly influenced most of the content of the patient transfer policy and will also have a strong influence on how its members comply with the policy.

At one point in time there will be a particular set of doctors making up the medical profession, at another point a slightly different set. It is often the interaction between the individual and the structure they are within that provides the explanation for a particular outcome. So, it is important to examine structure and agency separately; that is, "keep the social structure apart from the people who at a given point in time occupy its different positions and specific practices" (Danermark et al., 2002, p. 48). These social structures are not seen as being permanently fixed, but are seen as slowly changing over time. The structures affecting intensive care and the agents interacting with them will be discussed in Section 4.4.6.

A realist explanation aims to: identify what can produce a particular outcome (i.e., the causal mechanism); understand how that mechanism works; and in what conditions it works. Mechanisms act differently depending on the context, hence the importance of understanding the conditions. As Pawson and Tilley (1997, p. 34) say "one happening may well trigger another but only if it is in the right condition in the right circumstances." They propose a structured approach to realist study in which the mechanism, the context in which it is working and its outcome are each identified. This is the approach developed in the next section for use in a practical way to analyse the intensive care services. The approach used, as mentioned earlier, employs both quantitative and qualitative methods in an attempt to gain access to the objective and subjective dimensions of ICU/HDU provision.

4.4.5 Integrating qualitative and quantitative methods

Once it is accepted that both quantitative and qualitative methods are useful in a study, there is a further problem – how to combine the results to produce something useful? In this study a practical realist approach to investigation is developed and used to combine results.

Alongside this, triangulation is used to validate the results. Robson (2002, p. 371) comments that "triangulation, in surveying, is a method of finding out where something is by getting a 'fix' on it from two or more places." In analysis, triangulation means looking for the same results from different sources, or produced using different methods, or by applying different theories. In this case, results are accepted as valid if confirmed by three different sources or methods.

4.4.6 Developing a practical realist approach

How should the quantitative and qualitative data on intensive care be analysed? Pawson and Tilley's (1997) approach – in which the user identifies the mechanism, the context in which it is working and its outcome – might provide a way of structuring the analysis. However, in use it seemed oversimplistic for several reasons. First, it was important to consider very carefully what the terms "mechanism" and "context" were referring to. Second, this rather static model does not show the changes in structure that can occur when a mechanism is triggered or how important it is to consider that what happens

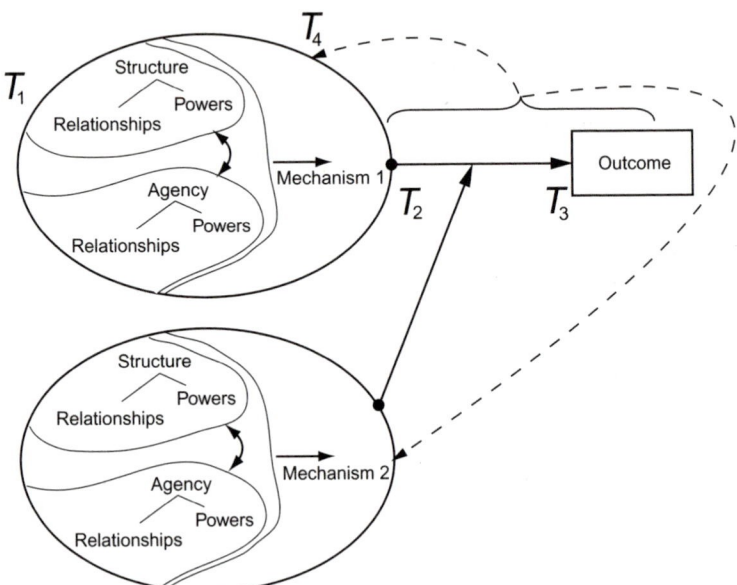

Figure 4.2—A practical realist approach to analysis.
Reproduced by permission of Routledge.

at one particular time may have effects much further down the line. Archer (1995) stresses both of these features and suggests that it is important to understand the structures at time T_1 (i.e., before the mechanism has been activated). The mechanism is then activated between times T_2 and T_3, followed by elaboration of the structure and potentially a changed structure at time T_4. Hence the approach taken attempts to combine Archer's and Pawson and Tilley's models.

The resulting model is shown in Figure 4.2, in which each structure is shown as interacting with a particular group of agents. The structures and groups of agents have their own powers to make things happen and their own relationships with other structures and agents. It is the interaction between structures and agents which triggers a mechanism; for example, the introduction of high-dependency care is the mechanism analysed later in this chapter, and the structures and agents that triggered its introduction will be identified. Context is made up of all the other potentially interacting mechanisms, in the diagram represented by "Mechanism 2" and "...", as well as the particular structures and agents interacting with these mechanisms. Note, though, that these may or may not be the same structures and agents that interact with the first mechanism. The mechanisms that interact with the introduction of high dependency will also be discussed in Section 4.5.3.

In the model, T_1–T_4 represent the stages in time referred to by Archer. Dashed arrows show feedback effects and the curly bracket is used to show that changes due to feedback effects may start to happen as soon as a mechanism has been triggered. Feedback effects include not only changes in structure but also the possibility that when a mechanism is triggered the mechanism itself or the agents involved may also be changed. These feedback effects apply equally to other mechanisms within the context of the one that is the main focus.

This diagrammatic approach is used to support analysis in two different ways: first, implicitly, in the background, to guide the user and make sure that all the different aspects are considered; or, second, explicitly as a template for analysis, as is the case when analysing the introduction of high-dependency care.

4.5 Analysing the introduction of high-dependency care

4.5.1 Quantitative analysis of high-dependency care

The quantitative analysis of this study was based on available data. The Intensive Care National Audit and Research Centre (ICNARC) collects detailed quantitative data on admissions to ICUs at a national level from 50% of ICUs in England and Wales. The Audit Commission had also recently carried out a survey of the management of ICUs, and anonymized, linked data were provided from the two data sets. This data collected by ICNARC came only from ICUs, so units treating only high-dependency patients did not appear in the data. However, ICUs could be divided into those that treated intensive care patients only and those treating intensive care and high-dependency patients (i.e., mixed units).

Multivariate statistical analyses of these linked data sets suggested that there were many different factors that affected successful provision of intensive care. Alongside these analyses, data envelopment analysis was also used to compare ICUs with others in similar circumstances and with similar levels of resourcing. For example, data envelopment analysis was used to compare mixed units with other mixed units rather than with those that nursed only ICU patients. When linked with the statistical analyses, these results could be used to show for a particular ICU areas where improvements could be made.

The quantitative analyses showed that these mixed IC/HDUs were relatively successful at providing care. In particular, mixed units achieved better survival rates, were more able to maintain the occupancy standards suggested by the Intensive Care Society, tended to provide bereavement counselling and had higher levels of post-basic nurse training. On the downside, though, mixed units had more transfers out and were less likely to be recognized as ICUs by the medical profession.

There are various reasons why mixed units may be more successful. They have greater flexibility in that the numbers of intensive care and high-dependency patients in the beds can vary. Another possible explanation is that they seem to have different priorities. ICUs focus more on treating patient illness and developing medical staff, while IC/HDUs focus on the patient as a whole in the context of their family and developing nursing staff.

4.5.2 Qualitative analysis of high-dependency care

Though the quantitative analysis was based on available data sets, the qualitative work involved a special investigation of one ICU. This included observation of ICU activity and directorate meetings and interviews with staff involved in ICU management at both operational and strategic levels – which provided much qualitative data. To provide comparative data, staff involved in ICU management at a strategic level were interviewed from four other ICUs. All five HDUs received patients from the wards and from intensive care. All of the units visited were either mixed IC/HDUs or an adjacent facility. In each case nursing staff were shared between intensive care and high-dependency care.

At the beginning of the study, initial interviews were used to find out the issues and problems that were important to intensive care specialists. The role of ICNARC and the presence of detailed quantitative data on admissions to ICUs came to light at this stage. Gaining and analysing the quantitative data then took place alongside further qualitative study at the first ICU. Suggestions made by interviewees could be checked out when analysing the quantitative data, and interviewees could be asked questions that arose from the quantitative results. Qualitative study at the four other ICUs came after the quantitative analyses, since these units were selected because of their data envelopment analysis results. These interviews could still be used to clear up any queries about the quantitative data and to identify further ideas for quantitative data analysis.

While quantitative results suggested that mixed units were relatively successful, qualitative results showed a negative response to the introduction of high-dependency care. The nurse staffing ratio is lower for high-dependency patients, and this can cause problems. As one directorate nurse (interview, February 2001) commented "a high-dependency patient can be incontinent, aggressive, confused, not able to get themselves washed, dressed." Thus, the workload for staff can be very high, leading to high levels of stress. Most intensive care nurses said that they disliked looking after high-dependency care patients – "I like looking after ICU patients because that's what I am trained to do and that's what I came to ICU for" (sister, interview, June 1999). Rotations between high-dependency care and the wards, where attempted, were not very successful. A directorate manager (interview,

December 2000) said "we have tried very hard to improve rotations of nurses from surgical specialties onto ICU. It has not so far worked very ... well. It's like two different animals."

4.5.3 Structures affecting intensive care

It is useful at this stage to look at the structures that affect intensive care and the agents that interact with them. These structures also affected the introduction of high-dependency care. It was suggested earlier that keeping structure and agency separate helps the researcher to work out the effects of each. A structure may have the power to trigger a particular mechanism (e.g., the implementation of a policy), but human agency means that choices may then be made by individuals or groups of individuals to influence how the policy is implemented and so its outcome. There are two structures that have had considerable influence in shaping the health service – the government's role as decision maker and the presence of professional hierarchies. In relation to intensive care, a particular structural feature – insularity – has had a major impact on the way intensive care has developed.

The main source of funding for health care is taxes, so the government is in a powerful position to dictate policy. Recent health policy explicitly aims to challenge the traditional values of the NHS, which have come from the medical profession, and to replace these with business-focused values. The reasons the government cites for health care policy making are usually about protecting the public's interests. Because public expectation is increasing, "the public" has an indirect influence on health care, as policies and practices are adapted to avoid public outcry. Government ministers and civil servants are responsible for developing health policies, while hospital managers are responsible for implementing them.

The medical profession had a central role in the creation of the NHS and remains a powerful force because of the widely held view that doctors, because of their training, are the only people able to make clinical decisions. There is a hierarchical relationship between the medical and nursing professions, with nursing gaining most of its power from its close relationship with medicine. Each profession has its own hierarchy, and within medicine certain specialties are held in higher regard than others. Intensive care specialists are usually anaesthetists and, as a supporting specialty, are much lower down the hierarchy than surgeons. The main people who are able to keep the professions as they are or change the way they work are the individual doctors and nurses who are part of them.

The third structure that has had a big impact on the way intensive care has developed is its insularity. The intensive care service is quite isolated from the rest of the hospital. As Franklin (1998, p. 1300) comments "In a sense, the ICU has become 'the black box of the hospital', viewed as an intricate

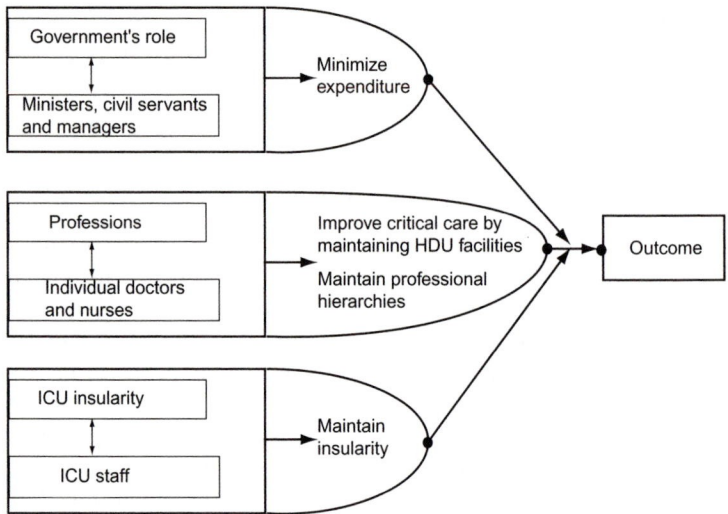

Figure 4.3—High-dependency care – mechanisms and interacting mechanisms.

assemblage of high-tech equipment where patients enter as 'input variables' at one end and emerge sometime later from the other end as 'outcomes'." The main people who help to maintain this insularity are the doctors and nurses within intensive care.

4.5.4 High-dependency care – success or failure?

Figure 4.3 is a much-simplified version of Figure 4.2, in which these structures and the agents associated with them are shown as triggering particular mechanisms. It is the interaction between the medical and nursing professions and their members that resulted in the introduction of high-dependency care, but interaction between these professions and their members also triggers actions that keep the hierarchical relationships within and between the two professions stable. This second mechanism is an example of a mechanism that interacts with the introduction of high-dependency care and affects its successful implementation.

4.6 Effects

4.6.1 The effect of structures

Despite the apparent success of the introduction of high-dependency care in achieving its aim of improving care, as shown by the quantitative results, the provision of such care has never achieved its full potential. Though the government agreed to the introduction of high-dependency care, it is a particularly costly service and the government's need to minimize expenditure took priority, leaving the service underfunded. This meant that not enough beds were provided and, therefore, high-dependency patients continued to be nursed in ICUs and on the wards. As one sister (interview, May 1999) commented "the nurses that we recruit from the surgical side do say that there are ... more seriously ill patients that they have recognized that probably should come to HDU and perhaps only get to HDU as a last resort when they go off and they end up on ICU."

The introduction of high-dependency care was a policy strongly supported by the medical profession (in particular, intensivists and surgeons). But, as suggested earlier, the medical profession has other agendas, and a competing mechanism in this situation was the desire of the medical profession to keep its hierarchical relationships stable. Hierarchical relationships are also present in the nursing profession and intensive care nurses are seen as the elite, partly because they are able to care for patients who have more complex illnesses than ward patients. They often keep themselves to themselves and ICUs are insular partly as a result of this, meaning that relationships between intensive care nurses and their ward colleagues may be strained. These relationships were made more difficult by the introduction of high-dependency care, because the two groups now had to work together much more often. One sister (interview, May 1999) provided an example of this friction: "Surgical wards not wanting to take patients back ... and senior nurses being deliberately obstructive and saying there's no bed, and people who I know coming back and saying 'Yes they have got beds'." So, another competing mechanism to the introduction of high-dependency care was the desire of intensive care staff to keep themselves apart from their colleagues and maintain intensive care's insularity.

4.6.2 The effect of agency

A policy to provide high-dependency care may be introduced, but the detail of its implementation is left to the individual managers, doctors and nurses in the situation. The hierarchical relationships within the medical profession affected the development of high-dependency care because often surgeons, with greater power, decided who should be medically responsible for high-dependency care. A directorate nurse (interview, September 2000) commented "there'd always been this thing that the admitting consultant didn't really want to hand over the care to the anaesthetist." In many units the clinical management of high-dependency patients, even when they were nursed in high-dependency beds in an ICU, was the responsibility of surgeons. High-dependency care had also been introduced in ways that kept intensive care insular by keeping high-dependency care either in the ICU itself or, if it is separate, by making sure the HDU is only staffed by intensive care nurses.

4.6.3   The effect of high-dependency care on skills

One of the possible problems that could be caused by introducing high-dependency care is that ward staff could lose their existing skills for looking after this type of patient on a normal ward. This did not seem to have happened, partly normal wards are often short of beds. One directorate nurse (interview, December 2000) said "the wards have increasingly acutely ill patients in them and are quite full ... So the patients they have in there are quite acute." It is possible that the gap between the skills of the intensive care nurse and the ward nurse has widened, but the increased level of acuteness of general hospital care makes this unlikely. The fact that intensive care nurses do not like nursing high-dependency patients and have problems with nursing two of them at the same time suggests that intensive care nurses as well as ward nurses need to develop the skills for nursing high-dependency patients.

4.7   Conclusions

To summarize, the introduction of high-dependency care succeeded in improving care by providing a level of care that matched patients' needs, but did so for only a small number of patients. Intensive care has had to become more integrated into the rest of the hospital. But the way in which this has happened has increased the problems between intensive care and the ward without providing the many benefits that could have resulted if this policy had been implemented differently. The skills needed to provide high-dependency care are still being developed.

The use of qualitative methods in operational research, particularly soft OR techniques, has become common. However, accounts of the combined use of quantitative and qualitative methods or of hard and soft OR are rare (Munro and Mingers, 2002). This study uses an approach that gives equal emphasis to quantitative and qualitative methods.

Quantitative and qualitative methods have different strengths and weaknesses, different types of questions they can best answer. In this study, quantitative methods were used to provide a broad overview of the success of the introduction of high-dependency care. Alongside this, qualitative analysis was used to look at this policy and how those within intensive care perceived it. To produce useful practical research, the choice of methods should match the research questions asked, rather than the method itself being the motivation for asking a particular question. An understanding of the framework in use and the ontology underlying the research counters the criticism that this approach is too pragmatic, by providing support for the methods used and guidance as to how they should be used.

In this study both quantitative and qualitative analyses are needed because of the complexity within the area of health care. This kind of complexity is equally visible in many other application areas. Ackoff (1979, p. 94) described OR as "mathematically sophisticated but contextually naive." Within complex areas the use of soft methods, including both soft OR and qualitative methods, enables the operational researcher to understand the context and the multiple perspectives of those involved.

Two ideas are particularly useful when drawing together the quantitative and qualitative analyses. The use of a diagram representing a realist approach to study helps to focus attention on the important features within the data, including the underlying structures, the agents associated with them, the mechanisms and their interactions, and, therefore, how outcomes occur. Triangulation is useful for validating the results gained from different sources, so drawing together the multiple perspectives, or gained using a variety of methods, so using different types of data to cast light on the analysis.

References

Ackoff R.L. (1979) The future of operational research is past. *Journal of the Operational Research Society*, **30**(2), 93–104.

Archer M.S. (1995) *Realist Social Theory: The Morphogenetic Approach.* Cambridge University Press, Cambridge, UK.

Berk R.A. and Rossi P.H. (1990) *Thinking about Program Evaluation.* Sage Publications, London.

Chelimsky E. (1997) Thoughts for a new evaluation society. *Evaluation*, **3**, 97–109.

Danermark B., Ekstrom M., Jakobsen L. and Karlsson J. (2002) *Explaining Society: Critical Realism in the Social Sciences.* Routledge, London.

Franklin C. (1998) Deconstructing the black box known as the intensive care unit. *Critical Care Medicine*, **26**(8), 1300–1.

Fulop N., Allen P., Clarke A. and Black N. (2002) Issues in studying the organisation and delivery of health services. In N. Fulop, P. Allen, A. Clarke and N. Black (eds) *Studying the Organisation and Delivery of Health Services: Research Methods.* Routledge, London.

ICS (1990) *The Intensive Care Service in the United Kingdom.* Intensive Care Society, London.

King's Fund Centre for Health Services Development (1989) Intensive care in the United Kingdom: Report from the King's Fund panel. *Anaesthesia*, **44**, 428–31.

Munro I. and Mingers J. (2002) The use of multimethodology in practice – Results of a survey of practitioners. *Journal of the Operational Research Society*, **53**(4), 369–78.

Pawson R. and Tilley N. (1997) *Realistic Evaluation.* Sage Publications, London.

Robson C. (2002) *Real World Research*, 2nd edn. Blackwell, Oxford, UK.

5 Complementarity in practice

George D. Paterson
Visiting Professor, Department of Management Science,
University of Strathclyde, formerly of Shell International

5.1 Introduction

This chapter looks at the question of complementarity from the point of view of clients of OR/MS (Operations Research/Management Science) who work in organizations making use of OR/MS to improve their businesses. As organizations change and develop, OR/MS resources are deployed in different organizational settings, leading to different relationships between the OR/MS practitioner and the client. In this way, OR/MS practice takes on different styles, depending on the context in which it operates.

To help understand this, two contrasting styles of OR/MS practice are examined. A traditional OR work style fits well where OR/MS resources are deployed in an *embedded* setting (Section 5.2.1), such as in an operational decision support process. However, when faced with complex issues or significant projects, large organizations typically take a multidisciplinary team approach, with different contributions being made by consultants in different areas. In this setting OR/MS practitioners are deployed in a *consultancy* work style (Section 5.2.2).

With this background, it is possible to understand the distinctive contribution that OR/MS makes compared with that of other consultants, which leads to some conclusions about the nature of OR/MS work. In particular, the use of models is seen as the common thread in all OR/MS practice. Hard and soft are seen as a spectrum of modelling approaches within the *consultancy* style rather than incommensurable paradigms.

The discussion is illustrated by some examples of OR/MS projects and activities within the oil and gas industry.

5.2 Organizational setting for OR/MS practice

Organizations continue to strive for efficiency by aligning their resources with their changing business activities. Needless to say, OR/MS resources have not been immune to the resulting waves of organizational change. Central OR groups in many UK companies have been realigned within their organization, have seen their activities dispersed within the organization or in some cases have been completely outsourced (Fildes and Ranyard, 1997). Though there are many different organizational settings in which OR/MS practitioners now work, the two idealized types described below capture the key characteristics of most situations.

5.2.1 Embedded

In this setting the OR/MS practitioner occupies a well-understood, well-defined role within an operational decision support process. Examples within the oil industry would be vehicle routing or refinery optimization – both of which are fundamental to the day-to-day operation of the business. In this type of setting, which could apply to a single OR/MS practitioner or a team of practitioners within a mainstream business department, the client is a colleague in the joint activity of that department. The practitioner may well see herself as a "business" person in the particular field of application rather than an OR/MS professional, or perhaps both. This allows OR/MS practitioners to work closely with their clients and to share their concerns.

5.2.2 Consultancy

The second idealized type occurs when the OR/MS assistance is provided by internal or external consultants. If the support is provided as part of an internal shared service, this is the situation that is most similar to the previously well-established setting of the internal OR group. However, it is now likely that OR/MS is only one of the skill sets available to clients in the portfolio of services offered. All consultants working in a shared service organization would see themselves as professionals, practising to professional standards. Work for clients is carried out on a (semi-)commercial basis, leading to more formal relationships with clients, albeit within the common culture and values of the parent company to which the clients also belong.

The greatest separation between practitioner and client occurs when the service is provided by an external consultant and applies to the lone independent consultant as well as to household name consulting firms. The OR/MS skill set competes within the whole marketplace of consultancy offerings, and any transactions with the client are on a fully commercial basis.

Although distinct, these latter two settings for a *consultancy* work style are quite similar: the internal shared service modelling itself on external consulting organizations, and the external consultants striving to achieve the closer client relationships of the internal shared service.

Consultancy-style OR/MS work is carried out on a client–consultant basis. In this type of engagement there is a *client*, the owner of the problem situation, who seeks assistance from one or more *consultants*, external to the problem situation, in bringing about improvements in that situation. Clients for OR/MS can come from any part of an organization, but the requirement for fees to be paid usually means that studies and projects will either come directly from or be sponsored by a client in a management position. The nature of managers as clients, their constantly evolving concerns and some of the motivations for seeking assistance are discussed by Eden and Ackermann in Chapter 9. It is important to realize that the client may have many different, potential sources of help and that OR/MS is just one of these. The client's understanding of what each of these different resources potentially offers is a key factor in determining how and by whom these issues are tackled, understood and moved toward resolution.

5.3 Types of assistance available

As shown in Figure 5.1 most managers would recognize the categories of potential assistance and skill sets discussed below. When tackling complex issues they would usually favour a team approach, involving an appropriate mix of resources.

5.3.1 People process

This category includes consultants skilled in organizational development, team working, facilitation and change management. These resources are usually favoured if there is a perceived need for more effective or different ways of

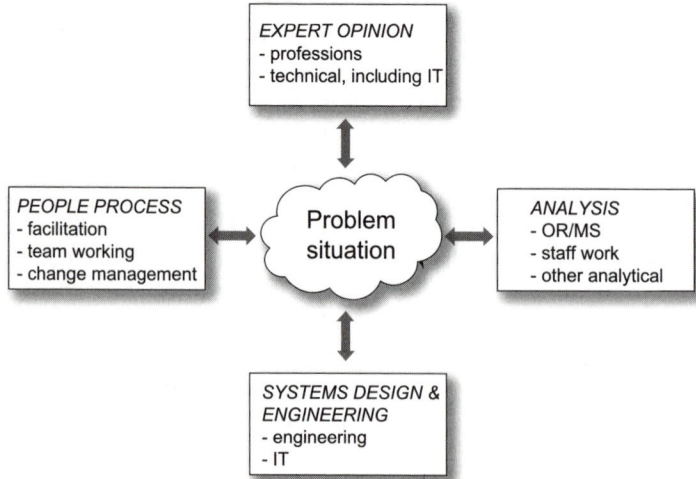

Figure 5.1—A common view of skill sets available from consultants.

people working together. Some senior management teams have this type of resource present on a permanent basis.

5.3.2   Analysis

OR/MS practitioners are usually seen in this category, along with management accountants, many "staff" jobs and a whole range of consultants skilled in (specialist) data analysis and interpretation. These resources would be called on when the perceived need is for distilled quantitative information related to the issue in question, or the answer to a well-posed question that requires analysis or problem solving.

5.3.3   Expert opinion

Many of the well-established professions fall into this group. It includes lawyers and accountants (finance and tax aspects) as well as technical, engineering and scientific consultants, including IT specialists. These are cast in the role of giving expert technical advice and would expect to be consulted for matters of fact, or for professional opinion.

5.3.4   Systems design and engineering

These include engineering, technical and IT resources available for analysing system requirements and producing system design specifications for a systems solution or a physical facility.

In the initial stages of tackling an issue, the client's world view, which will have been influenced by his own background and prior experience of using consultants, is a major factor in determining the type and scope of consultants to be engaged. Even later on, when the structuring of the problem is clearer, the client will often have a mental sketch of the range of professional help that will be required in a multidisciplinary team, even if that has not yet been articulated.

5.4   OR/MS in relation to other consulting offerings

Such a categorization by potential clients places OR/MS activities in the *analysis* category and is not helpful for the take-up of softer OR methodologies. It would after all be expected that these approaches have a strong contribution to make to the *people process* resource category. Such a classification, often encouraged by the way that consulting provision is organized, can clearly limit the effectiveness of all OR/MS work. To counteract this view a clear understanding of OR/MS's distinctive contribution is needed, and of soft OR in particular.

One of the potential difficulties that clients might have in categorizing soft OR is that discussed in Chapter 1 (i.e., the term is understood in different ways, even by OR/MS practitioners). As much of this book illustrates, the term soft OR can refer to a philosophy, a number of different methods, various different types of models using different sorts of data and to techniques, such as stakeholder analysis, facilitation or interviewing. For the client the techniques aspect is particularly confusing, because of the strong overlap with approaches used by the other identified consultant types in the *people process* resource category.

Taking a historical perspective, soft OR has developed a greater emphasis on consulting skills, so that in the OR/MS world these tend to be seen as features of soft rather than hard OR/MS. In practice, competence in consulting skills is necessary for consultants of all types, including hard and soft OR/MS practitioners. Commonality in consulting skills across a wide range of disciplines is recognized by the UK Institute of Management Consultancy (IMC), which has a well-developed competence framework for consulting. A description of this is available on the IMC website (http://www.imc.co.uk). It has three main areas, of which the IMC sets professional standards for the last two as part of their professional certification programme:

- technical discipline and sector specialism (e.g., OR in defence);
- consulting competence (client focus, building and sustaining relationships, applying expertise and knowledge, and achieving sustainable results);
- professional behaviours (including personal growth and ethics).

In the same vein, Eden and Ackerman (Chapter 8) also point out that all operational researchers require such competencies as developing customer relationships and understanding organizational politics.

However, the thing that is unique to OR/MS, including soft OR methods, is the use of models that, through analysis, enable the practitioner to make substantive contributions to the problem situation, and not just manage a process. Eden and Ackermann (Chapter 9) make a similar point "All of the well-established soft OR methods are designed to add value – each in different ways."

The use of models is thus a common factor in all types of OR/MS activity and, furthermore, is a distinctive characteristic when comparing OR/MS with other consulting approaches.

5.5 Models and modelling

The nature of models and modelling is discussed throughout this book; in particular, in Chapter 7 where Morecroft discusses a case in which a formal model became an instrument to link the different mental models of a management team. This view of a model as a *publicly shared representation of (aspects of) the problem situation* is powerful and has general applicability to OR/MS models, both hard and soft. Ackermann and Eden's account of using cognitive and cause mapping in Chapter 8 shows how individual cognitive maps are captured, merged and linked with other information to produce a model that is amenable to analysis and can be publicly shared in the process of the intervention.

Hard models have a natural integrative role, since one of the main reasons why people feel the need to resort to a hard model is the difficulty of understanding what the effect of multiple interacting factors might be in a particular situation. Logic and mathematics are the language of hard models, but the process of model building, both in structure and content, is similar to that for soft models. It is being based on the knowledge and experience of a number of different people, which the modeller has to extract, understand and represent in the model. Even the apparently straightforward process of data collection can be highly political, which underlines the broadly based consulting skills required by hard and soft OR/MS practitioners alike. That models should be publicly shared can be more of a challenge for hard models, but it is well worth the hard modeller pursuing transparency. This helps to generate trust and confidence in the operation and results of the model by those making use of the model for understanding or decision making.

The relationship between models and learning is also discussed in this book. It is important to consider whether the process of an OR/MS intervention contributes to organizational learning that reaches beyond the people immediately involved in the project. As Morecroft argues in Chapter 7, models can be "transitional objects" in this learning process, this being an example of modelling as learning (de Geus, 1992; Lane, 1992). However, if models turn out to have a strong reuse value, then there is an increase in the organizational capability to tackle similar problems, even if the people originally involved have moved on to other jobs. In general, it is more likely that hard models would have this property, as they tend to have some structure that would apply to another similar situation, although the specific content might not. An example where hard models have become the repository of organizational know-how in a major oil and gas company is discussed below. With soft models, both structure and content are more likely to be specific to the situation and so reuse is less likely.

5.6 Examples from the oil and gas industry

A characteristic of the oil and gas industry is that these natural resources are rarely found near to the centres of population where they are consumed. Both oil and gas therefore have to be transported long distances to come to market. In the case of oil and oil products, pipelines and vehicles of many types are used in transportation. In the case of gas, pipelines are the commonest means of transportation, but special purpose ships are also used to transport gas in a liquid form, either refrigerated or under pressure. For oil, ships for transportation are obtainable from the freight market, and there are also well-developed markets in crude oil and oil products themselves. Gas, however, is usually delivered under dedicated contracts. Development of a gas prospect is therefore complex, commercially and technically. Buyers have to be identified along with the means of delivery, whether by pipeline or dedicated ships, and long-term (25 to 30 years) contracts put in place before a gas field can be developed. Large gas development schemes are multibillion dollar projects.

Typically, in gas business development, a portfolio of possible prospects will be under consideration at any one time. Many factors, from host government interests and environmental considerations through marketing and customer demand and technical issues, will determine which prospects are progressed and at what speed. Often a decision point will be reached when a change in these external factors opens up a commercial opportunity for one of the prospects, and intensive evaluation of this opportunity is then required. While there are a number of different ways in which OR/MS can assist in the evaluation, the two specific types of OR/MS models – economic models and facility planning models – are discussed below.

5.6.1 Economic models

The purpose of an economic model is to estimate the cash flow for the whole life of a project and to derive estimated net present value and the likely return on investment. The model brings together all the cost aspects of gas field development, construction of facilities, normal operations, tax and royalties over time set against the revenue stream from gas contracts. The method of analysis is discounted cash flow, and spreadsheets are the usual tool for model building (see, e.g., Daellenbach, 1994; Dyson and Berry, 1998). If spreadsheet models are built in a very disciplined way with a clear layout and use of entity names for variables, transparency and adaptability is enhanced and in-built logic checking tools can be used to assist with internal validation.

5.6.2 Facilities planning models

The purpose of these models is to estimate the throughput of alternative configurations of facilities (pipelines, processing plant, harbours and ships) for transportation of gas from the well head(s) to the customer(s). In the case of transportation by ship, simulation models are used, due to the multitude of factors influencing journey times, and in the case of pipelines, network optimization models are used. These models integrate all the technical factors impacting the delivery of gas to customers.

5.6.3 The example of prospect evaluation

The first milestone in prospect evaluation is to establish a base case, which is a basic but feasible version of the prospect that serves as a reference for other variants that are considered later. The corresponding base case version of the models will have all relevant aspects captured and a complete set of data which is as realistic as possible. Sensitivity and risk analysis can be used with the economic model to understand the effect of uncertainty in base case data, particularly in project cost elements and timing of revenue streams. However, the base case is usually only a starting point, as during prospect evaluation many different variations will need to be considered. Some examples are discussed below.

- *Customers.* Concluding gas supply contracts takes time, as customers consider possible variations of price and volumes linked to forecast demand. Because of the need to deliver gas in particular volumes to different locations, adding or removing a particular customer has an impact on facilities back to the well head. Models are used to analyse these impacts and can assist in contract negotiations.
- *Partners.* Because of the huge capital cost of development, it is likely that partners will be involved in schemes of this sort, and there are many different types of partnership structure for the ownership (cost side) and revenue sharing. Economic models are particularly helpful in understanding the cash flow impact for different partners, and the use of a common economic model that has been validated independently by partners promotes shared understanding of the prospect economics and the development of trust between partners.
- *Facility options.* There will usually be a number of different options for the configuration of facilities to deliver the required amount of gas, and both types of model can contribute to the prospective designs. Forecasting capital costs for construction of facilities is a particularly difficult area that draws on previous experience, discussion with prospective contractors and on engineering judgement. Because of the inherent uncertainty, it is important to guard against optimistic assessments in the desire to construct a profitable prospect.

5.6.4 Hard and soft aspects

Both economic and facilities planning models contribute to evaluation of prospects and are used by the clients to support decisions about which

Table 5.1—Aspects of economic and facilities planning models.

Aspect	Economic models	Facilities planning models
Methodology	Mixed	Hard
Model type	Projection of future cash flows	Would-be initial design for project facilities
Model validity and validation	Internal logic and coherence checkable. Completeness of model a matter of judgement and prior experience of the many stakeholders involved	Technical components validated from the application of similar models in previous situations
Data	Some data are expert opinion (e.g., tax rates or cost of capital), some costs come from prior experience, sales data are forecast, some other items based on pure judgement	Gas availability at source has large technical variability. Some facilities' technical parameters are determined by expert opion. Required sales based on judgement, prior experience and forecasting
Value or outcome	Understanding of project economics and main sensitivities	Confidence in technical feasibility
Purpose	Support decision making and contract negotiation	Support decision making and initial design specifications

prospects are to be advanced to further development. Table 5.1 explores where each of these models lies on the hard–soft spectrum using the aspects discussed in Chapter 1.

Analysis shows that the models have different positions on the soft–hard spectrum, perhaps surprisingly so for the economic models, since their foundation in accounting logic might at face value give a different impression. Economic models have a significant element of subjective judgement involved in both model content and data input, and because of the importance of financial parameters in decision making OR/MS practitioners engaged in this type of work need to be fully aware of potentially vested interests in the choice of model structure and the estimation of data. However, as new aspects are considered and models changed and expanded to reflect these aspects, a shared understanding grows within the stakeholder group over a period of time.

The validation of the facilities planning models depends on the results of previous applications having been seen to be accurate. This reinforces the point made in Chapter 1 about credibility assessment, as client confidence in the models builds with repeated use. This can also be seen as a type of organizational learning. Models like this which are validated over a period of time become part of organizational capability, even if the people involved in working with the models (clients and analysts) change over time.

The above examples have been discussed from the OR/MS aspect, but the OR/MS practitioner would normally be working as part of a team involving many other consultants and experts (e.g., finance, legal, marketing, HR, country specialists, chemical engineering, petroleum engineering, marine engineering, and oil and gas traders). The uniqueness of the OR/MS contribution lies in the integrative nature of the models used, whether soft, hard or mixed. In addition, for the examples considered above, the OR/MS models provide a means of incorporating input from the other two resource categories of *expert opinion* and *systems design and engineering* into the prospect evaluation.

5.7 Complementarity of hard and soft

In this discussion of complementarity, two contrasting styles of OR/MS practice have been examined. The *embedded* style has seen to fit well with a traditional OR/MS practice, where the use of OR/MS models is an integral part of normal business operations.

The examples carried out in the *consultancy* work style have shown the defining distinctiveness of modelling for OR/MS approaches, compared with other consultancy offerings. The main outcomes are about understanding and confidence, and even with the harder facilities planning model quite a lot of subjective input is required. Both economic models and facilities planning models are used to inform decisions rather than make immediately implementable recommendations. Like the OR/MS approaches discussed in other chapters, such as SSM, cognitive mapping, system dynamics, simulation modelling and data mining, the examples discussed in Section 5.6 exist on a spectrum of modelling approaches, rather than in incommensurable paradigms. This leads to the conclusion that the hard and soft distinction is more about the types of models used by OR/MS practitioners, working in a *consultancy* style than about fundamentally different approaches. Hence, achieving any complementarity of hard and soft relies on in the blending of *people process* and *analysis* skills in ways that suit the problems at hand. This conclusion is illustrated in Figure 5.2 in which complementary OR/MS is shown as bridging the gap between *analysis* and *people process* skills. The challenge facing OR/MS consultants is to develop the understanding of their clients so that they also see OR/MS as offering these skills. Otherwise, the full potential of OR/MS will be unrealized.

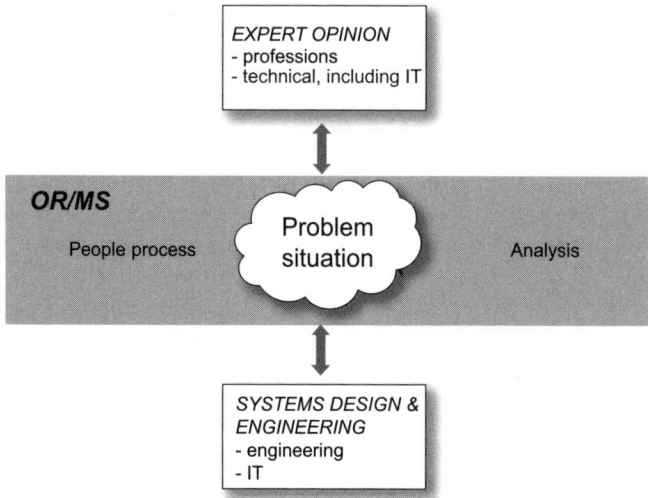

Figure 5.2—The importance of *people process* and *analysis* skill sets for systems modelling.

References

Daellenbach H.G. (1994) *Systems and Decision Making: A Management Science Approach.* John Wiley & Sons, Chichester, UK.

De Geus A. (1992) Modeling to predict or to learn? *European Journal of Operational Research,* **59**(1), 1–5.

Dyson R.G. and Berry R.H. (1998) The financial evaluation of strategic investments. In R.G. Dyson and F.A. O'Brien (eds) *Strategic Development, Methods and Models.* John Wiley & Sons, Chichester, UK.

Fildes R. and Ranyard J.C. (1997) Success and survival of operational research groups – A review. *Journal of the Operational Research Society,* **48**(4), 336–60.

Lane D.C. (1992) Modelling as learning: A consultancy methodology for enhancing learning in management teams. *European Journal of Operational Research,* **59**(1), 64–84.

6 The complementary use of hard and soft OR in developing tax policy*

Joyce Brown and Ceri Cooper
Inland Revenue

6.1 Introduction

This chapter illustrates how hard and soft OR (Operational Research) can be used in a complementary way in the development of public policy by using a case study from the Inland Revenue, a major department of the UK Civil Service. The case study describes a review of the UK personal taxation system that aimed to devise ways in which the operation of the UK's personal tax system could be improved.

OR was fundamental to the study and involved the carefully planned and complementary use of soft and hard methods. The hard OR was based on data mining to increase understanding of individual taxpayers and their changing needs within the personal tax system. The soft OR was based on soft systems methodology (SSM) with two aims in mind. First, to guide the review and, second, as an auditable approach for collecting the views of key internal and external stakeholders. The soft and hard OR were used alongside one another, rather than one providing a contextual scheme for the other. The experience reveals that soft OR is much more than common sense and that, used in parallel, soft and hard approaches have a powerful synergy. This chapter is based on a paper submitted to the *European Journal of Operational Research* (*EJOR*) (Brown et al., 2003).

6.2 Background

The Inland Revenue's original remit was to collect the taxes needed by the government to finance public services. Until recently its major task was the collection of income taxes from individuals and corporate taxes from businesses. Its remit is now broader and includes a number of other responsibilities, such as the payment of tax credits (e.g., to working families who are low paid) and the management of the system for collecting student loan repayments.

Formerly a department with the more or less single preoccupation of collecting taxes, it has become an agent of social change with tasks that include helping people to move into and to remain in work.

The Inland Revenue keeps its operations under continuous review, trying to find more efficient and effective ways of meeting the goals set for it by government. The study described here allowed some blue-sky thinking and analysis, set within the context of continuous review. The terms of reference for the overall study were set by the Board of the Inland Revenue and can be summarized as follows:

> *A study, in consultation with stakeholders, of the scope for modernising the operation of the UK's personal tax system. The study should take account of the current situation, developments elsewhere in the world, the possibilities for simplification and the opportunities provided by new technologies. It should take account of the need for a more "joined-up" approach to public policy and service provision.*

The study team took as its prime focus the impact of the personal tax system on people in employment, who pay tax on their earnings under the Pay As You Earn system (PAYE). In PAYE, employers deduct tax from wages and salaries using code numbers that reflect the individual circumstances of each employee and tax tables that specify the amounts to be deducted. Employees who are taxed through PAYE usually have very little direct contact with the Inland Revenue, since their employers do most of the work of calculating and deducting the tax on their earnings. Only those employees who have higher earnings, additional income from other sources or particularly complex affairs have to fill in a tax return at the end of the year.

The study team was a small group of tax policy experts that was able to draw on other resources it felt necessary. It chose to draw on the Inland Revenue's own OR resources and those of Lancaster University. This led to parallel work in both soft and hard OR. The hard OR was mainly based on data mining to establish profiles of customer groups and was conducted by in-house OR staff. The soft OR was based on Checkland's SSM, which was used to provide a structured and rigorous approach to the study and as a way of gathering stakeholder views. The interaction between the hard and soft OR was carefully managed so that the each gained from the insights generated by the other, which was of great benefit to the Study of Personal Tax (SPT). More detailed accounts of this work can be found in Brown et al. (2003).

6.3   The hard OR in the tax study

The study team wanted a better understanding of the types of customers served by the Revenue, to better appreciate their needs of the personal tax system. To do this, they used OR techniques to examine the types of individual served by the personal tax system and the heterogeneity in this customer base. Underlying this were two basic questions: "What would be required to meet customer needs?" and "What system(s) will be required if their needs were diverse rather than homogeneous?" These issues had become even more pressing with the changing role of the Revenue.

6.3.1   Data mining

The main "hard" OR approach used was data mining. This included basic data analysis (population counts, means, etc.), web/link analysis to understand linkages between events (e.g., the types of PAYE codes issued to individuals through time as their circumstances changed) and cluster analysis based on Kohonen self-organizing maps (Kohonen, 1990). The aim of the cluster analysis was to place individuals, as far as is possible, into homogeneous groupings based on input variables chosen by the analyst. Used in this way the data mining formed part of the problem structuring for the study and provided an evidence base that identified natural segments of the personal tax customer and their needs from the system.

The data mining used a random sample of just over 52,000 taxpayers based on the 1999/2000 tax year. For each of these taxpayers, data were extracted near to the end of December 2000, including age, employment history, sources of income and indications of their interactions with the tax system, such as the PAYE codes issued and repayments made in the previous year. The idea was to gain a snapshot of taxpayer characteristics and circumstances at that time. Extensive data validation and manipulation was carried out prior to clustering, since as is usually the case (Pidd, 2003) the available data were incomplete and needed some manipulation and analysis prior to the cluster analysis. This showed that some of the data were flawed, and where possible these were replaced by proxies. For example, age was not always present in the data set, but a person's National Insurance Number usually contains information that allows their age to be estimated approximately.

6.3.2   Basic analysis – population characteristics

The first aim was some overall understanding of the sample and an appreciation of how well the current system was working for different types of taxpayer. As an example, one driver for the study was a concern that the current system might not be meeting the needs of a changing workforce. The current tax system assumes that taxpayers are relatively homogeneous and enjoy stable employment, which may cause problems if a high proportion of people are switching employment during a tax year or because of an increase in portfolio workers. However, the data analysis showed the situation to be less extreme than this. For example, only about 5% of employees (excluding directors who accounted for 3% of the sample) had more than one consecutive job during the year, and as many as 40% had not changed jobs/main source of income within the last five years.

6.3.3 Cluster analysis

The cluster analysis was done with the Acustar software (package developed in-house by EDS) and employed Kohonen self-organizing maps (Kohonen, 1990), an approach based on neural clustering. The software was chosen because of the quality of output produced which is particularly good when explaining results to business experts. The approach is iterative, starting with initial clusters set up by the software that allocates a vector to each cluster based on random values for each input variable. The analyst specifies the number of clusters N into which the input data set is to be organized, the number of training cycles to be used (individuals being added to a cluster during each iteration based on the minimum distance between the individual and the cluster vector) and the extent to which clusters and neighbouring clusters are updated during the training. The extent to which clusters are updated also varies during training as specified by the analyst. As clusters are updated, the cluster vector changes to reflect the individuals allocated to that cluster. In turn, this may cause the cluster to attract different individuals during later training cycles. Toward the end of the training cycles the map hopefully converges in that there is very little updating of the vector as individuals are generally attracted toward the same cluster, and the cluster vector converges toward the vector means for the individuals within it.

Thus, clusters form as the training progresses, leading to a cluster map, with similar clusters placed contiguously. Though presented in two dimensions, the map is actually a torus (a doughnut shape) in which the extreme left and right-hand regions are joined, as are the top and bottom regions.

It is not sensible to try to develop a map from a single attempt. Hence, the process of clustering was gradual, and at each attempt important parameters, such as the size of map, training cycle and the inclusion of particular variables were amended as felt appropriate. In most cases a 5×5 cluster map was used, although on occasion this was thought too large, particularly when clustering on more homogeneous sub-groupings of the population (e.g., company directors), when a 3×3 map was used.

This clustering was part of an attempt to understand how heterogeneous was the customer base and, in turn, a wish to understand how well Inland Revenue processes mapped on to the clusters. Hence, once clusters were formed they were examined in the light of how individuals in the cluster interacted with the Revenue (e.g., number of changes to PAYE codes issued per annum, etc.). This showed how well or how badly the processes of the personal tax system (PTS) worked for the various customer groups.

The data mining identified several segments with very simple affairs, for whom the system works very well. However, other groups were not so well served. For example, transient workers, usually young people, whose affairs tended to be more complex and for whom PAYE may not operate very accurately. As expected the clustering identified other groups with complex affairs for whom, again, PAYE was not so well suited. The clustering and the attempt to understand the clusters in the light of Inland Revenue processes provided a useful basis for steering the SSM work in systems design.

6.3.4 Conclusions from the data mining

The main conclusion from this data mining is that the vast majority of taxpayers have very simple tax affairs and the system appears to work very well for them. But the system works less well for some segments, and as is discussed later the SSM part of the project sought to identify ways in which the needs of these customers could better be met. Another valuable insight from the cluster analysis was the extent to which traditional segments (e.g., company directors) were actually heterogeneous groups, containing people with very diverse characteristics and needs. Indeed some, directors had much more in common with employees with very simple affairs than with other directors with much more complex affairs.

Perhaps the major benefit of the data mining was that it provided solid, quantifiable evidence of the current operation of the personal tax system in the UK. It moved the debate away from subjective statements of interest and demonstrated that, for many UK taxpayers the system works well – though this does not mean that these people like paying income tax! It provided objective evidence of types of taxpayer, their needs of the tax system and the ways in which they interact with it.

6.3.5 Using the data analysis and data mining

The results of the data mining were presented at workshops with Inland Revenue business experts and statisticians to obtain their interpretation of the clusters. This was valuable in helping to interpret clusters and to ensure that the analysis was meaningful.

The data analysis and data mining formed part of the problem structuring for the study and provided an evidence base that identified natural segments of the personal tax customer and their needs from the system. Thus, it is not just soft OR methods that can be used for problem structuring, some hard techniques can also be drawn on for this. Pidd (1977, 2003) argued that problem structuring often involves more than soft methods and may include preliminary data analysis.

6.4 The soft OR

The soft OR approach in this study was based on Checkland's SSM (Checkland, 1981, 2000), which was used for two purposes. The first was as an overarching methodological guide. The second was used to gain understanding of how different stakeholders regard the personal tax system in the UK, an aspect discussed here in more detail. The SSM work was carried out by Inland Revenue staff, academic staff from Lancaster University (including Checkland) and external consultants well versed in SSM. The SSM was the basis for a series of consultations with internal and external stakeholders who might be affected by changes to the personal tax system. They were invited to comment on their opinion of its current operations and to suggest how it might be changed.

6.4.1 Workshops

SSM formed the basis for a series of workshops and interviews with a range of stakeholders. Each workshop aimed to elicit stakeholders' requirements and ideas by drawing comparisons between how they viewed the current tax system and what they would like to see in their ideal tax system. The idea, as shown in Figure 6.1, was that this comparison would generate ideas for change. As with many problem-solving approaches, this stage of the work allowed the divergent elicitation of many possible options for the future. However, it is important to follow this with a convergent phase in which fewer

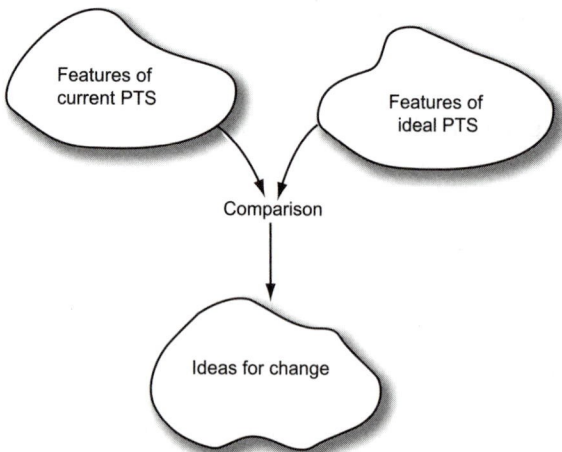

Figure 6.1—Generation of ideas for change.

main themes are examined in detail. SSM was used to support both the divergent and convergent phases.

Three broad groups of stakeholders were consulted through a series of workshops and interviews:

- external customer workshops were held with people, such as employees, tax credit recipients, pensioners, employers and accountants;
- internal (Inland Revenue) stakeholder workshops were held with groups such as operational staff, IT experts and tax policy experts;
- individual interviews were held with senior members of the Inland Revenue and representatives from other government departments.

With 14 workshops in prospect, which were to be conducted by a range of people including members of the Inland Revenue team, Lancaster University staff and external consultants, a consistent approach and format was needed.

A typical workshop began with an introduction to the study, its background and its aims and objectives. Once participants were introduced to the study, the workshop focused on eliciting their requirements and ideas. As mentioned earlier and captured in Figure 6.2, this was based on a comparison of participants' views of the current system and how they would like it to be.

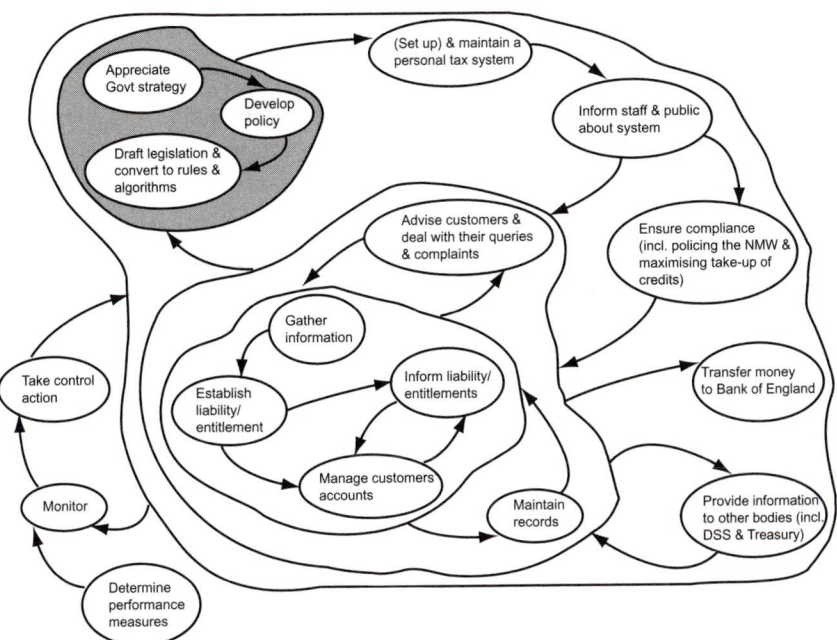

Figure 6.2—High-level system model for personal tax.

Such a comparison can be actually rather difficult in practice. Particularly as workshops covered a broad range of stakeholder groups, each with varying degrees of knowledge and experience of the PTS. Hence, each workshop used a core metaphor – the tax system as a car. Participants were asked what type of car, for them, represented the tax system and its features. If they suggested an old, barely reliable banger, this suggested that their experience of the tax system was less than positive. This simple device ensured that the discussions in the workshops remained at a strategic level and kept away from detailed issues. Once settled into this mode of thinking about the current tax system, participants discussed the features they would like to see in an ideal personal tax system. By drawing comparison between the two, participants were encouraged to come up with ideas for change that would deliver their ideal system.

These ideas were expanded, using a pro forma in everyday language, designed to elicit the components of a root definition in SSM. Following each workshop the ideas generated were converted into root definitions via *PQRs*, CATWOEs and 3Es (see Section 6.4.3 for explanations), providing a clear definition and an appreciation of the nature and scope of the ideas generated by participants. The understanding gained through this proved a useful precursor to the following stages of the SSM study. Using this approach proved to be very successful in encouraging participants to contribute their views and ideas. The workshops generated over 90 distinct ideas for changing the current system: some were aimed at improvements within the current system, while several proposed fundamental changes to the way the personal tax system is operated.

6.4.2   Clustering and reducing the range of ideas

The workshops produced far too many ideas to analyse in the time available, and there was considerable overlap. Thus, it made sense to cluster and prioritize them. This is a common difficulty in any problem solving that includes both divergent and convergent phases. Ideas are generated in the divergent phase, but these must be evaluated and some will be selected, which requires a convergent phase. This divergent to convergent shift was accomplished via a three-stage process. This included clustering together ideas that were extensions of or variations on other ideas. For example, a number of workshops raised ideas around improving the linkages between Inland Revenue computer systems, allowing easier access to taxpayers' records and a more complete picture of taxpayers' affairs. These ideas were grouped together to form a single cluster.

The clustered ideas were categorized as to their feasibility – excluding, for example, those that were already planned or too ill-defined – and evaluated as to the likely positive impact of ideas on the tax system. Clusters with a minor impact were excluded in favour of those expected to have a high impact, leaving 10 major themes to take forward.

Table 6.1—An example of a root definition.

Customers	Staff, individuals
Actors	Inland Revenue and its IT partners
Transformation	Takes and updates information from different systems and presents it in coherent ways
Weltanschauung	It would allow staff to operate more efficiently, would improve customer service. Further, treating an individual's tax affairs as a single entity is a good thing. The change could also lead to a paperless office and may improve compliance
Ownership	Inland Revenue
Environmental constraints	The IT resources available, the legislation on data sharing and resources to run such a system

6.4.3 Working with the major themes

A core concept of SSM is its use of root definitions to structure a debate about action that might be taken. A root definition expresses hypothetical activity that may later be represented in an activity model, given a particular world view. The analysis team developed root definitions for each of these themes. A root definition in SSM has six elements captured in the CATWOE mnemonic – customers, actors, transformation process, Weltanschauung, ownership, environmental constraints – (Checkland, 1981, 2000).

Since it is not always straightforward to go from a theme to a root definition, an intermediate step was employed in this study. This is often known as PQR, based on the following formulation for a proposal: that it would "do P, by Q, to achieve R". Hence, three fundamental questions were asked of each major theme. To illustrate this consider the proposal to provide a single interface linking the various Inland Revenue computer systems in use as illustrated in Table 6.1.

Finally, it is fundamental to SSM that such idealizations should be grounded in ways that allow their performance to be measured and controlled. This is usually captured in the notion of the 3Es shown in Table 6.2 (Checkland and Scholes, 1990), using the same example as before.

6.4.4 Activity modelling

In most SSMs the idea is to identify changes that are systemically desirable and culturally feasible (Checkland, 1981). Usually, this requires activity modelling, using systems concepts. In this study this was done by developing

Table 6.2—Performance measures from the root definition.

	Fundamental issue	Examples of performance measures
Efficacy	Does the system do what it is supposed to do (relates to P)?	Allows single edit revision Delivers information required reliably (i.e., correct information)
Efficiency	Are minimum resources used (relates to Q)?	Minimal resources to use and maintain
Effectiveness	Are the high-level aims of the system being met (relates to R)?	Improves customer service Accurate and coherent customer data available

the generic model of the UK PTS shown in Figure 6.2. It is important to realize that in SSM a model is not intended as a would-be representation of the real world, rather it is a vehicle to support debate – in this case among the tax policy experts of the Inland Revenue. The generic model identifies those activities that must be present in any modern personal taxation system in the UK. For example, the three activities within the shaded shape of the figure relate to the need to align the tax system with political priorities.

The ten root definitions were reduced down to the four that potentially had the largest impact on areas of concern to the study, such as current system strains and issues of great concern to emerge from workshops. While the others were not ignored, they were regarded as less pressing. Activity models, based on variations of the generic model, were then developed for the four systems encapsulated within the root definition.

At this stage the concern is less with how such activities might actually be implemented and more with gaining agreement that they must be present if the changes are to be systemically desirable and culturally feasible. That is, they accord with known principles for the operation of purposeful and purposive systems and that they are acceptable to the people involved.

These models were thoroughly evaluated, in terms of their impact on customers, how well they supported the various roles the department now plays and the extent to which the system exhibited the ideal features stakeholders described in workshops. They were also tested against possible future scenarios for the department to measure their robustness and adaptability to change. Finally, the implications of implementing and operating the proposed changes were elicited by drawing comparisons between activity models for the current and alternative systems. All this combined to give a rich account and understanding of the possible changes and to support further debate within the department.

6.5 Complementarity

6.5.1 Some general aspects

The preceding makes it clear that both the hard and soft streams of work contributed a great deal to the outcomes of the study in their own rights. SSM provided a consistent basis for the workshops, a methodology for analysing and interpreting the data they produced and a framework for taking the study forward. Similarly, the data mining provided learning on the operation of the current system, offered further insights into the needs of customer segments and ensured that these were objectively, rather than anecdotally, composed. However, the complementarity gained from combining the two further enhanced the value OR brought to the study. Using SSM to structure the process of carrying out the study also contributed to maximizing the benefit to be gained from complementarity. It proved to be a valuable tool in bringing together the various strands of work within the study and in surfacing opportunities for combining the hard and soft OR approaches.

Throughout the course of the study, the two approaches complemented each other in a number of ways. For instance, amalgamating the findings from the data mining and SSM enriched the team's understanding of customers, their requirements and problems they may face with the PTS. Combining the two approaches allowed an extended coverage of the customer base. Data mining provided detailed information on the employee population, allowing the investigation of some quite small subgroups or segments within this population that could not practically have been represented in the SSM consultation. For example, some individuals have several directorships and, therefore, fairly complex tax affairs, a segment given the name "career directors". On the other hand, the SSM consultation exercise allowed access to a much broader range of stakeholders in the PTS, including employers, tax agents and Inland Revenue staff in addition to employees.

Complementarity was also achieved where the approaches overlapped through merging the different perspectives offered by each approach. Data mining identified current behaviour and taxpayer characteristics; for example, pensioners who had simple tax affairs (i.e., one stable source of income) would require a PTS involving only minimal, straightforward contact with the Revenue. By contrast, SSM consultations identified customers' needs based on the views, opinions and experiences of workshop participants. For example, consistent with the data-mining evidence, some pensioners who were consulted wanted simplified forms to complete in line with their simple affairs. But others took this concept further, suggesting that the Revenue should assume continuity of a taxpayer's affairs, with pensioners having to fill in forms only when their circumstances changed. Hence, in this way, data mining indicated some of the requirements of the system, and SSM allowed for the investigation of stakeholder requirements and provided some of the potential systems appropriate to them.

However, the complementary use of hard and soft OR means more than this, for it offers a synergy in which the whole is greater than the sum of the parts. Running the two streams of work in parallel opened opportunities for interaction between the approaches. Feeding outcomes from the hard into the soft and vice versa was used repeatedly in the study both to enhance understanding and validate outcomes. As an obvious example, emergent findings from the data mining helped the team to understand how the different groups might view the current tax system, which informed the workshops. For example, the data mining highlighted the different pensioner segments. This was used in the pensioner workshop to ensure that the needs of those with simple affairs were not overlooked when considering the needs of pensioners with more complex affairs. Similarly, issues emerging from workshops, such as the burden of completing tax returns by those with simple affairs, could be investigated through data mining, which allowed the identification of customer groups most affected by this.

Another illustration of such complementarity was in testing the robustness of alternative systems developed through the SSM consultation. This testing was done by assessing the effect of the proposed changes on the customer groupings that emerged from the data mining. As well as checking for any unintended effects, this allowed the alternatives to be compared in terms of delivering the customer requirements expressed in workshops and derived from the data mining. The results of the data mining allowed the quantification of any issues, and where possible enhancements to the models were made. For example, one system developed to ensure taxpayers with multiple and/or frequently changing sources of income paid the right tax in each year also had the effect of increasing the compliance burden on employees in single stable employment. The results of the data mining allowed the team to compare the relative size of each of the segments, helping to resolve this trade-off.

Progressing the data mining and SSM in parallel, however, also had its drawbacks. One obvious way that the soft and hard techniques could have complemented each other would have been to use the customer segments from the initial cluster analysis to construct the stakeholder groups for consultation. This was not done due to the time pressure to get SSM workshops under way. Yet, it was possible later to check the composition of the workshops to ensure that all the significant customer segments were adequately covered. Synthesizing the material in this manner added a great deal of value to the project, providing a more detailed understanding of the problems raised and alternative systems considered.

6.5.2 Value and outcome of the study

Some form of quantified evaluation that allows option comparison is the hoped-for outcome of many hard OR studies. On the other hand, some form of agreement stemming from shared perceptions that will eventually inform learning and action is what comes from soft OR. What was the outcome from this study of personal taxation? Though it may be several years before the outcomes are seen in practice, it seems that both outcomes are evident. The data mining provided quantifiable estimates of taxpayer segments – for example, as mentioned earlier, 40% of taxpayers had remained in the same job for the last five years. This can clearly inform any decisions about the need to provide different treatment for different segments. Thus, even hard OR can lead to improved shared perceptions. The soft OR though clearly led to shared perceptions about the types of response that would be needed from the Inland Revenue were it to implement the ideas for improvement from the various stakeholders. Together, the potential impact on changes to the tax system is very large.

6.5.3 Purpose of the study

A different tack is needed when discussing the purpose of the OR component of this study, for it was intended to be a complementary mixture of hard and soft from the start. One interpretation of the terms of reference would have led to the study team to move as quickly as possible to statements of what changes were needed and how they should be implemented, using computer systems or whatever seemed appropriate. However, the team wisely chose to act otherwise by trying to understand the taxpayer segments, the ways in which current systems worked for them and the preferences of those segments as uncovered in the workshops.

Thus, though the terms of reference were taken as given, the interpretation of those terms was crucial to the success of the study. In this way the team allowed themselves to learn as the work proceeded. They learned about how data mining and SSM may be used in such work and they learned about the current operation of the tax system and how stakeholders wish it to be in the future. They also learned what conceptual elements would be needed in any attempt to develop systems to implement any changes that may be agreed.

Acknowledgements

Peter Checkland led the team through the application of SSM in this work, developing the particular approach used as the work progressed. Thanks are also due to the other members of the team who were helpful and supportive throughout. These are: Brian Mace, Mary Aiston, Angela Walker and Ian Casey of the Inland Revenue; Mike Pidd and Mark Westcombe from Lancaster University; and Steve Clarke, Mike Hayes and John Poulter, who were the consultants employed.

References

Brown J., Cooper C. and Pidd M. (2003) A taxing problem: The complementary use of hard and soft OR in public policy. Submitted to *European Journal of Operational Research*.

Checkland P.B. (1981) *Systems Thinking, Systems Practice*. John Wiley & Sons, Chichester, UK.

Checkland P.B. (2000) *Systems Thinking, Systems Practice*, revised edn. John Wiley & Sons, Chichester, UK.

Checkland P.B. and Scholes J. (1990) *Soft Systems Methodology in Action*. John Wiley & Sons, Chichester, UK.

Kohonen T. (1990) The self-organizing map. *Proceedings of the IEEE*, **78**(9), 1464–80.

Pidd M. (1977) OR methodology. In S.C. Littlechild (ed.) *OR for Managers*. Philip Allan, Oxford, UK.

Pidd M. (2003) *Tools for Thinking: Modelling in Management Science*, 2nd edn. John Wiley & Sons, Chichester, UK.

7 Mental models and learning in system dynamics practice

John Morecroft
London Business School

7.1 Introduction

System dynamics treats mathematical models as "transitional objects" – tangible, interactive and custom-built maps and simulators for individual and team learning. The approach is illustrated *with* a model of BBC World Service built with a management team directly responsible for strategy and planning. The managers provided objective knowledge of real operating constraints affecting international radio broadcasters as well as their insights into World Service operating policies. These factual and judgemental data were used to arrive at a feedback representation and simulator suitable for investigating the effect of new strategies and funding scenarios. Samples of model structure show how the team's knowledge was captured in diagrams and equations. The case sheds light on complementarity in model building and, in particular, the relevance of transitional objects to the hard-versus-soft modelling debate.

In a recent episode of a popular television programme called *Changing Places* a computer-gaming enthusiast who had clocked-up hundreds of simulated hours driving imaginary high-performance cars was invited to drive a real racing car around Silverstone. The experience was sobering. He spun off dramatically. Even when he stayed on the track he failed to achieve competitive lap times.

This story is quite revealing about the purpose, limitations and use of models and simulators. A common view is that models are representations of reality intended to be useful to someone charged with managing or understanding that reality. In this case reality has a well-defined meaning (the real racing car on the track at Silverstone), and it is clear that the computer model falls short of reality in some important ways. The natural temptation for the model user is to demand a better model – one that represents a racing car more accurately. More realism is better.

However, there are several problems with high-fidelity modelling. The most obvious is that realism requires ever more attention to detail. The model can become so large and complex that no one really understands it or has confidence in it. Slightly less obvious is that realism itself is often subject to debate if the system being modelled is ill-defined (suppose we're not really sure, before the event, whether the Silverstone challenge is to drive a car or a motorcycle). Finally, the elusive quest for realism can obscure the value available from having some kind of tangible model (even if it is much simplified) versus no model at all.

To appreciate the value of a deliberately simplified model it is useful to reconsider some positive but hidden aspects of the Silverstone racing experience. Most basically, the opportunity to "change places" and drive a real racing car at Silverstone would never have arisen without the gaming simulator. The gaming enthusiast was passionate about motor racing and knew much more about the sport than the average person. He had learned a lot about motor racing from hundreds of hours interaction with the simulator. He was familiar with the car's instrumentation and controls, he knew Silverstone's layout, he had acquired some expertise in cornering technique (even though he later spun off) and he knew competitive lap times.

7.2 Mental models, transitional objects and formal models

The would-be racer's success (albeit limited) calls for a new or expanded definition of a model. A model is a tangible aid to imagination and learning, a transitional object to help people make better sense of a partly understood world. This definition focuses particular attention on the interaction that takes place between the model that someone carries in their head of the way something works (their mental model) and a formal model. To illustrate let's use a much different example provided by mathematician and computer scientist Seymour Papert in his remarkable book *Mindstorms: Children, Computers and Powerful Ideas* (1980). He begins the book with an engaging personal recollection, "The gears of my childhood" (pp. vi–vii), a story of how he came to better understand the working of complex sets of gears and ultimately abstract ideas in mathematics:

> *[B]efore I was two years old I had developed an intense involvement with automobiles. The names of car parts made up a very substantial portion of my vocabulary: I was particularly proud knowing about the parts of the transmission system, the gearbox and most especially the differential. It was of course many years later before I understood how gears worked: but once I did, playing with gears became a favorite pastime. I loved rotating circular objects against one another in gearlike motions and naturally, my first "erector set" project was a crude gear system.*

Figure 7.1 shows the role of the formal model (in this case a crude gear system) in a learning process. On the left is the child's mental model of a gear system

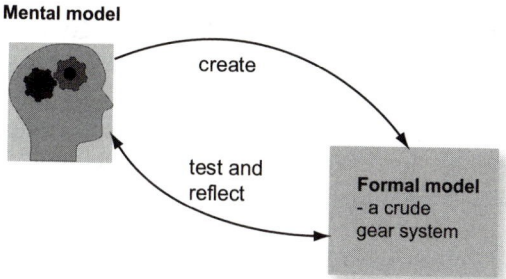

Figure 7.1—Formal model as transitional object for individual learning – "gears of childhood".

Based on an idea of Papert (1980).

depicted as gears in the mind. On the right is the formal model – a tangible set of gear parts that can be assembled, broken apart and reassembled in lots of different ways. At the start the child's mental model is primitive and naive. But the activity of repeatedly playing with the gear set leads to a much more sophisticated understanding and deeper appreciation of gearlike motions. The mental model goes through a series of "transitions" from naive to more sophisticated through repeated use of the gear set as a transitional object.

Papert fondly recalls his early learning experience:

[I] became adept at turning wheels in my head and at making chains of cause and effect: "This one turns this way so that must turn that way so . . . ." I found particular pleasure in such systems as the differential gear, which does not follow a simple linear chain of causality since the motion in the transmission shaft can be distributed in many different ways depending on what resistance they encounter. I remember quite vividly my excitement at discovering that a system could be lawful and completely comprehensible without being rigidly deterministic. I believe that working with differentials did more for my mathematical development than anything I was taught in elementary school. Gears, serving as models, carried many otherwise abstract ideas into my head.

Note that the definition of "model-as-transitional-object" suggesting a formal model achieves its value principally through creation and use. For a transitional object to be useful, it must obviously be an adequate representation but must also be tangible in a way that abstract ideas are not. As Papert comments, gears serving as models not only enabled him to think more clearly about gearlike motion but also carried abstract ideas about mathematics into his head.

7.3   Models of business and social systems

The significance of viewing formal models as transitional objects is the emphasis placed on aiding understanding rather than replicating reality. The idea there is a singular and objective world out there to be modelled is replaced with the softer notion that a formal model can help to improve mental models. It is through mental models that we interpret and make sense of the world around us. And in business and social systems mental models shape decisions and actions. As Forrester (1975a, p. 213) has noted:

> *[T]he mental image of the world around us that we carry in our heads is a model. One does not have a city or government in his head. He has only selected concepts and relationships which he uses to represent the real system. A mental image is a model. All our decisions are taken on the basis of models. All laws are passed on the basis of models. All executive actions are taken on the basis of models. The question is not to use or ignore models. The question is only a choice among alternative models.*

Figure 7.2 shows the alternative mental models of a management team. Like Papert's gears in the mind each member of the management team carries around an image of the organization. Individuals carry different mental images depending on their experience, responsibilities, power, ambitions and objectives. A formal model is an instrument to link these different mental models with the objective of improving the quality of the decisions and actions taken by the team.

The kind of formal model created depends on the kind of changes and refinements of mental models that are sought. System dynamics assumes that a competent management team can collectively describe the operating structure

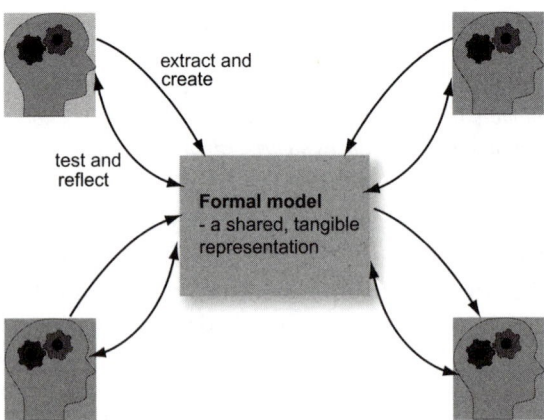

Figure 7.2—Formal model as transitional object for management team learning.

of their organization – how the different functions, divisions and regions work individually. Where the team needs help and where mental models are deficient are in:

1. seeing how the pieces fit together (taking an overview; seeing the forest while not losing sight of the trees); and
2. determining the performance over time (the dynamic consequences) when the parts of the organization interact with each other.

Like Papert's gear set the formal model is created to allow the management team to test, reflect and learn about some imperfectly understood aspect of their world – in this case the relationship between the operating structure and the performance over time of the organization. Obviously, the purpose of the formal model determines the kind of information included in the model and the resulting interaction between the formal model and mental models. In the next sections we review the construction and content of a model created for a management team at BBC World Service to illustrate the kind of representation appropriate to refine collective understanding of structure and dynamic behaviour. We then use this example to draw some general conclusions about hard and soft models for management.

7.4 The BBC World Service modelling project

The BBC World Service is an international radio broadcaster transmitting news, analysis and current affairs to a global audience. It aims to be the first choice for authoritative impartial news, a forum for the exchange of ideas, bringing benefit to the UK and acting as a showcase for British talent. While funded by the British government, World Service is editorially independent and managerially accountable to the Director General of the BBC.

At the time of the original study in the mid-1990s World Service operated a network of more than 50 transmitters covering 65% of the earth and 80% of the world population. It broadcast over 1,200 hours of programming per week in English and 43 other languages reaching 138 million people every week. In many respects the organization was highly successful. Its audience was more than double the size of its nearest rival and its cost per listener (a key performance indicator in radio broadcasting) was only 10% of rivals' cost.

Nevertheless, continuing pressure on public funding brought a more insecure environment with the need to seriously consider possible funding reductions and their implications for the organization. This environment provided the justification for an in-depth study. As a result a modelling project was launched by two senior members of the strategy development area with the

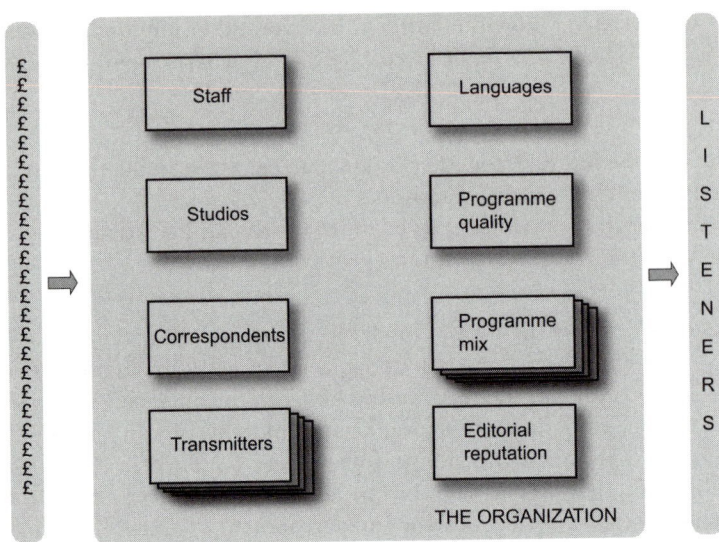

Figure 7.3—Resources in an international broadcaster – a list of tangibles and intangibles that convert funding into listeners.

intention of exploring funding, programming and technology scenarios over the interval 1995 to 2005.

The project required the active participation of an experienced management team of five people from World Service working with two modellers. The team met on four occasions spread over three months. Each meeting lasted for half a day and resulted in a shared representation of World Service suitable for thinking about funding scenarios.

Figure 7.3 shows the beginnings of a World Service model. On the left of the figure is the budget shown by "£" and on the right are listeners. In the centre, within the organization's boundary, is the list of resources that effectively convert the budget into listeners. There is a mixture of tangible and intangible resources identified by the management team as being particularly important for attracting and retaining listeners. The tangible resources include staff and studios in Bush House, correspondents in various regions and the number of transmitters (mostly short wave but also FM and long wave). The intangibles include the language portfolio (the menu of different languages broadcast), programme mix (the blend of news, factual services, music and drama), programme quality and editorial reputation.

At any point in time the number of listeners depends (in a rather complex way) on the amount and combination of resources. For example, if World Service were to purchase more short-wave transmitters its signal would reach new regions and attract more listeners. With extra staff the organization could offer additional hours of programming and again attract more listeners by offering new content at convenient times. In either case the extra resources require additional budget.

The system dynamics model helps the management team to visualize the network of resources, to examine how they are interrelated and to explore how they develop over time. But is there really just one model to represent how World Service builds resources, attracts listeners and achieves superior cost performance? Or does each member of the management team have a different mental model of the organization and, therefore, quite different views on how best to deploy the available budget? These questions lie at the heart of the distinction between hard and soft models. Here I want to show that the process of creating a system dynamics model with a management team, using the model as a transitional object, leads to a single shared representation specifically suited to the purpose of exploring funding, programming and technology scenarios. The result is a more complete image of the parts of the organization and how they work together cost-effectively over time to generate listeners. Some parts of the model are hard in the sense they represent natural, scientific or technical processes that cannot be altered by management. Other parts of the model are soft in the sense they represent policies and procedures devised and used by management to run the organization.

7.4.1   Asset stock accumulation – a real process

System dynamics directs management attention toward the performance of organizations over time. While Figure 7.3 is a list of the main resources that are believed to contribute to performance, it does not show how these resources change with time. Such change is the result of a real process of asset stock accumulation (Dierickx and Cool, 1989; Sterman, 2000, chap. 6; Warren, 2002). The level or amount of any resource in a business or social system is the accumulated difference over time between the inflow to the resource and the outflow. Figure 7.4 shows the process in BBC World Service. Each resource is shown with an inflow and outflow controlled by a tap, analogous to a tank of water being simultaneously filled and drained. So, for example, the number of staff at any point in time is equal to the number already there plus those recently hired (the inflow) minus those who have recently left (the outflow). Similarly, the number of transmitters at any point in time is equal to the number already there plus newly commissioned transmitters (the inflow) minus those taken out of service (the outflow).

Asset stock accumulation sets practical limits to the pace of change achievable in an organization. The only way to grow additional resources is through accumulation, which takes time. The only way to alter the balance of resources is to grow some or reduce others, which also takes time. Stock accumulation captures the real inertia of organizations. Mental models that ignore

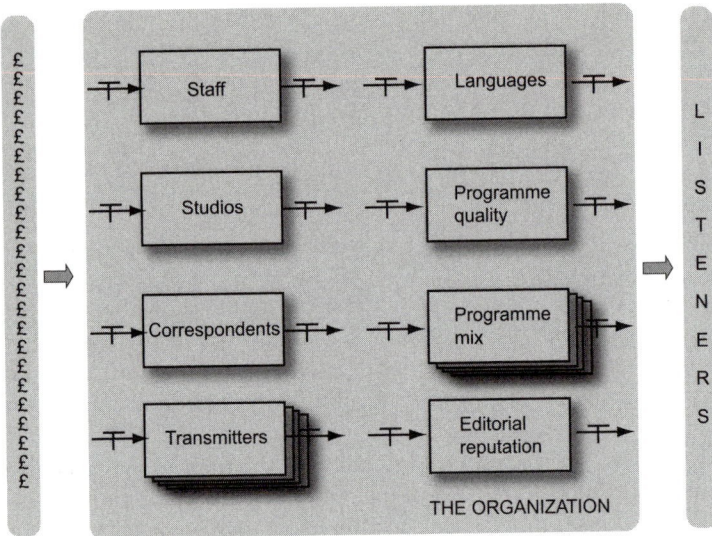

Figure 7.4—Resource accumulations in an international radio broadcaster that convert funding into listeners.

stock accumulation are flawed. Plans that overlook inertia will fail in much the same way that a racing car will spin off the track if cornered too fast.

7.4.2   Connections between resources – two types of causality

The rest of the model represents the web of connections that link the various resource accumulations (Wolstenholme, 1990, chap. 2). There are two distinctive types of causality in this web. There are operating constraints – practical rules for how resources combine to deliver products and services. There are also operating policies – management decision-making processes that guide resource accumulation. Many if not most operating constraints arise from well-understood constitutive laws that are similar for all organizations in the same industry. Where there are operating constraints there is an objective reality to be modelled. In contrast, operating policies can differ significantly between competing organizations. The connections that comprise operating policy are socially constructed. Unlike constitutive laws they can be modified and redesigned by management. Nevertheless, they are enduring and define the unique character of an organization.

7.4.3   Tracing practical causality

A management team can usually agree on the practical causality behind operating constraints. Consider, for example, the link between transmitters and audience in BBC World Service. Common sense suggests that more

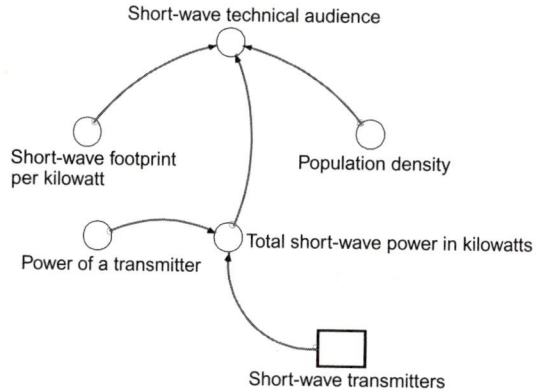

Short-wave technical audience

Short-wave footprint per kilowatt

Population density

Power of a transmitter

Total short-wave power in kilowatts

Short-wave transmitters

Figure 7.5—The link between transmitters and audience – an example of practical causality.

transmitters will lead to a larger audience. But exactly how does this relationship operate? Figure 7.5 shows the link between short-wave transmitters and the so-called technical audience that arose from conversations with team members. The map represents a shared mental model of how this particular part of the organization operates, accepted by all because it is consistent with expert opinion and established technical knowledge of short-wave broadcasting.

The number of short-wave transmitters is shown as a stock accumulation in the lower right of the figure (for visual simplicity the inflows and outflows are excluded from the picture). The short-wave technical audience at the top of the figure measures the number of people who could receive the broadcast signal, regardless of whether or not they wanted to listen. This measure of audience is a function of the number of transmitters, the footprint or area served per transmitter and the average population density in the regions served.

The technical audience is one component of a more complex web of causal connections that drives the listening audience. Another component is potential language listeners – the number of people with access to radios who could understand a radio programme regardless of whether or not they receive the broadcast signal. This number is a function of the current language portfolio, speakers per language and radio's share of language speakers.

Maximum audience measures the number of listeners who can understand at least one broadcast language, have access to a radio and can receive the signal. This number comes from combining technical potential audience and potential language listeners. Finally, the listening audience measures the number of listeners from the available pool who choose to tune in to programmes offered by World Service. This number is a fraction of the maximum audience and depends in part on the convenience of programme scheduling. Convenience can be traced through broadcast hours (the number of hours per day the station is on air) to staff hours available and, ultimately, to the number of staff.

This example shows how the practical knowledge of the management team (and expert advisers) is captured and shared to yield a reasonably objective and non-controversial representation of the causal links from three resources (transmitters, language portfolio and staff) to the listening audience.

7.4.4   Operating policy and goal-seeking feedback

The remainder of the connecting web represents the operating policies that management uses to adjust the level of resources. Here there is no one set of unambiguous causal connections because there are no physical laws that govern how much additional resource an organization should add to the existing stock. Policy is discretionary and under the control of management. Nevertheless, system dynamics provides guidelines for how to represent discretionary policies as goal-seeking feedback processes.

Figure 7.6 shows a general process of adjustment for a single resource in an organization (Forrester, 1961, chap. 10; Morecroft, 2002). Productive resource is a stock accumulation that increases due to an inflow from corrective action and decreases due to an outflow from attrition or loss. The focus here is on the inflow from corrective action. How much additional resource should the management add to the existing stock? The question presumes the organization is purposive – it is taking corrective action to achieve one or more goals. The goals may be implicit or explicit. An important though reasonable

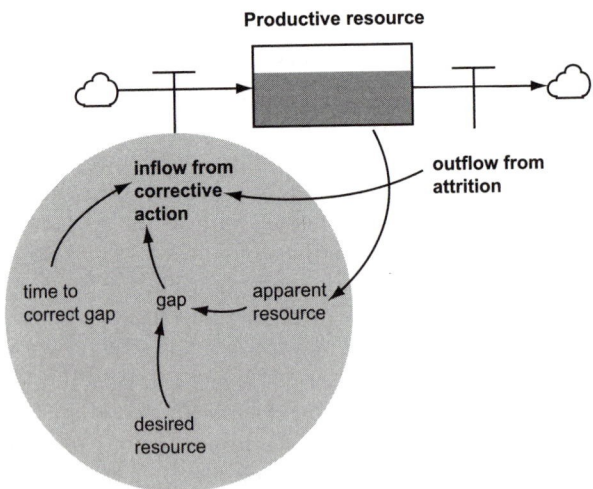

Figure 7.6—Operating policy and goal-seeking feedback – resource adjustment in a purposive organization. The grey area encloses the operating policy governing resource inflow.

assumption is that organizations pursue a variety of local operating goals that can be identified independently of broad strategic goals and intent.

Figure 7.6 shows that corrective action to acquire additional resource is influenced by three factors. In equilibrium the inflow is equal to the outflow. In other words a purposive organization with sufficient resources which is neither growing nor shrinking, will simply replace any resource lost through attrition. However, when a gap is recognized between the desired resource (the local operating goal) and the apparent resource (the current observed amount of resource), management takes additional corrective action to close the resource gap. The amount of corrective action depends both on the size of the gap and the time taken to correct the gap (the urgency attached to achieving the goal by those managers held responsible). The larger the gap the faster the inflow. The smaller the time to correct the gap the faster the inflow.

At first glance this general operating policy may seem rather simplistic and mechanical to capture the subtlety and variety of practical investment and resource adjustment. Nevertheless, it is capable of representing a very wide range of managerial behaviour from cautious to reckless, from highly co-ordinated and rational to unco-ordinated and speculative depending on the process of goal formation, the information that lies behind the choice of local operating goals, the accuracy with which current resource is known and the urgency attached to achieving the goal.

Figure 7.7 shows the operating policy that governs change in the language portfolio offered by World Service. Conversations with the management team revealed that World Service is deeply committed to broadcasting in a wide range of languages as part of the organization's mission to be the world's best known and most respected voice in international broadcasting. The current

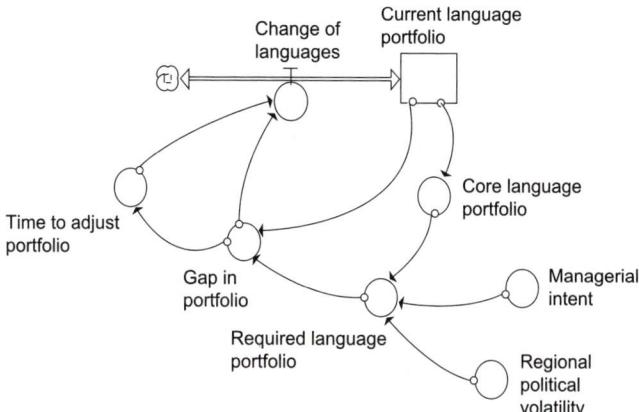

Figure 7.7—A changing language portfolio – an example of operating policy. The language portfolio reflects the history and traditions of the organization as well as current operating pressures.

portfolio of more than 40 languages reflects the history and traditions of the organization as well as current operating pressures. The language portfolio is politically sensitive, resistant to change and particularly difficult to reduce. The operating policy portrays the interplay of organizational pressures in this politically sensitive area of the business. Of course, there is a great deal of thinking that lies behind any one proposal to add or subtract a language. However, the map avoids the detail of individual languages. Instead, it shows the pressures that cause the portfolio to evolve in the aggregate.

The current language portfolio is shown as an accumulating resource in Figure 7.7. As languages are added or removed, the level of this resource will change. Change takes place when there is perceived to be a gap between the required and current language portfolio. The time to adjust the portfolio is assumed to be three months when adding languages and six months when removing languages, thereby capturing organizational bias against cuts in the portfolio. Deep-seated organizational resistance to change is captured in the goal formation process that lies behind the required language portfolio. The Figure shows the drivers of the required portfolio. An important driver is the core portfolio, those languages in the current portfolio that have attained a strong foothold because they have been in use for a long time. If the current portfolio has been stable for many years, then the core portfolio will be the same as the current portfolio. However, if short-term pressures result in language cuts, the core portfolio will retain an organizational memory of better times and thereby resist further cuts.

Short-term pressures on the language portfolio are represented by managerial intent and regional political volatility. Managerial intent to reduce the language portfolio can result from inadequate funding. In that case the required language portfolio will fall below the core portfolio, leading to language cuts. On the other hand, regional political volatility, such as a war in the Gulf or conflict in the Balkans, may call for additional languages so that news can reach the population in the affected region. When short-term pressures contradict each other, political volatility normally overrules managerial intent, reflecting the organizational importance attached to authoritative news coverage. Consequently, the required language portfolio can expand even in the face of inadequate funding.

We see here a policy for resource adjustment dominated by the history and tradition of an organization deeply committed to broadcasting and news. The process is behavioural rather than strictly economic. It is influenced by budget, but not fully determined by budget. The adjustment process is governed by goal-seeking feedback, but is not an optimal marginal adjustment. Inertia of the core language portfolio and bias toward language expansion from regional political volatility both contribute to the special status of the language portfolio within World Service.

It is important to appreciate that the feedback relationships governing change of languages are specific to World Service. Another radio broadcaster might adopt a much different approach to managing the number of broadcast languages, perhaps giving less weight to audience coverage and giving more weight to budgetary and economic factors, or else deliberately linking languages to planned growth of audience. Such alternative policies can also be represented by goal-seeking feedback, but the web of connections will be different depending on the information that drives goal formation. Operating policies are enduring, but they are not fixed by laws of nature in the same way as physical operating constraints.

On the soft–hard modelling spectrum, operating policies are soft because they are socially constructed by the organization that uses them. Policies embody the beliefs, culture, power and politics of organizations. They resist change, but can in principle be modified. They are therefore an appropriate topic for debate and redesign by management teams. By contrast, operating constraints are hard. They normally arise from scientific and technical laws about which there is widespread agreement.

7.4.5   An algebraic model

A similar mapping exercise was followed for all the other resources in World Service, leading to a shared map of the organization. A map constructed according to the principles of information feedback systems can be translated into an algebraic model and, ultimately, a simulator (Sterman, 2000). For many people the imperative to produce an algebraic model (typical of much applied system dynamics) is further evidence of hard modelling. Surely mathematical equations imply a very specific, singular and hard representation of business and social systems, far removed from the multiple worlds of soft modelling.

However, this conclusion is mistaken and oversimplifies the meaning both of soft modelling and system dynamics. As argued above, a system dynamics model contains both hard and soft elements. Asset stock accumulation and physical operating constraints are presumed to be hard, singular and real attributes of an organization. A management team must recognize and take proper account of the existence of these hard elements in order to sustain a feasible enterprise. You can't be an international radio broadcaster without transmitters. You can't send a radio signal to the Balkans or Baghdad from an FM transmitter placed on Bodmin Moor (because the normal range of FM is only about 50 miles). And you can't create new programmes without staff. These are but a handful of the many physical realities facing any broadcaster. On the other hand, operating policies are soft and socially constructed attributes of an organization. The number and type of transmitters ordered by a broadcaster is a discretionary operating policy under the control of management. Within the constraints of the available capital budget (which is itself a discretionary component of the overall corporate budget) there are a wide variety of different ways to spend the available money on FM, short-wave and long-wave transmitters.

Does a model containing hard and soft elements become harder when represented algebraically? Strictly speaking, the answer is no. The hard elements remain hard and the soft remain soft. The only difference is they are expressed more precisely than is normally possible in a diagram or with words alone. However, it takes time and skill to write good algebra. So what's the point of developing an algebraic model and simulator? The usual answer from professionals is that a simulator is a good way, perhaps the only reliable way, of deducing dynamic behaviour (and therefore performance over time) of a feedback system comprising the interacting hard and soft elements of the organization.

Another rather different way to express this advantage of a simulator is to say that it greatly extends the capability of a model as a transitional object. A simulator allows a whole variety of what-ifs and experiments that are not available from the map alone. To be sure, some conclusions about the adequacy of an organization's design may be derived from studying just the map (appreciating how the whole system fits together; seeing how one part depends on another; understanding the viewpoint and priorities of different divisions, regions and functions; overcoming the limitations of silo mentalities). But a simulator brings the map to life in new ways, making vivid and tangible the performance over time implied by the existing organization and enabling experiments on the results of policy change from re-designing the soft elements of the organization. These new interactions between mental models and a formal model are the prize for quantification. In this case the discipline of algebra creates a more playful model, stimulating rather than closing imaginative possibilities about the implications of strategy.

Figure 7.8 lists the equations for the World Service language portfolio. Technically, they are a set of difference equations (written in such a way as to

```
Current_Language_Portfolio(t) = Current_Language_Portfolio(t - dt) +
   (Change_of_Languages) * dt
INIT Current_Language_Portfolio = 43  {languages}


Change_of_Languages = Gap_in_Portfolio/Time_to_Adjust_Portfolio
Gap_in_Portfolio = Required_Language_Portfolio - Core_Language_Portfolio


Required_Language_Portfolio = Core_Language_Portfolio*Managerial_Intent
   *Regional_Political_Volatility
Core_Language_Portfolio =
   SMTH1(Current_Language_Portfolio,Time_to_Embed_Language)
Time_to_Embed_Language = 36 {months}
```

Figure 7.8—Equations for language portfolio.

closely approximate differential equations), governing the size of the language portfolio. This particular format for equations derives from the visual modelling language "ithink", one of several system dynamics modelling languages (Sterman, 2000, p. 904). Note the consistency of terminology between the equations and the corresponding map in Figure 7.7. This transparency is intended to build confidence in the algebraic model and show that it properly reflects the structural knowledge of the management team. The first equation is an algebraic restatement of stock accumulation. The current language portfolio at time (t) is identically equal to the language portfolio at an earlier point in time (t-dt) plus the change of languages over the interval dt. For example, this year's language portfolio contains all the languages from last year plus or minus any changes made during the year. The initial size of the portfolio is 43 languages.

The next two equations describe the process of adjusting the size of the language portfolio. A gap in the portfolio signals the need to add or remove languages from the portfolio. The size of the gap is simply the difference between the required language portfolio and the core language portfolio. The urgency with which management acts to close any gap is represented by the time to adjust portfolio. The organization's cultural preference to add rather than cut languages is captured by setting the time to adjust portfolio high (six months) when the gap is negative (too many languages) and low (three months) when the gap is positive (too few languages).

The final three equations represent organizational pressures influencing goal formation (Forrester, 1975b). The required language portfolio is anchored to the core language portfolio, itself a stable and long-term exponential moving average of the current language portfolio. This smoothing process represents the cultural inertia of the language portfolio, where the time to embed a language in the core portfolio is 36 months. The required language portfolio also responds to short-term pressure from both managerial intent and regional political volatility, represented as multipliers of the core language portfolio. According to this formulation, managerial intent and regional political volatility are quantifiable indices. They both assume a neutral value of 1, if there is no pressure to either increase or decrease the required portfolio. Managerial intent of less than 1 represents budgetary pressure for language cuts. Regional political volatility greater than 1 represents pressure to add languages in those regions affected by conflict or by war.

7.5 The impact of the World Service project on managerial thinking

The impact of the World Service modelling project is reported in Delauzun and Mollona (1999, pp. 369–70), who comment that the model building and simulation process influenced managerial intentions to pursue a number of strategic actions. This influence was achieved by elucidating the links between strategic actions and their dynamic consequences. Below are three examples cited in the paper. Notice in all these examples the reported role of the model in changing people's views and opinions, typical of a transitional object:

> [C]onsidering, for example, a very delicate issue such as the modification of control and measuring system, simulation of the model elucidated the possible advantages of moving towards total costing of activities and refining cost-driver analysis. By creating a positive attitude, the model developed in middle and top managers the intention and stimulated the course of action which led toward the introduction of total costing and the refinement and implementation of cost-driver analysis.

> [I]n the past, the language portfolio has been seen as too sensitive and political an issue to be touched except behind firmly closed doors. Whereas previously emphasis was on political costs of language portfolio reduction, the simulator highlighted the enormous benefits arising from the reduction of the number of languages in portfolio. The running of scenarios on the model and microworld led to more widespread and open discussion of languages broadcast by the BBC World Service, and in particular on the scope and consequences of reducing it and re-deploying the released resources. In this case, modelling, by illuminating costs and benefits arising from language portfolio reduction, changed attitudes to such a course of action.

> [T]he experience of running the microworld demonstrated to many staff and managers the difficulty of articulating a strategy sufficiently consistent to warrant public funding while at the same time maximising performance indicator targets (neither being sufficient on its own to ensure the survival of the organisation). Senior managers began to question the validity of a number of key indicators as a measure of account-ability to Government. They experienced through the simulations how revisions in accountability measures could have beneficial outcomes in terms of improved communication of organisational performances. As a consequence, senior managers developed the intention to re-bargain with Government indicators of performance and accountability.

7.6 Discussion

This final section provides an opportunity to reflect on complementarity in model building with reference to the World Service project and to system dynamics practice in general. The discussion contributes to the debate about hard-versus-soft modelling and, in particular, examines the role of transitional objects in model-based enquiry. Let's begin from the common sense view that mental models are the most ubiquitous and influential models in management and they are all soft models. However, this pragmatic view does not necessarily mean that all formal models must themselves be soft to handle unstructured management problems. What really matters is whether or not a formal model is a good transitional object for management thinking. Soft formal models are effective and so too are simulators, but for different reasons. Taking a slightly different tack I will also comment on the blend of hard and soft formulations normally found in system dynamics models to shed light on the important question of whether or not system dynamics should be described as a hard or deterministic systems approach.

7.6.1   Hard and soft in transitional objects

Formal models can be viewed as transitional objects for challenging, changing and improving mental models – tangible aids to enquiry, imagination and learning. Models that are effective transitional objects must somehow create an intense and engaging interaction with mental models whether through the model-building process itself, the use of the final model or both.

This view of models as incubators for knowledge and learning is relevant to the debate about hard and soft modelling. Are models-as-transitional-objects more likely to be soft than hard? Or could it be that transitional objects cannot be reliably placed on the hard–soft axis because some other attribute of the formal model (besides its hardness or softness) is responsible for the intensity of its interaction with mental models? To tackle these questions it is useful to bear in mind Figures 7.1 and 7.2 from the start of this paper, depicting interactions between a formal model and mental models.

One basic observation is that "softness" plays a vital role in any learning process. This is because softness resides in people's mental models of their shared world. In affairs of business and society these personal mental models differ from one another, sometimes radically. Yet, they can be changed, albeit with difficulty (Senge, 1990, chap. 10). So, in principle a formal model could be hard, singular and unchanging, and yet still accomplish a useful learning purpose if it led people to think and act differently. Papert's gears exemplify this point. A gear set is tangible. There is no ambiguity that a gear set comprises interlocking metal-toothed wheels. Yet, this set of wheels also contains within itself sufficient variety and hidden complexity to reveal secrets of gearlike motion to the patient and reflective learner. Moreover, this gearlike motion has relevance to abstract ideas in mathematics. As Papert recalls (pp. vi–vii):

> I saw multiplication tables as gears, and my first brush with equations in two variables (e.g., $3x \times 4y$) immediately evoked the differential (gear). By the time I had made a mental gear model of the relation between x and y, figuring how many teeth each gear needed, the equation had become a comfortable friend.

A similar argument applies to the racing car simulator. But there is a vital difference. The gear set is real whereas the racing car simulator is a representation of something real. We all know it is not a perfect representation. Nevertheless, like the gear set it is full of imaginative possibilities that engage the player and enable him/her to build some (rudimentary) understanding of the motor racing world. Through simulation the mental model of the would-be driver becomes better adapted to the racing world than it would otherwise be, even if it falls far short of Michael Schumacher's understanding.

When it comes to the world of business and strategy, management teams face unstructured problems characterized by the existence of multiple actors, multiple perspectives, incommensurable and/or conflicting interests, important intangibles and key uncertainties (Rosenhead and Mingers, 2001). All this seems far more ambiguous than gear sets or simulated racing cars. But these unstructured problems must still be approached and solved through the interaction of mental models, as implied by the communicating heads in Figure 7.2.

What kind of formal models can now serve as transitional objects? Soft formal models and related problem-structuring methods – such as soft systems methodology (Checkland, 1981, 1989) and strategic options development and analysis (Eden, 1989) – are well suited because they encourage exchange of viewpoints and thereby generate interaction between the team's mental models. As Mingers and Rosenhead (2003) argue, in order for problem structuring methods to provide effective decision support they must:

- *[e]nable several alternative perspectives to be brought into conjunction with each other;*
- *be cognitively accessible to actors with a range of backgrounds and without specialist training, so that the developing representation can inform a participative process of problem structuring;*
- *operate iteratively, so that the problem representation adjusts to reflect the state and stage of discussion among actors, as well as vice versa;*
- *permit partial or local improvements to be identified and committed to, rather than requiring a global solution, which would imply a merging of the various interests.*

Of these attributes the first three are directly concerned with interaction among stakeholders and, by implication, interaction of their mental models.

The BBC World Service project suggests another important dimension to interactivity not normally captured in the hard–soft modelling debate. The usual assumption of this debate is that singular hard models cannot shed light on alternative perspectives precisely because they are singular representations. However, the World Service model does to some degree embody alternative perspectives within its separate goal-oriented feedback processes controlling the accumulation of each resource. The perspectives associated with managing each component part of the organization are aired and discussed during the mapping process that precedes algebraic modelling. Moreover, and perhaps most important, the algebraic model allows simulation – with all the interactive learning advantages already identified for Papert's gear set and for the racing car simulator.

A multi-function strategic simulation model enables several alternative perspectives to be brought into conjunction with each other, and it is cognitively accessible to actors with a range of backgrounds and without specialist training. The crucial difference between a simulator and a normal problem-structuring method is that the simulator's representation (the "final" model) is usually fixed (except for design changes to operating policy). A finished simulator is not developed "to reflect the state and stage of discussion among actors" (although the simulator itself may have arisen from an interactive modelling process, as in the case of the World Service model). Nevertheless, the simulator is a potent transitional object capable of stimulating discussion among actors and altering their viewpoints.

Here (in the influence of a simulator on debate and discussion) lies an important message for the hard–soft debate and for the field of system dynamics. Many people mistakenly believe that efforts to quantify a feedback representation, to turn causal loops or stock flow diagrams into working simulators, are wasted because the resulting model is a more singular and hard representation of the situation being studied. The presumption is that soft modelling preserves variety of opinion (thereby allowing productive dialogue), while hard modelling destroys it. This line of reasoning overlooks the playful characteristic of simulators – their ability through repeated use to engage attention, to spark new ideas and to generate shared understanding. The considerable effort required to develop a credible algebraic model is worthwhile because it allows all sorts of new interactions between mental models and a formal model that are not available from qualitative problem-structuring methods alone. That's not to say one modelling approach is always better than another, but rather to recognize the different ways in which formal models can achieve value as transitional objects for management teams.

The same advantage-from-playfulness may also be true of traditional hard modelling approaches. I am reminded of an operational research project for a manufacturer making gigantic tyres for earth-moving equipment (Degraeve and Schrage, 1997, 1998). The authors, who specialize in applied optimization, describe the development of a model to optimize production scheduling. Historically, production was controlled by four schedulers of varying expertise and experience. The most experienced scheduler had been in the job for over 25 years and his colleagues respectively for 13, 7 and 4 years. They decided independently on the daily scheduling of the scarce and extremely expensive capital equipment (ovens and moulds) required to produce such enormous specialist tyres. At the end of their shift they would then sit together in a meeting room to review each other's schedules and develop the final production plan for the next 24 hours, effectively trying to solve a complex combinatorial optimization problem. With such long cumulative experience they had developed quite sophisticated mental models of the plant. Consequently, during the development of the optimization programme the modellers learned a lot from the comments and feedback of the schedulers. However, the schedulers were also learning from initial model results about how to improve their manual production plans. At the end of the development phase, the most experienced scheduler, Tom Lykens, proclaimed to his management "... this scheduling programme is great ... I like this ... you people have no idea what I am up against every morning ...."

Although the schedulers were sceptical initially, they became fascinated with the similarities and differences between the optimizer's schedules and their own judgemental schedules. Often there was little difference, which built the schedulers' confidence both in the formal model and themselves. Sometimes the differences were significant, which then forced the schedulers to re-examine their thinking. For example, the schedulers normally created stacks of three or sometimes four tyres before placing them in ovens. However, the programme identified highly efficient stacks of five tyres never discovered before. The immediate reaction of the schedulers was to question the feasibility of this solution. Then, after only a few minutes, having thought about the solution, they were coming up with their own stacks of five. An important part of the value of the project lay in the interaction between the mental models of the schedulers and the formal model. Through use and experimentation, the optimizer alerted the schedulers to interesting new scheduling options. In other words it was an effective transitional object.

7.6.2   Simulation and realism

Models are effective as transitional objects when they help people to amplify thought experiments, stimulate imagination and question accepted wisdom. But adequacy of representation is surely important too. Common sense demands that a useful model bears some resemblance to the situation at hand. Simulators of fantasy worlds do exist (such as Lara Croft in *Tomb Raider*), but presumably intense interaction with a fantasy world does not enhance understanding of practical policy and strategy.

Nevertheless, it is an interesting question where to draw the line on realism. Consider, for example, how to use modelling to understand the puzzling dynamics of resource allocation inside a firm. Internal competition between departments for shared resources, such as manufacturing capacity or skilled salesforce, is common and is often dysfunctional. Business units can find themselves in an expensive and fluctuating tug-of-war for scarce capacity in order to meet local performance targets. Surprisingly, a simulator representing hotel showers (Morecroft et al., 1995), in which two players (unbeknown to themselves) share a fixed supply of hot water, proves to be an effective metaphor for the dynamics of organizational resource sharing. The comfort-seeking shower takers become locked into an escalating battle for hot water. The result is wild and persistent temperature fluctuations and deep frustration because neither shower taker achieves a comfortable temperature, rather like infighting departments that underperform. The shower simulator sparks lively debate among experienced business people about how best to control such infighting through improved communication and greater tolerance of temporary performance shortfalls.

The hotel shower model is obviously not a realistic model of a multi-department firm. Yet, it stimulates thinking about organizational dynamics. A well-known passage by Herbert Simon (1999, chap. 1, pp. 18–21) about "simulation as a source of new knowledge" addresses the relationship between the realism and usefulness of a simulator:

> *[T]his brings me to the crucial question about simulation: how can a simulation ever tell us anything we do not already know? The usual implication of the question is that it can't ... [T]here are two related ways in which simulation can provide new knowledge – one of them obvious, the other perhaps a bit subtle. The obvious point is that, even when we have correct premises, it may be very difficult to discover what they imply. All correct reasoning is a grand system of tautologies, but only God can make direct use of that fact. The rest of us must painstakingly and fallibly tease out the consequences of our assumptions ... [T]he more interesting and subtle question is whether simulation can be of any help to us when we do not know very much initially about the natural laws that govern the behavior of the inner system ... [A]rtificial systems and adaptive systems ... [h]ave properties that make them particularly susceptible to simulation via simplified models ... [R]esemblance in behavior of systems without identity of the inner systems is particularly feasible if the aspects in which we are interested arise out of the organization of the parts, independently of all but a few properties of the individual components.*

So a hotel shower simulator is arguably a good transitional object for managers interested in dysfunctional dynamics of organizational resource sharing because it captures (in a vivid and amusing way) the essential structure and organization of interdependent, competing and goal-oriented feedback processes.

7.6.3 Soft and hard in system dynamics models

The following contribution by my London Business School colleague Kim Warren to a web discussion of the System Dynamics Society evoked lots of online debate (note that his comment is limited to the real physical constraints that exist in organizations and is not intended to imply that all relationships in business and social systems are "hardwired"):

> *[I]t has become rather fashionable, not just in system dynamics but in management generally, to adopt the position that "the world is as you see it". Much top team facilitation works at trying to elucidate the overlaps and similarities between each person's mental model, so as to assemble a shared mental model to which they can all sign up. But this view has some big problems. First, there is a lot of basic "physics" that operates according to its own laws, regardless of what our mental model might say about what is going on — we can't lose people we haven't got, if we add more products than we discontinue then our product range increases, and so on. Second, the only part of the system one person can affect directly is the part where they are personally involved ... [S]o what exactly are we capturing when we surface these mental models, and what exactly are we creating when we help a group merge these into a shared mental model? Should we not be seeking to specify the physics, and to identify and represent the actual behaviours of other players in the system, rather than conceptualise our own view of the system, which will almost certainly be largely fictitious? The risk (which seems to arise in many practical cases) is that the management team move to a strong consensus on a "shared vision", and enthusiastically pursue a strategic plan to do precisely the wrong thing!*

Among the many responses was one from Finn Jackson who (as someone with a first degree in physics, a second in business administration and experience of both consulting and of industry) was especially intrigued by "the physics of business". In answer to the two closing questions he observed that:

1. *if the firm contains conflicting mental models it will not move far (infighting);*
2. *if the firm contains a single mental model (consensus) it can move in that direction (until it comes up against the "basic physics");*
3. *over time, the firms whose mental models most closely match the "basic physics" will survive, while others fail.*

This sample from a system dynamics web discussion is part of the hard–soft OR debate. If reality is sufficiently complex and ambiguous, then disagreement among mental models is to be expected. As Pidd (1996, pp. 21–22) has noted:

> *[O]ur impressions of the world are always partial, both in the sense that we do not experience everything and also in the sense that we may well be biased ... [T]he task of the modeller is to take these ill-defined and implicit views of reality and cast them in some form well enough defined to be at least understood and argued over by other people.*

Soft modelling methods pragmatically use the modelling process to bring about better mutual understanding of alternative views, recognizing (as Checkland has observed) that consensus and accommodation, or at least mutual appreciation of differences, is an essential ingredient of success in human activity systems. In a sense, political support for strategy is an integral part of any model of strategy. Strategies can fail and firms underperform because there is conflict, mistrust and misunderstanding among those who have the power to act. One might therefore argue that a good strategic model should include "political support for strategy" as a variable from the reality the model represents. But this requirement is confusingly recursive and misses the essential point that the process of modelling itself generates mutual understanding and support for action.

System dynamics occupies a very particular position in the hard–soft spectrum. It assumes that people in organizations can describe with reasonable accuracy the operation of parts of the organization for which they are responsible (Forrester, 1994). Where individual's mental models often fail is in:

1. understanding the operation of other parts of the organization (for which they are not responsible);
2. seeing how the parts fit together; and
3. reliably inferring how the parts interact to generate performance over time.

These limitations of mental models can easily lead to strong differences of managerial opinion over strategy even when the parts of the system can in principle be accurately described and represented.

The assumption that the operating parts of an organization can be accurately (or at least adequately) represented has led some critics of the field to suggest that system dynamics takes a hard and deterministic view of business and social affairs. A thorough review and rebuttal of this criticism is provided by Lane (2000), who also convincingly positions system dynamics as far more than a mechanistic approach within the broad domain of social theory (Lane, 1999). I will not replicate his arguments or evidence here. Rather, I will address the specific point that the ability to create a single agreed representation of an organization does not necessarily imply the resulting model is hard or deterministic. Nor does it mean such models are soft and entirely subjective. The predominant philosophical view within the field is that basic "constitutive laws" and regularities *do* exist in business and social systems – some regularities are natural and some are socially constructed. The influence of these laws and regularities will limit the range of feasible strategy and will therefore be captured in a good model regardless of whether or not they can be elicited (whole and intact) from anyone's mental model. Asset stock accumulation is one such law (together with the requirement for rigorous conservation of quantities in stock-and-flow networks). Practical operating constraints of the kind describing the geographical reach of short-wave transmitters in the BBC World Service model are also examples of constitutive laws.

Although asset stock accumulation and operating constraints are intended to represent hard structure in business and social systems, they are not the entire structure. The remaining structure resides in the information feedback network. This network is socially constructed, subject to the loose yet binding constraints of bounded rationality. Bounded rationality is a principle of social system structure (Simon, 1976, 1978), but unlike stock accumulation and operating constraints it is not an "iron law". The principle of bounded rationality (as it applies to information feedback models) merely suggests that managerial operating policies (to guide asset stock accumulation) are parochial by nature (Morecroft, 1985; Sterman, 1989, 2000 chap. 15). They use much less co-ordinating information than is available from the organization as a whole, because normal flesh-and-blood humans simply cannot process all the information that might conceivably be relevant. As a result the co-ordinating information feedback network is sparse (much sparser than an optimally controlled network). For example, in BBC World Service very little information is needed to establish the required language portfolio. Essentially, the operating policy-in-use is to offer the same languages in the future as have been offered in the past (rather than fine-tuning the portfolio, say, to match changes in transmitters, staff or programmes). The only modification to "business-as-usual" comes from internal short-term budget pressures and external regional conflict. The apparent independence and inertia of language management reflects the organization's long-standing tradition of broadcasting many different languages. Adherence to this tradition greatly simplifies the resource co-ordination task.

In general, the most influential information links in a business model are discovered by investigating the rationale of managers responsible for particular operating policies. Interviews, workshops and even formal longitudinal field studies (Repenning, 2000) are used for this purpose. The investigation reveals which information sources these managers pay attention to and why? Which information sources do they ignore? System dynamics models capture the resulting pattern of the information network. This pattern is enduring, but it is also socially constructed. In other words, system structure controls the decisions of human agents, but a part of that structure (the co-ordinating information network) is itself amenable to change and redesign by organizational leaders. Herein lies the essential "structural softness" of system dynamics models (separate from the influence of simulators on soft mental models). The philosophical conclusion here is the same reached by Lane (2000). System dynamics models are not rigidly deterministic models. They do not "relegate humans to mere cogs in a machine, passive respondents who have no autonomy."

In conclusion, any organization has a unique character or personality that arises from its special combination of hard, lawful processes and soft, socially constructed (yet enduring) processes. This character is amenable to modelling. Just as a political cartoonist captures the enduring and recognizable features of a celebrity face in a few bold pen strokes, so a system dynamics modeller captures the enduring and recognizable operating structure of a firm in a few bold feedback loops. Simulations, then, reveal the performance implications of this structure comprising asset stock accumulations and a semi-lawful (hard-and-soft) co-ordinating network. Intensive and repeated use of a well-constructed simulator by a management team can lead to new insights about strategy and greater collective confidence in a proposed course of action.

References

Checkland P. (1981) *Systems Thinking, Systems Practice.* John Wiley & Sons, Chichester, UK.

Checkland P. (1989) Soft systems methodology. In J. Rosenhead (ed.) *Rational Analysis for a Problematic World.* John Wiley & Sons, Chichester, UK.

Degraeve Z. and Schrage L. (1997) A tire production scheduling system for Bridgestone/Firestone off-the-road. *Operations Research*, **45**(6), 789–96.

Degraeve Z. and Schrage L. (1998) HOP: A software tool for production scheduling at Bridgestone/Firestone off-the-road. *European Journal of Operational Research*, **110**(2), 188–98.

Delauzun F. and Mollona E. (1999) Introducing system dynamics to the BBC World Service. *Journal of the Operational Research Society*, **50**(4), 364–71.

Dierickx I. and Cool K. (1989) Asset stock accumulation and sustainability of competitive advantage. *Management Science*, **35**(12), 1504–10.

Eden C.L. (1989) Using cognitive mapping for strategic options development and analysis (SODA). In J. Rosenhead (ed.) *Rational Analysis for a Problematic World.* John Wiley & Sons, Chichester, UK.

Forrester J.W. (1961) *Industrial Dynamics.* MIT Press, Cambridge, MA (reprinted by Pegasus Communications, Waltham, MA).

Forrester J.W. (1975a) Counterintuitive behavior of social systems. *Collected Papers of Jay W. Forrester.* Wright-Allen Press, Cambridge, MA.

Forrester J.W. (1975b) Planning and goal creation: Excerpts. *Collected Papers of Jay W. Forrester.* Wright-Allen Press, Cambridge, MA. (This paper is an excerpt from: Planning under the dynamic influences of complex social systems. In E. Jantsch (ed.) *Perspectives of Planning: Proceedings of the OECD Working Symposium on Long-range Forecasting and Planning, Bellagio, Italy.* Organization for Economic Co-operation and Development, Paris, 1968.)

Forrester J.W. (1994) Policies, decisions and information sources for modelling. In J.D.W. Morecroft and J.D. Sterman (eds) *Modeling for Learning Organizations.* Productivity Press, Portland, OR.

Lane D.C. (1999) Social theory and system dynamics practice. *European Journal of Operational Research*, **113**, 501–27.

Lane D.C. (2000) Should system dynamics be described as a "hard" or "deterministic" systems approach. *Systems Research and Behavioral Science*, **17**(1), 3–22.

Mingers J. and Rosenhead J. (2003) Problem structuring methods in action. *European Journal of Operational Research*, **152**(3), 530–554.

Morecroft J.D.W. (1985) Rationality in the analysis of behavioral simulation models. *Management Science*, **31**(7), 900–16.

Morecroft J.D.W. (2002) Resource management under dynamic complexity. In J. Morecroft, R. Sanchez and A. Heene (eds) *Systems Perspectives on Resources, Capabilities, and Management Processes.* Elsevier Science, Oxford, UK.

Morecroft J.D.W., Larsen E.R., Lomi A. and Ginsberg A. (1995) The dynamics of resource sharing – A metaphorical model. *System Dynamics Review*, **11**(4), 289–309.

Papert S. (1980) *Mindstorms: Children, Computers and Powerful Ideas.* Basic Books, New York.

Pidd M. (1996) *Tools for Thinking.* John Wiley & Sons, Chichester, UK.

Repenning N. (2000) A dynamic model of resource allocation in multi-project research and development systems. *System Dynamics Review*, **16**(3), 173–212.

Rosenhead J. and Mingers J. (eds) (2001) *Rational Analysis for a Problematic World Revisited.* John Wiley & Sons, Chichester, UK.

Senge P.M. (1990) *The Fifth Discipline: The Art and Practice of the Learning Organization.* Doubleday Currency, New York.

Simon H.A. (1976) *Administrative Behavior*, 3rd edn. The Free Press, New York.

Simon H.A. (1978) Rational decision making in business organizations. *American Economic Review*, **69**(4).

Simon H.A. (1999) *The Sciences of the Artificial*, 3rd edn. MIT Press, Cambridge, MA.

Sterman J.D. (1989) Modeling managerial behavior: Misperceptions of feedback in a dynamic decision making experiment. *Management Science*, **35**(3), 321–39.

Sterman J.D. (2000) *Business Dynamics: Systems Thinking and Modeling for a Complex World.* Irwin/McGraw-Hill, Boston, MA.

Warren K. (2002) *Competitive Strategy Dynamics.* John Wiley & Sons, Chichester, UK.

Wolstenholme E.F. (1990) *System Enquiry: A System Dynamics Approach.* John Wiley & Sons, Chichester, UK.

8 Using causal mapping – individual and group, traditional and new

Fran Ackermann and Colin Eden
Strathclyde Business School

8.1 Background to mapping

The benefits of using diagrammatic forms for structuring qualitative informa-tion have been the object of researcher and practitioner interest for a number of decades. A wealth of material has been produced, focusing on its use in many contexts; for example, in the political science and managerial world (Axelrod, 1976; Eden et al., 1979; Huff, 1990; Huff and Jenkins, 2002). However, when reviewing this research and practice, it is clear that there is not one single method, but rather a range of different forms from causal mapping in its many guises (Axelrod, 1976; Conklin and Begeman, 1989; Eden, 1988; Laukkanen, 1994) to mind mapping (Buzan and Buzan, 1993) and influence diagrams (Richardson, 1991; Wolstenholme, 1990; Wolstenholme and Coyle, 1983). Each of these techniques aims to provide the user with the means of capturing not only a set of nodes (usually text) but also some means of representing ways in which they are connected together. These diagrams thus permit exploration of both the detail (how particular nodes relate to other nodes) and, in some cases, the holistic properties (patterns emerging from the overall representation that in turn yield further insights into the subject at hand).

However, while all essentially comprise words and arrows, each of these different forms of diagrammatic "note-taking" techniques has, or has not, its own theoretical basis, purpose/objectives and coding rules which need to be taken into account if practised properly. In addition, for many of the forms listed above (e.g., causal mapping) there are also subvarieties, each stemming again from a different theoretical basis or set of objectives, making the use of these techniques a trap for the unwary.

For the purpose of this chapter we are focusing on cognitive mapping based theoretically on the work of psychologist George Kelly (1955) and developed as cause mapping by Eden (1988), Eden and Ackermann (1998b, see also Rosenhead and Mingers, 2001; Pidd, 2003). We chose cognitive mapping because it has a well-established record of use for problem structuring and solution development by operational researchers, both on its own and with other operational research techniques.

This form of cognitive and cause mapping aims to produce manual or electronic representations of how people perceive a situation in the form of a means–ends diagram (a directed graph). As such the map may reveal issues of concern, how these issues relate to one another and how changes in the character of one issue may have repercussions for another. The technique can be used with an individual allowing both the surfacing and exploration of a single person's construal of the issues and producing a cognitive map (a depiction of an individual's cognition). This examination may be sufficient to support thinking and action. In addition to this the map can be woven together with other cognitive maps focusing on the same issue/area of concern to produce a group cause map, which can subsequently be used to provide the basis for a group workshop designed to help the group agree action. (The group map cannot be called a cognitive map because cognition belongs to an individual.) Alternatively, mapping can be used directly with groups to build up a causal model where all in the group develop a sense of shared understanding and a common language as the capturing and structuring of material takes place during group working. Thus, in both cases, although typically more so in individual interviews, mapping facilitates an increased surfacing of ideas, assertions, assumptions and facts enabling the individual or group to widen their exploration, tapping into the richness and depth of individual expertise and knowledge. From this it is possible to more effectively represent and manage the complexity of the issue/concern being explored and be better positioned to begin to resolve it.

Cause mapping has also been used in the mode of analysing text to discover the robustness or otherwise of a body of argument.

Typically, individual maps have 90–120 nodes following a 45–60-minute conversation (Eden and Ackermann, 1998b) and group maps several hundred nodes. Thus, the maps are seeking to capture the subtlety of complex problems rather than representing generic or archetypical characteristics of the problem situation with 10–20 nodes (as is the case for some types of mapping).

Understanding is gained through the additional meaning being given to a node (statement) not only from its content but also its context (i.e., the consequences and explanations that are linked to that statement). Therefore, emphasis is placed on ensuring that each node/statement contains around 6–8 words and is phrased in a way that suggests possible action. Where a contrasting element is provided (e.g., "publish in leading research journals rather than professional journals"), this too is captured as it provides further insight into what was meant by the person. Arrows (links) illustrate chains of argument and, therefore, through providing detail in terms of the material linking in (options/explanation, etc.) and linking out (consequences/ramifications) of the statement more insight into what is meant is revealed. Through this means–ends structure implied possible actions, and outcomes as suggested by the "theories" a person uses to explain the world as they see it, can be captured (Eden and Ackermann, 1998b).

Over the last decade or so mapping has moved from its traditional roots – that of messy complex problem solving (Eden, 1989) – to supporting work in a number of other arenas. This chapter commences with an exploration of the different modes of use (i.e., individual, group based or textual) before describing two different application areas: prospective modelling to result in agreed action – problem solving and strategy making, clarifying multiple aims and objectives, performance measurement and modelling; and retrospective modelling – for forensic analysis and organizational learning. Finally, some consideration is given to the implications and issues associated with these applications.

8.2 Modes of use

As noted above, mapping can be and has been used in different modes: with individuals, groups and for the analysis of argument. Which mode is used depends as much on the skills and confidence of the operational researcher as the context within which the piece of work is being undertaken.

8.2.1 Individual mapping

Individual cognitive maps can either be made by an "interviewer" using the technique to elicit information from another individual (i.e., two parties are involved) or undertaken to resolve a personal issue where the interviewee and interviewer are one and the same person. While the authors and others have used mapping to great effect to help them resolve personal issues (Bryson et al., 2004), most of the operational research/management science use has focused on using cognitive mapping as a means of eliciting and structuring information through interviews (although with multiple purposes).

In the one-to-one mode, good interviewing and good mapping enables interviewees to be freer of peer pressure and other conformity constraints, encouraging them to open up and discuss issues as they really see them rather than follow a party line (Eden and Ackermann, 1998b). Consequently, it is possible to bring to surface "theories in use" rather than "espoused theories" (Argyris and Schön, 1974) and, therefore, begin to model the situation as it is rather than as some sanitized form. In addition, as a result of this ability to be more open (without penalty) interviewees often experience a sense of relief as the interview itself acts as a cathartic process.

Interviews carried out using the cognitive-mapping technique also provide interviewees with the ability to say what concerns them in a manner that allows the interviewer to develop an appreciation of the situation before making judgements. The implied lack of a prescribed set of questions is relieved through the developing map and visual analysis providing the agenda. Nodes can be further explored by asking questions focused on teasing out details regarding options, consequences and constraints. For example, statements that appear unconnected are easily identified and can be followed up during the interview thus reducing the likelihood of discovering, post interview, areas of uncertainty. Rough visual analysis identifies those statements that are busy (lots of links in and out of the statement), those that appear potential goals (at the top of chains of argument) and those that are possible options (at the bottom of chains of argument). Interviewees are therefore provided with added value through both an enhanced understanding of their own view of the world as illustrated through the map and through the analysis of the structure of the map, yielding some insight into emergent properties. As a result a more thorough understanding of the interviewee's world is created as a model in the form of the map. Thus the map becomes a vehicle for purposeful dialogue about the problem situation.

As a consequence of the mapping process teasing out consequences and explanations, it is possible to get beyond the rehearsed script often given to enquirers and start to surface the richness and knowledge of the individual. From this both parties benefit, the interviewer through gaining a deeper understanding of the issue and the interviewee through understanding their own thinking better and becoming aware of possible actions. This resonates with Weick's (1979) statement about sense making: "how do I know what I think until I see what I say."

Given that the mapping technique requires some practice in order to gain confidence, one means of providing a degree of security is to carry out the interview using two interviewers. Here one interviewer takes responsibility for directing the flow of the interview (so as not to confuse the interviewee), but both capture the information. At appropriate intervals it is possible for the lead interviewer to ask the other whether there are any further questions or elaborations he or she would like to raise. This mode of working provides two benefits. The first is that it allows at least one interviewer to concentrate solely on getting down the information (rather than considering the social process, and next question). Second, comparison of the maps can then take place after the interview and any contractions or uncertainties identified can subsequently be raised with the interviewee.

8.2.2 Group mapping

Group mapping can take many submodes, depending on the organization and client requirements (Ackermann and Eden, 2001a). One mode is the use of a simple interactive modelling approach referred to as the oval mapping technique (OMT) – using oval Post-its (Ackermann and Eden, 2001b; Bryson,

1995; Eden and Ackermann, 1998b). Another mode focuses on a facilitator using specially designed mapping software – *Decision Explorer* – to capture the statements and relationships as they are surfaced through debate and conversation and so develop the maps in real time (Ackermann and Eden, 2001b). A third mode provides each participant with a computer, enabling them to enter their contributions directly into the computerized version of the map (the model) as well as allowing them to allocate preferences to particular statements (usually options) and rate statements against one another.

The manual mode is best used when the group is unfamiliar with technology (and therefore likely to view the computer-based system with some anxiety) and where other less overt objectives exist (e.g., a deliberate effort at team building). The method requires only flip chart paper, pens and oval Post-its (see www.ovalmap.com) and a lot of flat wall space; it is easy to set up and is therefore flexible in terms of location. Individuals are given a number of ovals and asked to write their understanding of the problem situation onto the ovals – one statement per oval (applying the same coding rules as noted above). As the ovals are placed on the wall in front of the rest of the group, participants are able to piggyback off one another, increasing their range of views about the issue. This generation stage of the process is followed by the structuring stage which not only enables participants to understand how one another construes the situation (through becoming aware of the different links possible) but also surfaces further material as explanations for particular relationships are suggested. The aim is to gradually negotiate a group view of the problem situation – one that at least most participants have some ownership of, if not agreement about.

Where the mode of using a facilitator and *Decision Explorer* to capture and structure the material is chosen this can be either for surfacing material (in a manner similar to the oval mapping or interviewing) or for exploring material already captured (though using either interviews or oval mapping) and beginning to *negotiate* a way forward (Eden and Ackermann, 1992). Using the software increases flexibility, as statements and links can be captured, amended and deleted easily allowing subtle negotiations to take place through the gradual shifting of the wording of equivocal statements (Eden, 1992). Although not providing the same ability to see the "big picture" as the oval mapping technique does, the software does allow the group through the facilitator to see as much or as little of the captured material as required, further helping the management of the complex picture that is unfolding. Real time analysis (Eden, 2004) can also be undertaken, providing the group with insights into the emergent properties of the model and helping them make decisions.

Using the fully computerized mode (*Group Explorer*) of a network of linked laptop computers as the method of capturing input from participants provides them with the means of being completely anonymous in their contributions (thus providing them a similar environment to the interviews) as well as making most effective use of time (through parallel entry). The disadvantage is that of the overhead of requiring an independent local area network of computers using *Internet Explorer* (or the use of a "normal" existing network) to be available (not always possible). In addition, *Group Explorer* provides participants with the facility to allocate preferences against possible options or issues and rate items (e.g., assessing leverage) – a significant aid to gaining political feasibility (see Chapter 9). However, the system is typically used for only 20–30% of the duration of a workshop as the remainder of the time is allocated to moving from the divergent contributions to a shared perspective – thus working in the second mode (i.e., facilitator-driven).

In all three modes the intention is to enable participants to surface all of their contributions, ensuring that it is clear what these statements mean and how they relate to other statements captured. This ability to capture, structure and analyse contributions from participants assists not only in ensuring "procedural rationality" (Simon, 1976) takes place but also that "procedural justice" is served (Kim and Mauborgne, 1995), encouraging participants to feel more ownership for the outcomes and therefore increasing the likelihood of implementation.

8.2.3 Analysing text

The third, and perhaps least used, mode of mapping is the mapping of text (i.e., documentary material: Axelrod, 1976 reported on studies of this type in the field of political science). In instances where this has taken place, there exists typically a considerable amount of written material that needs to be made sense of (Eden and Ackermann, 2003). For example, in many public sector bodies there are a plethora of governmental initiatives to be met, and finding some means of understanding not only what these initiatives comprise but also how they relate to one another can be an important task (Eden and Cropper, 1992).

Mapping text and then analysing the map is also sometimes a useful preface to strategy work, where the existing strategy document is mapped. In these instances it is usual to find that the map reveals how the existing strategy is incoherent, plans and policies are not clearly related to goals, operational programmes are not clearly linked to strategies and so on.

Its use in typical OR (Operational Research) projects derives from the ability to pull together into a model amenable to analysis a variety of proposals from different parts of the organization and analyse their interconnections, contradictions and possible systemicity that shows feedback loops. The map so created offers itself as a vehicle for pulling together a group of people from different parts of the organization, where the map acts as a way of facilitating constructive debate and negotiating agreements. The outcome of such workshops is often the commissioning of further traditional OR modelling to analyse in more depth aspects of the qualitative soft OR model.

However, working with text is perhaps the most difficult application of mapping. This is partly due to the fact that there is little if any ability to ask for clarification from the sources. As a result the maps often emerge as relatively sparsely linked with isolated islands of material and no clear indication as to their role within the overall direction. In addition, the temptation to personalize the map, through adding links that are "obvious", is also a trap. When working in this mode, care therefore has to be taken.

8.3 Applications of mapping

This section examines two common application areas: the more common proactive work of resolving problems and/or developing strategic direction, and forensic work where events have already occurred and an understanding of complex occurrences, the causes and consequences, is required prior to simulation modelling.

8.3.1 Mapping for problem "solving" and strategy development

Mapping that is used to structure messy complex problems or develop strategy frequently commences with one of the group-based submodes. This is often because the nature of the issue(s) being tackled is such that there is urgency and sometimes because the situation demands negotiation in order to reach agreements. Nevertheless, while our experience suggests that group mapping predominates, the purpose of each group intervention should direct the mapping approach (Ackermann and Eden, 1997). For example, where managers are seeking views from a broad spectrum of the organization, then the OMT can be a good place to start as it focuses on opening up the discussion (asking participants to take a "yes, and" stance). By using the workshop to influence and inform thinking, it is possible to work on intelligence and design: the first two phases of decision making identified by Simon (1997). This attention to representation will also help in reducing the likelihood of missing critical areas as well as increase ownership and understanding through attending to procedural justice requirements.

Once these OMT workshop(s) have occurred, then the resultant material can be woven together using *Decision Explorer* and analysis undertaken. Here the emphasis is to identify goals (those statements that express good outcomes in their own right) and so a "goal system", which is supported by issues that in turn are supported by potent options (options contributing to the resolution of a number of issues − hence potent). This process of categorization not only assists in tidying up the model and providing added value (through aiding the management team navigate through the model) but also familiarizes the analyst with the content – aiding subsequent workshop design and facilitation.

The resultant analysed model then provides the means for the decision-making group to explore the material and move to a more "yes, but" stance, where alternatives are explored alongside their ramifications and issues relating to resources and leverage take place – the choice/evaluation stage of Simon's model. Where necessary – perhaps to resolve issues or add depth – further views are collected from other staff and added to the model. Alongside viewing these additional contributions of staff, managers continue to add their own views (either using the facilitator-driven method or the multi-user *Group Explorer* system), ensuring their ownership of the outcomes. This ability to explore, consider, amend and refine the material is aided by the model's interactive capability, allowing it to act as a "negotiative device" (Eden, 1992).

One of the biggest problems with working with maps, particularly with software support, is managing the amount of material captured. As the map aims to capture the complexity of the issue at hand it becomes very rich. However, while this richness better informs decision making a balance needs to be had between the debilitating impact of complexity (Eden and Sims, 1981) and the increased ownership and practicality of extensive considerations. The software provides a number of ways of managing the material. Providing an overview of the material by using the analysis tools enables an easy understanding of the whole. This is similar to a road map for a country – highlighting the major points (cities in the case of road maps) and the links between them. As with the road maps, where routes between cities appear direct (rather than passing through towns) the overview map depicts the links between goals and issues showing both direct and indirect routes (Eden and Ackermann, 1998b). In addition, using the facility of having "windows" or "views" depicting user-defined areas of the map/model provides a way of seeing each important part of the map: that is, the goals system, the interacting issues, each issue in turn, potent options as they relate to the resolution of a number of issues and feedback loops (positive and negative). The software thus supports the creation of a number of views of the model (similar to sheets in Excel), and so it is possible to build up a picture of the whole over a number of views.

Stakeholder analysis and management   As part of the strategy process (for more detail of the entire strategy approach known as "Journey Making" see Eden and Ackermann, 1998b) stakeholder mapping can assist both in the process of identifying and analysing stakeholders and in determining means for their management (Ackermann and Eden, 2003). Through a range of mapping-based processes it is possible to identify the different power and interest bases in relation to a particular proposed direction, examine in more depth the sanction and support mechanisms, and surface and attend to the informal and formal network links between identified stakeholders. This process can provide valuable insight into:

(a) composition of workshop attendees, ensuring that the right constituencies are involved; and
(b) how best to enhance implementation success through consideration of those external and internal to the organization who will need careful management.

Exploring alternative futures   Another area that has benefited from the use of mapping is the development of alternative futures or scenarios (Eden and Ackermann, 1999). Here the process commences with the surfacing of events – triggers – that are outside of the control of the organization and yet will significantly influence the environment within which it is operating. These events, encompassing elements relating to politics, economics, technical developments, regulatory effects, social trends, etc., are then explored through considering their multiple implications – which would be difficult to appreciate and capture without cause mapping. As the many chains of causality are built up, a number of properties are revealed. First, the events rather than working in isolation interact with one another, escalating the resultant impact on the future. Second, dynamic behaviour emerges where particular events cause particular actions from stakeholders, which in turn reinforces the behaviour.

8.3.2   Clarifying multiple aims and objectives

Clarifying the objectives of a study or project can also be undertaken using mapping. For example, in working with the UK National Audit Office (NAO) the group involved wished to determine exactly what the client wanted from the study. Through using the OMT, the client group with two members from the NAO team surfaced concerns, issues and implications and developed a clear set of goals and actions. From this material the NAO team were able to design the audit far more effectively and undertake the audit in a more collaborative setting, rather than the slightly adversarial climate often caused due to the nature of audits. Whenever there was concern over the audit's direction, reference could be made to the map (Ackermann and Eden, 2001b). Similarly, when considering purchasing strategies the group involved used a combination of oval mapping (to surface material) and facilitated computer mapping (for negotiation and agreement) to develop a set of goals (objectives) and actions (alternatives), which were then further analysed using a Multi-Criteria Analysis model (Belton et al., 1997).

8.3.3 Performance measurement

An area that is gaining interest both from an OR (Shuttler and Storbeck, 2003) and a strategy perspective (Kaplan and Norton, 1992) is performance measurement. To date, mapping has been used to assist with strategic performance measurement in a number of ways. First, as actions and strategies are agreed, those made responsible are not only given the task but also the rationale, thus enabling them to understand the "what" and "why". Through understanding this, there is an increased likelihood of implementation, as those further down the organization are able to understand how they too contribute to the overall direction. This can be critical to ensuring that not only is the task achieved but also that it is achieved for the purpose that gave rise to its adoption. Second, mapping has been helped to explore how different performance measures impact on one another, thus building up coherent portfolios rather than sets that are discrete and at times in contradiction with one another.

This ability to develop coherent portfolios of performance measurements enables the organization to focus both at the macro and micro-level and thus facilitates triangulation across measurements. For example, as those responsible for specific detailed actions report back on their progress, detailed notes regarding the level of attainment can be captured. These can then be compared with the results of more macro-analysis of progress (e.g., exploring how successful a particular strategy is against a range or performance indicators). From this comparison it is possible to test for inconsistencies (Eden and Ackermann, 1998b, p. 177). One common inconsistency is having lots of progress being reported at the micro-level and yet little progress being made regarding the strategy in question. Here questions relating to the appropriateness of the strategy actions can take place, determining whether the link between action and strategy does in fact have any efficacy. Likewise, where considerable progress is seen against the performance indicator of a strategy but those actions supporting the strategy have little progress noted against them, then questions regarding the accuracy of the performance indicator's position as well as possible alternative actions occurring can take place.

Finally, through building strategy maps with associated performance measurement indicators and testing these out using continuous simulation models, managers are able to be alerted to the fact that often the performance of the organization will dip before improving – what Pettigrew et al. (2003) have referred to as the "J curve" (i.e., performance plotted over time – performance commences at point X, drops to point Y before increasing up to point Z which is greater than that of point Y, thus providing the shape of a "J"). This early recognition can reassure managers and prevent them from falling into the trap of changing the strategy and subsequently seeing more progress drops.

8.4 Some considerations in usage for problem "solving" and strategy development

Although mapping, as presented in the above application areas, typically provides benefit to those adopting its use, nevertheless it is worth being aware of some of the notable additional considerations associated with their use. Noted below, against each application area, are a number of those most commonly experienced as well as some suggestions regarding management:

1. When carrying out interviews it is important to set clear expectations at the beginning with regards to the outcome (i.e., how the map's contents will be used). Given that in many circumstances those interviewed have rare experiences of being taken seriously, being interviewed in depth may raise their expectations regarding the significance of their role in the strategy process. This is partly because the technique's ability to help them think through their views more thoroughly and, therefore, become more convinced about the way forward and partly because of the emotional experience of being listened to effectively.

2. Throughout the entire process – from initial surfacing of material through interviews or group mapping to running workshops – care has to be taken regarding navigation of the model's richness and complexity. Consequently, as we suggested above, participants can often become overwhelmed with the amount of information they have generated. Therefore, while rationally they are persuaded that seeing the big picture is important, emotionally they feel "out of control" and tend toward a desire to reduce rather than manage complexity. One means of helping participants during workshops is to use a "route map" and overview as well as different views depicting discrete aspects of the model, showing how the issue is made up of interacting problems.

3. A sense of uncertainty regarding what has been achieved is exacerbated when producing maps as feedback from workshops. First, sometimes they don't show a clear unambiguous route forward (in contrast to using more quantitative models) and, therefore, participants aren't sure where to start – both in terms of "reading" the maps and understanding what might determine actions (working with maps is likely to be a new process for participants). Second, many participants find that explaining the feedback maps to those not at the workshop is problematic – maps are often cryptic and owned by those involved in the process, whereas they are not so easily accessible to others only familiar with text-based formats.

4. There is a considerable load on the facilitator of a workshop (Eden and Ackermann in Chapter 9). The facilitator is required to manage the processes of group working (Phillips and Phillips, 1993), capture material and code it according to the formal mapping guidelines, and manage the

mapping software, apart from helping the group gain added value from the emerging maps. Thus gaining familiarity with both the technique and the software (in low-risk environments) obviously helps, as does developing a set of process scripts (Andersen and Richardson, 1997).

5. When working with multiple OR methods, managing the interface between the different modelling methods must be seamless to those attending. However, this is not always easy to achieve. As many of the more quantitatively based techniques demand a reduction in the amount of information, focusing on bare bones (e.g., criteria and alternatives), participants need to understand the process of managing the complexity into a reduced format (procedural rationality) and feel comfortable with the reduction of richness required (procedural justice). As mapping is for many a very transparent technique focusing on natural language, this lack of detail and subtlety that is the result of transference into the quantitative model can sometimes be difficult.

6. Finally, using mapping as a means of monitoring performance has some similar issues. The process of working with even a "reduced model" containing goals, strategies and actions, and monitoring the performance of each can be seen as "too complicated" – particularly as a very important part of the process is testing the performance of the links as well as nodes. Further, keeping these performance models up to date and integrated with any other methods of performance measurement can add further workload, particularly as the entities in the strategy map tend toward more qualitative measurements (e.g., performance indicators for strategy), making data collection problematic as there isn't a clear and indisputable result.

8.5 Organizational learning and forensic analysis through mapping

Mapping has been used to understand and explain the consequences of disruptions and delays (Eden et al., 2000) experienced on large manufacturing projects, particularly where the contractor is considering litigation against the client (Ackermann et al., 1997). However, this type of examination of existing knowledge to explain and understand the past has been the basis for organizational learning about projects in general (Williams, 2003). In the case of litigation, mapping has been used as the first stage of the modelling process, providing the structure to guide, for example, the construction of simulation models and as a means of visually demonstrating to the contractor, lawyers and mediator the causality for complex outcomes.

As projects of this nature often span a range of disciplines, interviewing individual project participants is the most common starting point for organizational learning. By using cognitive mapping in interviews it is possible to begin to identify critical incidents (Flanagan, 1954), what caused them and what were their consequences. In the case of manufacturing projects, this might include interviews with participants from design engineering, methods engineering, manufacturing, testing and commissioning. It is necessary to capture experiences from all these disciplines to gain a holistic view of the entire project – particularly concentrating on the interfaces between each discipline. In addition, the mapping process may additionally include an analysis of available documentary records – memos, meeting minutes, "hard" data, etc.

One of the difficulties in carrying out forensic mapping is that the interviewee inevitably is taking a retrospective viewpoint and, therefore, implicitly if not explicitly succumbing to *post hoc* rationalization. Thus, the resultant map does not reveal what actually took place, but rather a "sanitized" version. There are at least two reasons why this might occur:

(i) staff seek to understand what has occurred and gradually make sense of it through the construction of "urban myths"; and

(ii) those interviewed – typically managers – are nervous about their own performance.

In particular, when organizational learning is about failed projects, there is a temptation to provide a neat and tidy explanation, and omit certain details.

Interviews give members the chance to reflect on the project and begin to understand its complexity. Often they gain some sense of relief as they realize that the difficulties were far greater than could be managed successfully and that given the circumstances their actions were not incompetent (Ackermann and Eden, 1998). Gradually, managers become more inclined to open up and provide further material, revealing areas not previously covered and surfacing information on those issues that potentially could be seen as contentious, and which unless known about can produce anomalies when simulation models are required. Here simulation modelling can be used as an important way of checking out certain aspects of a cause map. The possible "sanitized" version becomes more reliable through (a) triangulation between interviews and (b) triangulation through the examination of documentary evidence. Moreover, the process of mapping – of exploring both explanations and consequences – reveals inconsistencies, challenging the urban myths, as the logic doesn't add up.

An aspect of this form of modelling which is different from when mapping is used prospectively is the increased level of importance placed on ensuring that the maps are rigorous, comprehensive and most of all accurate. While triangulating information gained between interviews and with documentary evidence goes some way toward achieving this, a second method of ensuring that the interview is as effective as possible is the use of two interviewers (see above comments on interviewing using mapping). The point here is that in prospective modelling it is particularly important that agreements for action are negotiated, where as here in retrospective modelling the cycling between qualitative and quantitative modelling techniques is an important validation exercise that needs to be balanced with the need for some ownership of the material if the learning is to be used. Therefore, in the case of mapping for organizational learning there is less emphasis on negotiation.

Following the interviews and mapping of relevant documents the material captured is then carefully woven together to form a single computer-based causal model, which can contain upward of 2,000 nodes. As the statements and relationships are entered into the model, *Decision Explorer* allows a log to be kept, noting the proponent of the statements and allowing for audits to be carried out at any stage. Once all of the contributions are captured in the model the process of weaving the different representations together takes place.

This process of weaving together interview material and documentary material is managed in the same manner as merging many cognitive maps in a problem-solving/strategy development project. First, the process of identifying the common themes is helped by the need to ask cross-referencing questions of interviewees (assisting with triangulation). Second, as the software has built into it a number of powerful analyses (see Eden and Ackermann, 1998b) that reveal emergent themes, similar areas can be detected and inconsistencies resolved. Third, word searches can be carried out to find similarly expressed statements. Once potentially related (or identical) statements have been identified, they can then be examined in more detail and the appropriate action taken to forge links and/or merge nodes (the software automatically merges associated links). Where uncertainty exists regarding a link, then a different form – a tentative link – can be entered (dotted rather than solid) which can later be validated with specific managers or through a group workshop. An important analysis, particularly in the analysis of past projects, is the identification of feedback loops (Chapman, 1998; Lynesis et al., 2001; Rodrigues and Bowers, 1996), which are then subsequently examined in detail to check accuracy/validity. When feedback loops are identified they can provide the structure for a system dynamics simulation model. In addition, *Decision Explorer* supports further examination of themes raised in interviews by investigation of their structural properties. This can help to identify key, critical incidents or disruption triggers – the latter being exogenous variables that drive the simulation model. In addition, the creation of categories to aid with the management of complexity (so as to be able to easily recognize the status of statements) allows potential variables to be distinguished from trigger categories, additional context and strategic ramifications.

Within the overall iterative approach, group workshops usually follow map creation and subsequent analysis. As with the strategy work, this is where the resultant model is reviewed; however, unlike strategy workshops where nego- tiation of agreed actions is the outcome and therefore statements will change as the process unfolds, mapping of past projects demands a more critical consid- eration by the group of the validity of the statements, their relationships and results of the analysis. Here the focus is on accuracy, coherence and comprehensiveness. Through being able to capture the richness and yet manage the complexity, in a manner similar to strategy making, the capacity to allow participants to see the "wood from the trees" helps stimulate thinking, further surface material and refine the model. The modelling process also demands that participants work to resolve contradictions revealed through the weaving together of the interview maps and/or document-based maps.

Once the model is seen to be as accurate a representation as possible, further analysis can be undertaken. Here the feedback loops are re-examined and reduced to their "bare bones" (i.e., additional information stripped out to provide structure for the simulation model). Likewise, the trigger categories are reviewed, ensuring that each category is mutually exclusive to avoid double-counting, and used to inform the simulation model. The model can also be used as a valuable source to refer back to when data do not fit the structure proposed, and meditation efforts are required. The modelling process outlined above is usually the most significant vehicle for organizational learning, rather than the final model (Lane, 1992). Although the demands of simulation modelling often unravel important organizational learning, as in the case of the demands within the model for recognizing significant endogenously generated discontinuous events, such as changes in the project manager (Howick and Eden, 2001). Nevertheless, in many instances the model becomes a reference point for learning for those who never participated in the modelling process (e.g., the induction of new staff: Eden and Sims, 1981).

8.6 Some considerations in usage for organizational learning

Having a clear link between different modelling techniques is particularly important when the simulation model is to act as proof of the consequences of noted behaviours, but is to be based on witness views. Not only does the client group need to understand how the qualitative map gives rise to the quantitative simulation model output but so too do other stakeholders (Howick, 2003). As each party has varying levels of knowledge of projects, of modelling and of the notion of feedback, ensuring how the different techniques complement each is critical. Experience has shown that intermediate models can assist here. For example, the move between the cause map to the system dynamics model can be facilitated through providing the more formalized influence diagram model that shows only those nodes that are to be quantified.

The benefits of using two interviews was raised above; however, working in pairs is time-consuming and may be socially intimidating, especially when considering that managers are already feeling vulnerable (due to past decisions being examined). A balance between eliciting what actually occurred, exploring ramifications and explanations, teasing out problems and providing an atmosphere that is conducive to sharing is therefore important.

8.7 Summary

This chapter has sought to present both examples of the range of modes of working with maps and examples of the application areas where mapping has recently and extensively been used for both prospective managerial action in problem solving and strategy development, as well as retrospective analysis for organizational learning. The chapter only reflects those areas where there is a reasonable body of author experience to draw on, and so it seems worth briefly mentioning some other more recent explorations into mapping. In these instances the benefits are less well understood, and yet initial results appear to suggest that there is potential value. These three areas include:

- Mapping as a means of facilitating conversation, sharing experiences and aiding decision making with participants that are working across time and space (i.e., geographically separated with different time zones). Initial findings suggest that maps can help in problem structuring when circumstances make same time/same place working difficult.
- Mapping as a means of surfacing knowledge and structuring it as a part of knowledge management projects. This use of mapping has potential to inform the knowledge management community both in terms of the manner in which contributions are raised (Shaw et al., 2003) and in the valuable material that is captured in the model as an organizational memory.
- Mapping to support risk assessment. Through being able to surface risk events across a wide range of aspects (e.g., political, technical, financial, environmental, social, etc.), along with their consequences, some comprehension of the systemicity of risks can be attained (Ackermann et al., 2004; Williams et al., 1997). When adding to the map possible actions for mitigating these risks/risk consequences as well as the ramifications stemming from these actions, a better understanding and therefore more accurate assessment of the project's viability can be determined. Carrying this out in a *Group Explorer* computer-supported workshop not only ensures a comprehensive view is gained but also enables those involved in the project to be aware of what the risks are and what ramifications might emerge from particular mitigating actions.

While it is appreciated that learning to map is not easy, there is evidence that "novices" can use mapping – either in interviews or in a group setting – to great effect. For example, over the last 10 years, students studying for either an MBA or MSc in Operational Research have successfully used mapping in order to carry out projects based on mapping where significant organizational change has followed, and there is a continued demand for courses providing mapping instruction.

References

Ackermann F. and Eden C. (1997) Contrasting GDSSs [group decision support systems] and GSSs in the context of strategic change: Implications for facilitation. *Journal of Decision Systems*, **6**, 221–50.

Ackermann F. and Eden C. (1998) *The Role of GSS in Developing the Case for Entitlement in Disruption and Delay Litigation*, Working Paper No. 98/13. Dept of Management Science, University of Strathclyde, UK.

Ackermann F. and Eden C. (2001a) Contrasting single user and networked group decision support systems for strategy making. *Group Decision and Negotiation*, **10**, 47–66.

Ackermann F. and Eden C. (2001b) SODA – Journey making and mapping in practice. In J. Rosenhead and J. Mingers (eds) *Rational Analysis in a Problematic World Revisited*. John Wiley & Sons, Chichester, UK.

Ackermann F. and Eden C. (2003) Stakeholders matter: Techniques for their identification and management. *Proceedings of the Academy of Management Conference, Seattle, 3–6 August.*

Ackermann F., Eden C. and Williams T. (1997) Modeling for litigation: Mixing qualitative and quantitative approaches. *Interfaces*, **27**, 48–65.

Ackermann F., Eden C., Williams T., Howick S. and Gill K. (2004) 'Systemic Risk: a case study. International Journal of Risk Assessment and Management', Working Paper 03/18, Department of Management Science, University of Strathclyde.

Andersen D.F. and Richardson G.P. (1997) Scripts for group model building. *System Dynamics Review*, **13**, 107–30.

Argyris C. and Schön D.A. (1974) *Theories in Practice*. Jossey-Bass, San Francisco.

Axelrod R. (1976) *Structure of Decision*. Princeton University Press, Princeton, NJ.

Belton V., Ackermann F. and Shepherd I. (1997) Integrated support from problem structuring through to alternative evaluation using COPE and VISA. *Journal of Multi-Criteria Decision Analysis*, **6**, 115–30.

Bryson J.M. (1995) *Strategic Planning for Public and Nonprofit Organizations*. Jossey-Bass, San Francisco.

Bryson J., Ackermann F., Eden C. and Finn C. (2004) *What to Do When Thinking Matters*. John Wiley & Sons, Chichester, UK.

Buzan T. and Buzan B. (1993) *The Mind Map Book*. BBC Books, London.

Chapman R.J. (1998) The role of system dynamics in understanding the impact of changes to key project personnel on design production within construction projects. *International Journal of Project Management*, **16**, 235–47.

Conklin J. and Begeman M. (1989) gIBIS: A tool for all reasons. *Journal of the American Society for Information Science*, **40**, 200–13.

Decision Explorer – see www.banxia.com

Eden C. (1988) Cognitive mapping: A review. *European Journal of Operational Research*, **36**, 1–13.

Eden C. (1989) Strategic options development and analysis – SODA. In J. Rosenhead and J. Mingers (eds) *Rational Analysis in a Problematic World*. John Wiley & Sons, Chichester, UK.

Eden C. (1992) A framework for thinking about Group Decision Support Systems (GDSS). *Group Decision and Negotiation*, **1**, 199–218.

Eden C. (2004) Cognitive maps to help structure issues or problems. *European Journal of Operational Research*, forthcoming.

Eden C. and Ackermann F. (1992) Strategy development and implementation – the role of a Group Decision Support System. In S. Kinney, R. Bostrom and R. Watson (eds) *Computer Augmented Teamwork: A Guided Tour*. Van Nostrand Reinhold, New York.

Eden C. and Ackermann F. (1998a) Analysing and comparing idiographic causal maps. In C. Eden and J-C. Spender (eds) *Managerial and Organizational Cognition*. Sage Publications, London.

Eden C. and Ackermann F. (1998b) *Making Strategy: The Journey of Strategic Management*. Sage Publications, London.

Eden C. and Ackermann F. (1999) The role of GDSS [group decision support systems] in scenario development and strategy making. Presented at *6th International SPIRE /5th International Workshop on Groupware Proceedings, 22–24 September, Cancun, Mexico*. IEEE Computer Society, Los Alamitos, CA.

Eden C. and Ackermann F. (2003) Cognitive mapping for policy analysis in the public sector. *European Journal of Operational Research, 22–24 September*.

Eden C. and Cropper S. (1992) Coherence and balance in strategies for the management of public services: Two confidence tests for strategy development, review and renewal. *Public Money and Management*, **12**, 43–52.

Eden C. and Sims D. (1981) Computerized vicarious experience: The future of management induction? *Personnel Review*, **10**, 22–5.

Eden C., Jones S. and Sims D. (1979) *Thinking in Organisations*. Macmillan, London.

Eden C., Jones S., Sims D. and Smithin T. (1981) The intersubjectivity of issues and issues of intersubjectivity. *Journal of Management Studies*, **18**, 37–47.

Eden C., Williams T.M., Ackermann F. and Howick S. (2000) On the nature of disruption and delay. *Journal of the Operational Research Society*, **51**, 291–300.

Flanagan J.C. (1954) The critical incident technique. *Psychological Bulletin*, **51**, 327–58.

Group Explorer – see www.phrontis.com

Howick S. (2003) Using system dynamics to analyse disruption and delay in complex projects for litigation: Can the modelling purposes be met? *Journal of the Operational Research Society*, **54**, 222–9.

Howick S. and Eden C. (2001). The impact of disruption and delay when compressing large projects. *Journal of the Operational Research Society*, **52**(1), 26–34.

Huff A. and Jenkins M. (2002) *Mapping Strategic Knowledge*. Sage Publications, London.

Huff A.S. (ed.) (1990) *Mapping Strategic Thought*. John Wiley & Sons, New York.

Kaplan R.S. and Norton D.P. (1992) The balanced scorecard – Measures that drive performance. *Harvard Business Review*, January–February, 63–72.

Kelly G.A. (1955) *The Psychology of Personal Constructs*. W.W. Norton, New York.

Kim W.C. and Mauborgne R.A. (1995) A procedural justice model of strategic decision making. *Organization Science*, **6**, 44–61.

Lane D. (1992) Modelling as learning. *European Journal of Operational Research*, **59**, 64–84.

Laukkanen M. (1994) Comparative cause mapping of organizational cognitions. *Organizational Science*, **5**(3), 322–43.

Lynesis J.M., Cooper K.G. and Els S.A. (2001) Strategic management of complex projects: A case study using system dynamics. *System Dynamics Review*, **17**, 237–60.

Pettigrew A.M., Whittington R., Melin L., Sanchez-Runde C., van den Bosch F.A.J., Ruigrok W. and Numagami T. (2003) *Innovative Forms of Organizing*. Sage Publications, London.

Phillips L. and Phillips M.C. (1993) Facilitated work groups: Theory and practice. *Journal of the Operational Research Society*, **44**.

Pidd M. (2003) *Tools for Thinking: Modelling in Management Science*. John Wiley & Sons, Chichester, UK.

Richardson G. (1991) *Feedback Thought in Social Science and Systems Theory*. Pennsylvania University Press, Philadelphia.

Rodrigues A. and Bowers J. (1996) Systems dynamics in project management: A comparative analysis with traditional methods. *System Dynamics Review*, **12**, 121–39.

Rosenhead J. and Mingers J. (2001) *Rational Analysis for a Problematic World Revisited*. John Wiley & Sons, Chichester, UK.

Shaw D., Ackermann F. and Eden C. (2003) Sharing and building knowledge in group problem structuring. *Journal of the Operational Research Society*, **54**(9), 936–48.

Shuttler M. and Storbeck J. (2003) Special issue: Performance management. *Journal of the Operational Research Society*, **53**.

Simon H.A. (1976) From substantive to procedural rationality. In S.J. Latsis (ed.) *Method and Appraisal in Economics*. Cambridge University Press, Cambridge, UK.

Simon H.A (1977) *The Science of Management Decisions*. Prentice Hall, Englewood Cliffs, NJ.

Weick K.E. (1979) *The Social Psychology of Organizing*. Addison-Wesley, Reading, MA.

Williams T. (2003) Learning from projects. *Journal of the Operational Research Society*, **54**, 443–51.

Williams T.M., Ackermann F. and Eden C. (1997) Project risk: Systemicity, cause mapping and a scenario approach. In K. Kahkonen and K.A. Artto (eds) *Managing Risks in Projects*. E&FN Spon, London.

Wolstenholme E.F. (1990) *System Enquiry: A System Dynamics Approach*. John Wiley & Sons, Chichester, UK.

Wolstenholme E.F. and Coyle R.G. (1983) The development of system dynamics as a methodology for system description and qualitative analysis. *Journal of the Operational Research Society*, **34**, 569–81.

9 Use of "soft OR" models by clients – what do they want from them?

Colin Eden and Fran Ackermann
Strathclyde Business School

9.1 Introduction

The chapter will be based on the authors' experience of over 200 interventions using "soft OR" (Operational Research), often coupled with visual interactive quantitative modelling, within the context of senior management teams in public and private organizations, large and small, national and international.

The intention of the chapter is to highlight learning from these experiences and indicate the impact of this learning on our and others practice. We start with a discussion of the nature of senior managers as clients and the organizational setting for this type of OR work. This discussion is followed by some commentary on the kind of modelling work undertaken, with particular attention given to the issues of delivering added value, the nature and significance of problem structuring in a group setting and the need for flexibility in modelling approaches. The chapter closes with an exploration of the implications of interactive modelling for the facilitation skills of an operational researcher and a discussion on the issues in closure for projects that involve the direct interaction of analysts with senior management teams.

9.2 The nature of clients

Most senior managers are busy people, they are dealing with a portfolio of issues that vary enormously in significance and are often unrelated to each other. Some issues are urgent, some are interesting, some are strategic and some are tedious but require immediate attention. This means that there appears to be a shifting aspect to a manager's attention span. This is significant because the issue presented for the project is presumed by the OR analyst to be central to the manager's life (or at least as far as the analyst is concerned, it ought to be central). In fact, a client will often give the impression that the issue is crucial and indeed, will believe this to be the case – at that particular moment. However, later on, when the work of the analysts is presented, it often will have apparently lost importance. This is because the salience and surfacing of issues comes and goes within the complex milieu of organizational life (Dutton and Ashford, 1993; Dutton et al., 1983).

It is unusual for any project to address only the needs explicitly expressed in the contract – the visible objectives. Typically, because managers are involved in addressing issues that engage both the "rational" need of the organization and the need to make things work, there will be undeclared/"invisible" objectives related to persuading staff, helping negotiate change with more senior managers, encouraging compromises, negotiating order (Strauss and Schatzman, 1963) and so on. (See Friend and Hickling, 1987, pp. 103–4, for an interesting discussion of invisible and visible objectives, and Eden and Ackermann, 1998, pp. 393–8, for an example of a workshop design that explicitly shows invisible, as well as visible, outcomes.)

Analysis is wanted, but only at the time when attention is on the topic – afterwards attention moves on. Boredom levels can rise quickly as one issue is traded for another as a result of the shifting demands of the organization (Eden and Sims, 1979).

In addition, it is rare for any serious OR project to involve a single player. Rather, the client sits within a team of powerful actors, each with a stake in the outcome of the project. These stakeholders have a social life within which the project is one, often small, part of the conversations that ensure the dynamics of problem definition. It is important to accept that senior management teams can be fast-moving (in terms of problem redefinition) – they talk about the issues in corridors, over lunch, travelling to work, and they tend not to adhere to tight definitions of their role/task. By accepting that versions of the problem are continuously changing, then the corollary is that the analyst as consultant is also there to help the client change his/her mind continuously, rather than just at the end of a project through a final report.

Therefore, although a consultant must attend to the needs as expressed in the formal contract, the need to help the client will nevertheless be paramount. The work of a good analyst *will* be continuously changing the mind of the client about the nature of the problem. The politics of the problem setting, the emergence of new data and new ways of construing the problem situation mean that the problem definition/structure will continuously change. Ideally, the formal contract needs to change to reflect the changes in problem definition, but this is rarely possible. At least, analysts must not get upset when their interventions during a project change the nature of the problem being addressed, and hence the nature of the analysis required.

The implications of these realities of organizational life are that the analyst has to make sure that the output of the modelling process meets all of the needs of the client and recognizes the *changing* salience of different aspects of the project. This implies that the OR analyst has well-developed skills in eliciting expectations and goals (both visible and invisible) from the client.

9.2.1 Relating to the client

A good way to start is by finding the "pain" – that which is of real concern to the client, which "keeps them agitated" and works as a distraction from other duties. If a project does not deal with the "real pain", whatever else it does becomes irrelevant and may not be heard. It is like finding a person lying in the street bleeding from a fight and giving them a talk on strategies for avoiding fights *before* helping them stop bleeding! This focus on "pain" helps to identify with, and gain some empathy for, the client, and achieving this gain is non-trivial (Eden and Sims, 1979). It is the person with the issue ("pain") and power that will look for assistance and will judge the outcome (and therefore will implement, or not, the recommendations). Nevertheless, attention to the other participants in relation to their power to influence the outcome is also necessary. This means identifying:

(i) the person who is the *sponsor*;
(ii) persons who are *key actors* – powerful players with an interest in the project;
(iii) those who are *sources of expertise*, knowledge or protectors of important data; and, if possible
(iv) someone in the client organization who can act as a *partner* to the operational research team.

The client, therefore, is the person who has commissioned the project, is responsible for approving its design, signs off or requests resource usage, calls participants to workshops and acts as the focus of attention for the analyst. "The client is not the organization, division or department. It must be somebody or a small group who can be related to as if in normal conversation" (Eden and Ackermann, 1998, p. 475). Whereas, a sponsor is the person who has agreed that the client may pursue the project (where this is necessary). They will have some ownership of the project and wish to protect it, even though they may have no direct involvement.

The operational researcher will need to form a "psychological contract" with the client as well as respond to the formal contract. This will involve explaining the proposed process and the roles and contributions expected from all the players (including the operational researcher's role). Most importantly, it involves demonstrating to the client that the analyst has at least some awareness of the political setting that constrains the actions of the client. Where other key players are to be involved in working on the problem, the analyst will need to discuss not just the benefits of group working but also some of the dangers (Ackermann, 1996). For example, good problem structuring usually means many interconnected issues get "out in the open", and often a client might prefer these to have remained dormant. However, they are difficult to "push back under the carpet" once surfaced explicitly.

There may be implications for the client having to hand over temporarily a degree of authority to the operational researcher – particularly when group workshops are required. Not surprisingly, this is often a sensitive part of the "contract", and a conversation about the implications is essential – managers do not take kindly to analysts grabbing such authority as if it were their right! Discussing the mechanics of how the client can retain control is important (Ackermann, 1996).

At the same time, and if possible, the formal contract should show an overall route plan that recognizes that the plan may be diverted, from what was intended, to reflect the realistic contingencies of blockages or fast progress. However, the contract should also set some expectations about what has to be done, why this is appropriate, how long it will take and what the milestones there will be on the way – process milestones as well as content agreements. Continual review of this route plan against declared "milestones" will not only allow an illustration of progress made but also enable consideration of next steps in the light of what has already been achieved, thus ensuring that the design of the intervention continues to be appropriate to the situation.

Finally, the analyst needs to remember that the key actors are only human and, therefore, not to expect them to know the answer to apparently obvious questions. Unless there is sympathy, and empathy, for the realities of managerial life, then the client may end up feeling embarrassed and possibly trapped by the expectations of the analyst. It is worth recognizing that even such supposedly simple questions as "what are your objectives?" or "what are your priorities?" can be wholly unhelpful (Sims, 1993). Managers are supposed to know what their objectives/priorities are – they know this and so does the analyst. Because managers are supposed to know these, objectives/priorities managers will sometimes be trapped into finding a way of answering the question, whether or not the answer was readily available or reliable thereby, resulting in unintended misinformation being given. Furthermore, the crucial issue for clients may be that they are not sure of their objectives/priorities and may have hoped that the OR project would help in developing them. This need is therefore not raised and not resolved.

9.3 Politics and political feasibility

Attempting to gain at least some understanding of the politics related to the issue and to the situation faced by the client will enable analysts to demonstrate that they are realists rather than someone just living in a world of symbols and models. If the analyst is prepared tactfully to discuss some of the politics in a manner that is practical – related of course to the realistic resolution of the issue – then it will act as the first steps in building trust. The conversation can show that the analyst accepts that compromises will be implied by the need for political feasibility rather than just the "right" answer – that the "best" answer will be the one that is politically feasible.

OR "solutions" are usually expected to change, sometimes by large amounts, the way an organization works. Change of any sort will always be seen to have winners and losers by those who are the recipients of change. Indeed, most of the key actors in implementing the solutions will see themselves, rightly or wrongly, as potential winners or losers. As soon as an OR project is believed to be potentially influential, rather than "just another investigation", then the project will generate significant organizational politics. For example, new coalitions will form and reform, key actors will be seeking to position themselves for an uncertain future and managers will be forced to live within the stressful environment of increased uncertainty and ambiguity. If this is not so, then "sleeping dogs" will continue to sleep. Organizational politics must be accepted as going hand in hand with successful OR – if it does not, then nothing will happen and the OR will be a futile exercise.

Modelling some aspects of the politics can be helpful for the analyst team and, at least, will allow reasoned debate about what each analyst is picking up about the issue and situation. Three simple techniques are:

(i) Constructing a stakeholder grid of all of the key actors, where they are each positioned on the basis of their relative power with respect to the issue and the extent of their interest in the outcome of the project (see Ackermann and Eden, 2003; Eden and Ackermann, 1998, pp. 344–50). Those with both high power and high interest are likely to be crucial to the implementation of any OR proposals.

(ii) Labelling each of the actors on the grid as anticipated winners or anticipated losers. It is not important to assess who will actually be winners or losers, the political dynamic derives from whether actors *believe* themselves to be winners or losers. This process focuses on the potential for support or sabotage of the OR work. Discussing potential anticipated winners and losers with the client can be a very effective way of opening up a conversation about the political situation in a practical way.

(iii) Exploring the influence structure between key actors by mapping out both formal and informal influences on the grid (see Ackermann and Eden in this book – Chapter 8). Often this shows how power has been over or under-estimated – an actor may show up as being a centre of influence (an "opinion former") and so have more power than originally thought.

Sometimes the stakeholder modelling can be declared to the client and become a helpful dialectical tool that can also become a part of the problem-structuring process as well as helping determine the make-up of the client group. However, although clients may be prepared to discuss the politics they may be uncomfortable with any explicit record.

The single most important consideration in managing change in organizations is that of determining the extent of the political feasibility for change and that of making the likelihood of change more politically feasible.

For operational researchers, political feasibility is usually expected to be the result of paying attention to means/ends or substantive rationality only (Simon, 1976) – it makes sense, a case can be made, reasons can be stated. The majority of attention is focused on the capture of the substantive material, or data, and the associated forms of analysis and data manipulation. It is attention to these processes that is taken to be the test of whether or not the OR analysis/modelling outcomes are correct. Little or no attention is paid to the social processes of delivering, discovering and negotiating the data, determining and manipulating its meaning for action and change, and agreeing the changes required.

Thus, the approach to content management must be informed by process management issues, and vice versa (Eden, 1990; Huxham and Cropper, 1994). This means that the content of issues cannot be understood without an understanding of politics, power, personalities and personal style; similarly, process design cannot be done without understanding the nature of the substantive issues faced by a problem-solving group. There is no separation between the work of the rational analyst/operational researcher and the work of the social process facilitator (Eden, 1978).

Political feasibility is not only about managing the delivery of OR proposals but also about carrying out change that creates co-ordinated and co-operative action. Using methods that support and acknowledge a negotiation process is fundamental (Eden, 1989).

Brewer (1981) and Feldman and March (1981) noted the symbolic use of analysis to deflect attention away from issues and yet give the impression of action. Adopting the symbolic analysis route may be the result of groups being unable to manage their social relationships and so failing to find ways of opening up the "real" issues. The deflection is often something that no one wants and yet it is the only way the group can find of proceeding:

> *Every negotiator has two kinds of interests: in the substance and in the relationship – in fact, with many long term clients, business partners, family members, fellow professionals, government officials, or foreign nations, the ongoing relationship is far more important than the outcome of any particular negotiation* (Fisher and Ury, 1982).

9.4 Delivering "added value": problem structuring in groups – modelling as "structuring", negotiating and agreeing

Clients and consultants like to see progress. The most impressive way of building trust and demonstrating progress is to be able to relieve at least some of the "pain" fast. "Quick and dirty" (dirty as in rough and accurate, but not unnecessarily accurate) problem structuring that is turned round within a couple of days can be very impressive. However, the problem structuring must show added value rather than being only a reflection back of what is already known (e.g., providing added value accrued through being able to see the whole and determining emergent properties). Although reflecting back is also important because it provides reassurance that the analysts have been doing a good job of listening and researching and provides a basis on which to work. All of the well-established "soft OR" methods (Rosenhead and Mingers, 2001) are designed to add value, but each in different ways.

Because of the changing demands on managers, managers sometimes need to decide on a way forward ahead of the originally planned timescale. The analysts must be aware of this likelihood and be prepared to respond to the need for assistance before a project is complete. This means that the analysts must be acutely aware of how things are changing in the client's world – moving "out-of-touch" with client pressures can have the consequences that the client is forced to decide without any helpful input from the operational researchers. Thus, adhering to at least some form of interaction (telephone or face to face) with the client within a "psychological week" (Monday of one week to Friday of the next week) is important. This enables the analysts to be in a better position to respond to the request for help "now rather than when contracted". This means that analysts must be prepared to undertake their work on an incremental basis where added value can be provided on an almost continual basis, rather than only at the end of stages in the project. A useful question to have in mind at all times is: "if the client were to call me now, because they have to decide now, what can I usefully tell them as a result of my work to date?" This requirement means that a "cascade" approach to the contract is important, where the analysts do not pursue in depth any avenue until all avenues have been evaluated at the broad level, and so on down the cascade.

Delivering added value against short-term milestones encourages the location of more tractable problems amenable to analysis and, so, continues to add value as these are addressed as part of the contract. Given the shifting attention of clients, regular progress and regular interaction means that the analyst is able to keep in touch with what is going on in the client's setting.

9.4.1 Problem structuring

There is a need for co-ordinated and coherent problem-solving processes, which require some degree of commonality of problem construal by all members of the "client group". This does not mean that the detailed construal of the problem is similar, but rather that there is some agreement about what to see and not to see, to the extent that there is a reasonable level of negotiated problem ownership. In any case an effective team depend on each team member offering different ways of understanding (even though they may use the same problem label). However, it will at the very least mean a commitment to some shared values.

Nevertheless, let us not overemphasize the problem-structuring process as focusing only on building emotional commitment; without designing processes it will also reinforce high-quality rationality (Collins and Guetzkow, 1964). But, without emotional commitment to delivering agreements the rationality of the reasoning becomes irrelevant and so politically infeasible. The value of high-quality thinking is close to zero without a willingness of managers to co-operate in the implementation of its implications for action (Woolridge and Floyd, 1990). Indeed, there is a great danger of deliberate sabotage of highly rational decisions that have not taken any account of the social needs of the group (Guth and MacMillan, 1986). The social relationships of members of an organization are mostly expressed through their everyday ways of working together, their patterns of interaction, their social dependencies. OR proposals that focus only on rationality are at risk, regardless of their reasoned goodness, because team members will sabotage them in subtle ways in order to retain social equilibrium and comfort levels. And in implementing the proposals a lack of commitment to one part of them will always have repercussions for other parts (Eisenhardt, 1989).

Ensuring "procedural justice" (Thibaut and Walker, 1975) is, therefore, an important consideration for OR practice. For example, a particular decision may be unfavourable and yet a team member will support it because the process of arriving at it was procedurally just. Procedural justice is concerned with attending to the fact that people are concerned about the fairness of the procedures used to arrive at a decision, as well as the decision itself (Folger and Konovsky, 1989; Kim and Mauborgne, 1995; Korsgaard et al., 1995; McFarlin and Sweeney, 1992). It relates to an involvement in issue formulation, being listened to and having a voice. It also involves an understanding from some participants that there is a difference between being heard, and taken seriously, and being responsible for deciding.

However, in addition, establishing that the procedure itself makes sense for the particular circumstances means managers are able to feel that they have embarked on a process that is "procedurally rational" (i.e., that the procedure itself is the outcome of a publicly stated set of reasoning and so can gather cognitive commitment from most participants). Procedural rationality is an extension of the notion of procedural justice, as well as contributing to the negotiation process in its own right. Procedural rationality suggests that the procedures used for problem structuring and resolution make sense in themselves – they are coherent, follow a series of steps where each step is itself understood (not opaque) and relates to prior and future steps. "Behaviour is procedurally rational when it is the outcome of appropriate deliberation" (Simon, 1976). Furthermore, it requires that it is not too time-consuming or too hurried, and that conclusions and agreements are closed off with an appropriate balance between emotional and cognitive commitment (i.e., no paralysis by analysis and yet the "ground was covered").

Thus, in designing and working on problem structuring, attention to both procedural justice and procedural rationality is likely to increase the likelihood of political feasibility in the implementation of agreements. It also reinforces the need to see problem resolution as both a negotiation about "facts" and their implications, and about social relationships.

We have identified above that good problem structuring is a crucial part of building a good relationship with the client. But, more obviously, for good OR, it is crucial to good analysis as it forms the basis on which the analysis is carried out. A transparent depiction of the problem situation, and one that is amenable to analysis (as is an OR model), enables the client to gain ownership of the progress of the analysis and, therefore, increase the likelihood of usage. Because it is amenable to analysis the modelling proffers added value.

The highest level of ownership comes from being actively involved in the model building. The modelling therefore has to be transparent. The common currency of organizational life in group meetings is that of verbal exchange through conversation and debate. Participants present arguments of their interpretation of the situation – their explanations of how it came about and their propositions for doing something about it. This process is the basis for the social process of problem structuring. It is for this reason that our preference has been to develop a modelling technique – cognitive and cause mapping – that reflects this social process and reflects a problem-structuring view of cognitive psychology (Personal Construct Theory: Kelly, 1955, where people seek to make sense of their world and act in it). The essential features of the approach follow from the assumptions that:

- We make sense of a problematic situation by explicitly or implicitly making contrasts. We do this by suggesting ways in which an event, situation, person or object is different from another. For example, often the contrast is between a past and possible future situation, as in "the queue length is too great rather than being less than five minutes", or contrasting the past with the present or the present with the future.
- We use explanations of how the situation came about as a way of suggesting possible actions. For example, "sales have dropped because the competitors dropped their price – so we might consider dropping our price".
- We consider the consequences of situations – how a desired outcome is attacked, or a disastrous outcome is possible. For example, "if this situation continues, then the number of customer complaints will be untenable."
- We consider many possible explanations and consequences, some of which are in conflict and may be inconsistent.
- We make assertions about "the facts of the matter" and in doing so have in mind reasons why these facts matter, even though we sometimes do not

make these clear. For example, "productivity has dropped by 11%", implying rather than stating that the workforce has become badly managed.

All of these features are the components of a cause map (or cognitive map, when it is a model of one person's thinking about a problem situation) (see Ackermann and Eden in this book – Chapter 8). An analyst can build a cause map as a group discusses a situation, or the group members can build it directly (Ackermann and Eden, 2001). In either case the map can be too much of a reflection of the views of socially dominant members of the group – not necessarily those who have given the situation the most thought, or who have the best ideas for its resolution, or those who are not concerned to push their own personal ends, etc. (although good facilitation can aid in eliciting a more comprehensive view). Thus, in designing group workshops and choosing tools and techniques, attention needs to be paid to these issues.

In any event the analyst is using a model to intervene in *group* problem structuring and problem resolution. Yet, analysts must become concerned with the management of group processes as a crucial part of their task of problem structuring. Most "soft OR" methods, as well as cause mapping (as a part of Strategic Options Development and Analysis – SODA) or Journey Making (Eden and Ackermann, 2001a), involve group processes: most obviously Soft Systems Methodology and Strategic Choice (see Rosenhead and Mingers, 2001).

9.5   Flexibility of tools and techniques – having a wide range and being able to use them contingently

The key requirement is for visual interactive modelling to provide absolute transparency, so that the participants become involved in the growing model, have enough ownership of the group-developed model and so have some ownership of the analysis and consequences of the analysis. We commented above that managers at least believe themselves to be short of time and, so, demand that their time is engaging and filled with added value results. Thus, progress must be almost continuous – senior managers will not be involved for long on the basis of grand promises of added value, they need to "see it coming". Developing solutions will be regarded as "robust" or not (including in the sense presented by Rosenhead, 1980, 2001 as a part of Robustness Analysis) rather than accurate. A spurious sense of accuracy is not usually required. Thus, the analyst must have skills in requisite modelling (Phillips, 1984).

Given this process requirement, hard and soft modelling are almost indistinguishable to clients – appropriateness is the key test. In our own case, as a cause map develops the analyst and client group appreciate the need for different types of models to be developed from aspects of the cause map – albeit the possibilities need to be introduced gently to the group by the analyst (see also Ackermann and Eden in this book – Chapter 8). These possibilities arise with greater ease when the mapping is undertaken using the special purpose mapping software *Decision Explorer* as a visual interactive modelling tool:

- The identification of feedback loops can introduce the benefits of system dynamics modelling. In many cases we have conducted visual interactive modelling using system dynamics (typically using *Vensim*). This might often include the group being guided through interactively developing a system dynamics "plumbing diagram" and with some parameter estimation by the group, as well as suggesting "back room" work on a system dynamics model for introduction at a later group session.
- Dipping into, and out of, interactive spreadsheet models is very common as a way of exploring the numerical consequences of attractive options. In strategy development this often involves testing out a business model by building the spreadsheet to replicate the cause map aspects of the business model (see Eden and Ackermann, 1998, pp. 108–10).
- The "top" part of a cause map, which depicts the "goals system", can sometimes be depicted helpfully as multiple criteria and the options evaluated using Multiple Criteria Decision Analysis tools (Belton et al., 1997).
- Similarly, decision trees bring about a way of helping evaluate options.
- Although we have little experience of aspects of a cause map suggesting the structure for a discrete event simulation model, we know others have successfully pursued visual interactive models using such tools as *Simul8*. (The airport queuing model one of the authors constructed many years ago – Eden, 1991 – is a good example of a problem structure suggesting discrete event simulation.)

Therefore, successful interventions with management teams depend on accepting the flexible use of OR tools and techniques. They need to be used contingently and must be chosen alongside or following structuring, not in advance. Working directly with management teams cannot be a way of selling easily the current technique "fad" of the OR group. What it does mean is that the analyst must be equipped to know how to choose from a variety of tools and be able to summon help, if necessary, in their delivery to the group.

Working with groups of senior managers over 20 years has led to the development of processes and software tools to aid the cause-mapping problem-structuring process, the productivity of the group processes and the better management of the social and political processes. Most recently, the continued development of a group support system for direct interactive cause mapping has enabled group sessions to be set up and conducted easily. The original version of a group support system known as *Group Explorer* was first used in 1990 when laptop computers were uncommon and operating systems were not amenable to ease of set-up with a mix of computers using different operating systems. The current version uses *Internet Explorer* and, so, is now operating system independent. It has also become easy to "borrow" a set of laptop computers from the client group at short notice. These developments mean that cause maps can be developed using anonymous processes, Nominal Group Techniques (Delbecq et al., 1975) and other group processes (Shaw et al., 2002) that can help in the management of dysfunctional politics. In addition, techniques to help assess the political feasibility of possible action portfolios as well as analysis options are available (Eden and Ackermann, 2001b).

Nevertheless, although the use of computer technology has helped in providing greater productivity and higher chances of negotiated agreements, as well as ease of group problem structuring, success is still dependent on good facilitation. As we have suggested above, working with senior management teams demands that an operational researcher must be a good analyst experienced in the use of a wide range of modelling techniques (both "soft" and "hard" OR techniques). But, as we have also suggested above, the operational researcher must also be a good process facilitator able to get the extra leverage that can derive from process management skills being informed by content management skills, and vice versa.

9.6 Visual interactive modelling means workshops which means facilitation

The main role for a facilitator is to add value by managing the process as well as structuring content. This activity of managing process and of managing content together acts to reinforce each. The facilitator typically has no decision power. Performing this role effectively is one of the key challenges for the operational researcher.

Creating a "transitional object" (de Geus, 1988) or negotiative device is the purpose of the model – which does nevertheless need to be socially valid, robust (by testing the sensitivity of the conclusions) and "hard data"-valid. This aspect is discussed in more detail by Morecroft in Chapter 7.

The facilitator needs to be able to handle the interaction that goes on between the members of the group and guide this toward getting the best contribution from everyone, promoting better thinking through the interaction and ensuring that there are, as appropriate, visible and invisible outcomes (Ackermann, 1996).

An additional important outcome of group work is the creation of an "organizational memory" which is strongly owned by the group. The use of computer support to the group (a group decision support system – GDSS – such as *Group*

Explorer: Ackermann and Eden, 2001) enables the group to build the transitional object that can help negotiation within the group and allow the group to create their own organizational memory.

The most usual, flexible and dynamic form of communication between people is conversation. In meetings of managers the normal mode is talking. Talking, however, puts an enormous burden on listening and remembering. Visual aids like flip charts are used in presentations to help manage this difficulty. It is then possible to listen and remember "through the eyes" as well as the ears. However, traditional visual media of flip charts, whiteboards (even those that are electronic) and overhead projector slides are not flexible enough to allow for problem structuring and restructuring. During the process of thinking, thoughts need to be rearranged as more views are heard and other people's ideas need to be built on. In facilitation of shared thinking it is necessary to be able to capture ideas visually, and as they are contributed to reflect those back to the group and to make changes very easily which correspond to new *patterns* of insight and a new visualization of the problem.

The negotiation of new insights, new knowledge and new options, around which group members can agree, needs different perspectives to be shared (Fisher and Ury, 1982; Nutt, 2002) and for interaction between diverse ideas to take place in order to generate new knowledge. Thus, when designing a facilitated workshop the aim is to provide circumstances for people to share their ideas and, if possible, to "change their mind" and generate innovative new ways of understanding the issue.

The quality of facilitation is very dependent on "trivialities", such as the environment, the type of pens used, the lighting and so on (see Eden, 1990; Hickling, 1990; Huxham, 1990). There are several ways in which the optimum physical situation for facilitation differs from most meeting room situations. This often leads to a battle with furniture that should not be overlooked. The environment sets the tone of the workshop and influences the flow of exchange. Some useful guiding principles are:

- ensure comfortable but "alert" seating with freedom to move around easily;
- an open circle is best with primary visual aids at the open end of the circle ensuring ease of readability for everyone;
- ensure all participants can have eye contact with each other;
- wall space to allow for surrounding the team with the products of each stage of the workshop and which can therefore be referred to as and when needed (Friend and Hickling, 1987);
- space for someone to capture (on a computer – using *Decision Explorer*, *Group Explorer* or other visual interactive modelling tools) the output of the workshop;
- a data projector to review the output as a team is important.

Our work in training analysts in the use of "soft OR"-type tools and techniques has shown that most trainees underestimate the impact of such trivialities, and when asked what they would pay more attention to after early experiences they consistently discuss the above principle (Ackermann et al., 2004).

It is the nature of any problem-solving activity that however carefully it is designed there are unknowns that will make carrying it out unpredictable. Good problem structuring enables the participants to explore and develop their own thinking in interaction with one another. The model as a transitional object or negotiative device provides the basis for this psychological and social negotiation. The facilitator will not follow a fixed script, as in a presentation or lecture, but rather act in relation to the shifting patterns of social negotiation (Andersen and Richardson, 1997; Eden, 1989).

The facilitator must also take into account the nature of the group in determining the form of modelling approach to use. For example, should manual methods be used or can computer support be included? This decision is not only influenced by participants' general comfort levels toward computers but also the duration of the workshop and thus the need to provide mental refreshment and further stimuli toward creativity (for further discussion regarding different forms of mapping-based modelling approaches see Ackermann and Eden in this book – Chapter 8). This flexibility will also assist when there is the need to change direction according to the group's objectives and interests.

9.7   Issues of closure

Formal contracts usually demand a formal closure and, so, a final report becomes an important milestone. However, across all the interventions that inform this chapter, no more than 10% of occasions have resulted in a final report, even though in most cases a final report was expected. We stated earlier that this process of continually influencing the views of the client and key actors led to agreements being made and actions taken throughout the life of the project. Because of the use of visual interactive modelling technology the progress of the work was always visible and, so, the "minutes" of each part of a project were always being automatically generated (Ackermann and Eden, 1994). Even in instances where the dominant technology was flip charts these became the minutes and were recorded photographically using, more recently, digital cameras so that participants could walk away from the session with a hard copy (Friend and Hickling, 1987). If "instant" feedback is not possible, then providing feedback the next day based solely on the visual interactive material produced with a client group retains ownership. In addition, providing the client group with some social photographs shows a record of the process and helps them recall not only the content of the workshop but also the social process that led to agreements.

Perhaps the most difficult aspect of modelling work with senior management teams is that of recognizing that politically feasible agreements are often reached before analysis is complete (as far as the operational researcher is concerned). The client, in particular, as an experienced manager will be looking for a balance of emotional and cognitive commitment: the right analytical decision in balance with preparedness to deliver action from members of the team. Whereas the analyst usually wants to push the analysis further and create a more certain decision – sometimes leading to "paralysis by analysis" accusations from the client group. This is different from any notions of "solution" or "decision" or "optimizing", emphasizing settlement, harmony, progression and arrangement all of which lie close to the notion of "satisficing" and "problem finishing" (Eden, 1987). Using the term "problem finishing" includes the idea of a satisficing procedure for decision making as well as an outcome that satisfices.

Providing added value means providing the modelling that helps members of a client group change their mind and reach an informed consensus where each member of the key actor group believes the agreement to have been based on sound analysis and consideration of good options: the combination of procedural justice and procedural rationality. It does not necessarily mean delivering a traditional final report, although there will usually be some requirement for a document that signals closure (and so an opportunity to invoice for work done!).

9.8 Summary

This chapter has attempted to reflect on the processes of carrying out "soft" OR with senior management teams. To that end it has concentrated:

(a) on considering issues as continually shifting entities;
(b) on acknowledging the need to attend to both the analytical contribution to problem solving as well as the social and emotional requirements;
(c) on highlighting the importance of being able to interactively model material allowing for negotiation;
(d) on providing effective facilitation of workshop-based interventions; and
(e) on understanding the complexities of closure.

References

Ackermann F. (1996) Participants perceptions on the role of facilitators using group decision support systems. *Group Decision and Negotiation*, **5**, 93–112.

Ackermann F. and Eden C. (1994) Issues in computer and non-computer supported GDSSs. *International Journal of Decision Support Systems*, **12**, 381–90.

Ackermann F. and Eden C. (2001) Contrasting single user and networked group decision support systems for strategy making. *Group Decision and Negotiation*, **10**, 47–66.

Ackermann F. and Eden C. (2003) Stakeholders matter: Techniques for their identification and management. Presented at *Proceedings of the Academy of Management Conference, 3–6 August, Seattle, WA.*

Ackermann F., Eden C. and Brown I. (2004) *The Practice of Making Strategy*. Sage Publications, London.

Andersen D.F. and Richardson G.P. (1997) Scripts for group model building. *System Dynamics Review*, **13**, 107–30.

Belton V., Ackermann F. and Shepherd I. (1997) Integrated support from problem structuring through to alternative evaluation using COPE and VISA. *Journal of Multi-Criteria Decision Analysis*, **6**, 115–30.

Brewer G.D. (1981) Where the twain meet: Reconciling science and politics in analysis. *Policy Sciences*, **13**(3), 269–79.

Collins B. and Guetzkow H. (1964) *A Social Psychology of Processes for Decision Making*. John Wiley & Sons, New York.

Decision Explorer – see www.banxia.com

de Geus A. (1988) Planning as learning. *Harvard Business Review*, March–April, 70–4.

Delbecq A.L., Van de Ven A.H. and Gustafson D.H. (1975) *Group Techniques for Program Planning*. Scott Foresman, Glenview, IL.

Dutton J. and Ashford S. (1993) Selling issues to top management. *Academy of Management Review*, **18**, 397–428.

Dutton J.E., Fahey L. and Narayanan V.K. (1983) Understanding strategic issue diagnosis. *Strategic Management Journal*, **14**, 307–23.

Eden C. (1978) Operational research and organizational development. *Human Relations*, **31**, 657–752.

Eden C. (1987) Problem solving or problem finishing? In M.C. Jackson and P. Keys (eds) *New Directions in Management Science*. Gower, Aldershot, UK.

Eden C. (1989) Operational research as negotiation. In M.C. Jackson, P. Keys and S.A. Cropper (eds) *Operational Research and the Social Sciences*. Plenum Press, New York.

Eden C. (1990) Managing the environment as a means to managing complexity. In C. Eden and J. Radford (eds) *Tackling Strategic Problems: The Role of Group Decision Support*. Sage Publications, London.

Eden C. (1991) Working on problems using cognitive mapping. In S.C. Littlechild and M. Shutler (eds) *Operations Research in Management*. Prentice Hall, London.

Eden C. and Ackermann F. (1998) *Making Strategy: The Journey of Strategic Management*. Sage Publications, London.

Eden C. and Ackermann F. (2001a) SODA – The principles. In J. Rosenhead and J. Mingers (eds) *Rational Analysis in a Problematic World Revisited*. John Wiley & Sons, Chichester, UK.

Eden C. and Ackermann F. (2001b) Group decision and negotiation in strategy making. *Group Decision and Negotiation*, **10**, 119–40.

Eden C. and Sims D. (1979) On the nature of problems in consulting practice. *Omega*, **7**, 119–27.

Eisenhardt K.M. (1989) Making fast strategic decisions in high velocity environments. *Academy of Management Journal*, **32**, 543–76.

Feldman M.S. and March J.G. (1981) Information in organisations as signal and symbol. *Administrative Science Quarterly*, **26**, 171–86.

Fisher R. and Ury W. (1982) *Getting to Yes*. Hutchinson, London.

Folger R. and Konovsky M.K. (1989) Effects of procedural and distributive justice on reactions to pay decisions. *Academy of Management Journal*, **32**, 115–30.

Friend J. and Hickling A. (1987) *Planning Under Pressure: The Strategic Choice Approach*. Pergamon Press, Oxford, UK.

Group Explorer – see www.phrontis.com

Guth W.D. and MacMillan I.C. (1986) Strategy implementation versus middle management self interest. *Strategic Management Journal*, **7**, 313–27.

Hickling A. (1990). "Decision spaces": A scenario about designing appropriate rooms for group decision management. In C. Eden and J. Radford (eds) *Tackling Strategic Problems: The Role of Group Decision Support*, pp. 169–77. Sage Publications, London.

Huxham C. (1990) On trivialities in process. In C. Eden and J. Radford (eds) *Tackling Strategic Problems: The Role of Group Decision Support*. Sage Publications, London.

Huxham C. and Cropper S. (1994) From many to one – and back: An exploration of some components of facilitation. *Omega*, **22**, 1–11.

Kelly G.A. (1955) *The Psychology of Personal Constructs*. W.W. Norton, New York.

Kim W.C. and Mauborgne R.A. (1995) A procedural justice model of strategic decision making. *Organization Science*, **6**, 44–61.

Korsgaard M.A., Schweiger D.M. and Sapienza H.J. (1995) Building commitment, attachment, and trust in strategic decision making teams: The role of procedural justice. *Academy of Management Journal*, **38**, 60–84.

McFarlin D.B. and Sweeney P.D. (1992) Distributive and procedural justice as predictors of satisfaction with personal and organizational outcomes. *Academy of Management Journal*, **35**, 626–37.

Nutt P.C. (2002) *Why Decisions Fail: Avoiding the Blunders and Traps that Lead to Debacles*. Berrett-Koehler, San Francisco.

Phillips L.D. (1984) A theory of requisite decision models. *Acta Psychologica*, **56**, 29–48.

Rosenhead J. (1980) Planning under uncertainty. II: A methodology for robustness analysis. *Journal of the Operational Research Society*, **31**, 331–42.

Rosenhead J. (2001) Robustness analysis: Keeping your options open. In J. Rosenhead and J. Mingers (eds) *Rational Analysis in a Problematic World Revisited*. John Wiley & Sons, Chichester, UK.

Rosenhead J. and Mingers J. (eds) (2001) *Rational Analysis in a Problematic World Revisited*. John Wiley & Sons, Chichester, UK.

Shaw D., Ackermann F. and Eden C. (2002) Sharing and building knowledge in group problem structuring. *Journal of the Operational Research Society*, **54**(9), 936–48.

Simon H.A. (1976) From substantive to procedural rationality. In S.J. Latsis (ed.) *Method and Appraisal in Economics*. Cambridge University Press, Cambridge, UK.

Sims D. (1993) Coping with misinformation. *Management Decisions*, **31**, 18–21.

Simul8 – see www.simul8.com

Strauss A. and Schatzman L. (1963) The hospital and its negotiated order. In E. Friedson (ed.) *The Hospital in Modern Society*. Macmillan, New York.

Thibaut J. and Walker J. (1975) *Procedural Justice: A Psychological Analysis*. Lawrence Erlbaum, Hillsdale, NJ.

Vensim – see www.vensim.com

Woolridge S.W. and Floyd B. (1990) The strategy process, middle management involvement, and organizational performance. *Strategic Management Journal*, **11**, 231–41.

10 The status of models in defence systems engineering

Sean Price and Philip John
Cranfield University at the Royal Military College of Science

10.1 Introduction

This chapter considers the nature of modern systems engineering in the defence sector and the role that models play within the discipline. It discusses how this systems engineering (SE) relies heavily on models to develop understanding and to aid decision making and communication throughout its application. These system considerations and modelling approaches lead directly to a design for a purposeful system or process that is implemented in the real world.

In the past, systems engineering was associated with hard, well-bounded, well-precedented and it seemed well-understood problems. However, modern, highly integrated applications require a greater systems consideration and understanding than was previously the case. Considering the changing nature of modern systems and the obvious difficulty of the early stages of any system design process shows how approaches from other systems disciplines enable modern systems engineering to deliver complex systems and capabilities in the defence sector.

10.2 What is systems engineering?

Systems engineering is the application of *systems thinking* to real world systems problems in the field of *engineering* in order to achieve successful solutions to such problems. Engineering is a discipline that aims to solve real world problems through the application of scientific and technical solutions. The *Collins Dictionary* defines engineering as "... the profession of applying scientific principles to the design, construction and maintenance of engines, cars, machines, buildings, roads, electrical machines, communication systems, chemical plant and machinery or aircraft" (*Collins*, 1995). Systems thinking involves the realization that many of the things dealt with in day-to-day existence can be considered as systems (i.e., sets of entities related in some way, often organized or designed to achieve some purpose). These systems can contain any combination of people, processes, technology, hardware, software and organizations. They generally contain subsystems and are themselves part of wider systems. Indeed, these systems, subsystems and wider systems can be conceived in different ways and from different perspectives. The remit of systems engineering is hence broader than in traditional engineering disciplines. When dealing with systems it is crucial to consider such issues as boundaries, viewpoints and emergence – behaviour manifest at the system level that is not apparent at the subsystem level. Systems engineering is hence the discipline that deals with *designing and implementing systems composed of people, hardware, software, processes and procedures to meet user requirements, within a great variety of wider environmental influences.*

Since modern systems engineering is based on systems principles it is best to consider a variety of systems methodologies when looking at its practice. The earlier definition, which considers systems engineering to be a discipline that applies the principles of systems to the practice of engineering, is not accepted by everyone. Many people see it merely as a "systematic" process for the development of large, complex systems. Although, of course, process plays a large part in it, this view misses the "systemicity" of the subject itself, leading to a view that "traditional" systems engineering is systematic, not systemic. Some would argue that "SE is a process not a discipline." This leads them to regard systems engineering as dominated by process and the production of "hard" outputs, such as formal documents and hard engineered products. In turn, this leads to an emphasis on corresponding "hard" methods and tools, such as information management tools and formal system design methodologies. In good systems engineering the notion of system should pervade both the process and the product. It is through a systemic consideration of the problem in its domain together with a systematic approach to its solution that designed systems, meeting a variety of stakeholder requirements, can be developed and fielded with confidence.

What is in a name? A key achievement of Peter Checkland is that he was able to coin an enduring phrase for his approach to problem solving in managed systems – Soft Systems Methodology (SSM). The term systems engineering has existed for 50 years, during which both the subject and the object have changed substantially; in essence the words are the same, but the meaning has changed. Thus, two people can have a conversation about systems engineering without realizing that they are talking about what are in effect different things. This is a besetting problem – the term can mean almost anything. Perhaps the time is right for a re-evaluation of what is meant by systems engineering.

10.3 The nature of modern systems challenges

This process view of systems engineering is reinforced, for some, when dealing with well-precedented systems problems and solutions. In these situations it is dominated by the systematic application of these processes, methods and tools to situations that are apparently so well understood that there is no need to focus much attention on explicitly developing an understanding of the systems problem, relationships, influences, interdependencies and potential solutions. Further, in the defence sector, systems engineering has traditionally dealt with well-bounded systems, such as tanks and aircraft. This has led to a view that there is no need to build up an explicit understanding of different stakeholder views, wider systems and related systems. In fact, many of the problems that have been experienced when dealing with such apparently well-bounded problems have arisen because too many issues were taken for granted and not fully understood.

This traditional view is changing because of the nature of modern systems challenges. First, modern systems are highly integrated, complex amalgams of people, processes, hardware and software, where decision making is often embedded and failure modes are far from simple and clear. They have multiple stakeholders and complex interrelations with other systems. These systems present much more open, unbounded, unprecedented problems (and opportunities) and demand a much more explicit systemic understanding of the systems problems, issues and solution to be developed and communicated. Second, these challenges force systems engineers to think much more in terms of meeting a variety of (different) stakeholder requirements, rather than merely developing new variants of old systems. These challenges require the development and communication of an early, clear and explicit systems understanding with a variety of stakeholders and then throughout the development process. Models are key to the development of this understanding, its communication and ultimately its realization into a fieldable physical system.

Though people have been engineering systems for thousands of years, systems engineering is a relatively new discipline. Various standards have been issued over the last few decades, but it is only in the last 10 years that an international professional society has been set up to provide a forum for discussion of SE issues. In the UK there is no single body for the accreditation of systems engineering courses. The latest work is represented by the development of an international standard in the discipline: ISO 15288, "Systems Engineering – System Life Cycle Processes". This document identifies six stages in the SE life cycle. They are: concept, development, production, utilization, support and retirement. Table 10.1, which is drawn from ISO 15288, illustrates these stages and identifies the purpose that underlies it.

As discussed earlier, systems engineering has traditionally been seen as a process that systematically enables a number of key phases in the development

Table 10.1—The systems life cycle.

Life cycle stage	Purpose	Decision gates
Concept	• Identify stakeholders' needs • Explore concepts • Propose feasible solutions	Decision options: • Execute next stage • Continue this stage
Development	• Refine system requirements • Create solution description • Build system • Verify and validate	• Go to previous stage • Hold project activity • Terminate project
Production	• Mass-produce system • Inspect and test	
Utilization	• Operate system to satisfy users' needs	
Support	• Provide sustained system capability	
Retirement	• Store, archive or dispose of system	

of systems solutions (such as development and production). These phases have been hard, well defined and clear, allowing the utilization of well-defined engineering processes. For example, Computer-Aided Design, Computer-Aided Manufacture (CADCAM) modelling can allow the investigation of design concepts which helps to clarify the real world ability to develop them. Simulation modelling can be used to inform and ultimately enable efficient manufacturing processes.

However, systems engineering should *systematically and systemically* enable all phases of the life cycle. It is important to consider all stages of the system life cycle at every stage, and this can only be done in a systemic way (i.e., systems engineering should provide a systematic and systemic approach to problem solving and the design and integration of systems). Life cycle phases, such as concepts and utilization, are less well defined and demand a clear systemic consideration of requirements, related systems and the wider system of interest. This is critical because the whole systems engineering endeavour (and in particular its success) is crucially dependent on the quality and robustness of the systemic understanding on which decisions are made. This expands the traditional, hard process view of systems engineering and demands that its practitioners tackle the "less well exposed" early phases of its life cycle in a much more explicit and creative way.

10.3.1 The reaction chamber model of systems engineering

In these terms, systems engineering can be seen as a process that allows initial understanding of requirements through the development of concept solutions, their evaluation, the making of trade-offs, selection and ultimately their implementation. This process is in many ways characterized by the early stages,

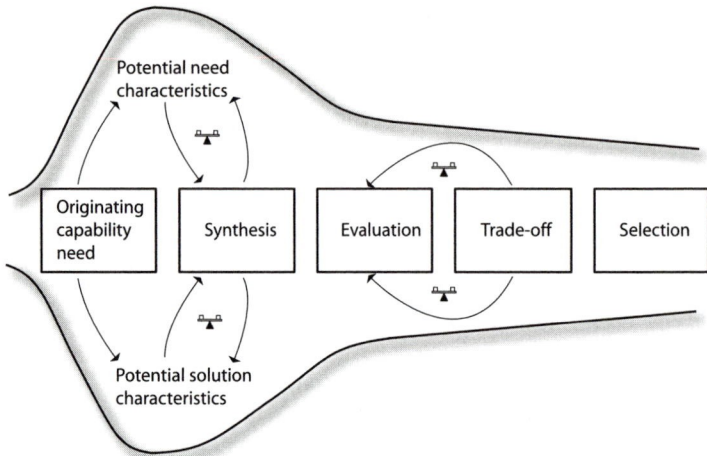

Figure 10.1—Early stages of a systems engineering life cycle: reaction chamber view.

which represents an explosion of information and conflicting requirements before, through a process of refinement and the subsequent focusing of ideas and concepts, models are generated that can be used to drive a hard engineering process. The "reaction chamber model" illustrated in Figure 10.1 illustrates this view of the early stages of the systems engineering life cycle.

This development of understanding thus proceeds through a series of phases, which can broadly be characterized as:

- a *divergent phase*, in which the problem is formulated in a broad systems context and an initial understanding of the characteristics of potential solutions is developed;
- a *convergent phase*, in which requirements and potential solutions are refined within the systems context.

It is important to note that these phases are iterative and concurrent rather than sequential. Potential solutions will need to be considered within the context of wider systems, which will force a new consideration of the whole system. Useful methodologies will enable both phases.

Exploration of these early stages of the system life cycle, reflected in the left-hand area of this model, requires a broader set of techniques than in the past, techniques that are generally not seen as being part of the systems engineer's tool kit. Examples of such techniques that have been found to be useful include:

- SSM;
- completeness and whole system modelling;
- influence diagramming and qualitative system dynamics modelling;

- mind mapping; and
- data modelling.

In addition there are other techniques where the output is not substantive (as in much of engineering design), but objective in that the systems engineer learns about the problem space. Thus, in these areas the model can be seen as a transitional object. These techniques allow the development of understanding in the initial phases of the project and its subsequent "hardening" into concepts and designs as the system life cycle evolves. This is the essence of divergence and convergence as discussed above.

10.4 Traditional problem domain boundaries

There is great commonality between the methods of approaching problems applied by modern SE and soft operational research (OR) – and, indeed, other disciplines where system modelling is fundamental. This is driven by a belief that the context of a practical discipline, such as systems engineering, should be defined by the problem rather than a set of methods "developed" for the domain. To a certain extent, mature disciplines develop sets of recognized tools, methods and techniques through a process of evolution and over time (i.e., different disciplines are often bounded by the methods and tools that are employed by their practitioners). However, in an evolving discipline this can be counterproductive, since it can emphasize differences that are not really there, the differences are in the applications (or problems) themselves rather than the methods. Systems engineering is to a certain extent a method for looking at the world and trying to solve real world problems to meet requirements, and a broad set of methods and tools is admissible in this quest. Indeed, rather, as in early OR, no method is inadmissible if something is potentially to be gained from its use.

Systems engineers design and oversee the implementation of complex systems to meet varied and diverse user requirements. Operational researchers apply scientific and rational methods to assist with decision making related to the operations of organizations. Both disciplines support decision making in complex environments. Both disciplines rely on simplifying initial complexity in order to gain insights into the way systems are organized, and in both disciplines models are central to the problem-solving approach. In SE it is through the use of models that user requirements are exposed, that concepts are visualized and ultimately (through design documents) that systems are built. In OR it is through the development of models and their investigation that inferences can be drawn about how to behave in the real world.

10.5 The uses of models

Models may be characterized according to the use to which they are put. It is arguable that all modelling is done in the light of a problem and to drive behaviour or action – else why conduct the modelling activity? Yet, models may generate many things – "answers", common understanding, insight and so on. An often-used taxonomy for describing the use of models is to consider them as being:

- *Descriptive*. Models that explain or describe a problem, phenomena or system. An example of a model used in a descriptive sense might be an organization chart. Such a model is useful for system understanding and communication.
- *Prescriptive*. Models that indicate courses of action which are in line with our requirements. An example of a model used in a prescriptive sense might be a linear programming or optimization model designed to inform something like factory throughput.
- *Predictive*. Models that indicate how the world may evolve in the light of certain decisions or actions. An example of a model used in a predictive sense might be a war game designed to illustrate the consequences of particular combat options or force mix decisions.

However, this taxonomy is not particularly clear, nor do models belong to a single one of these types. Rather, depending on why they are being developed and on where, when and how they are being used the use to which models are put will emphasize different aspects of each. Consider, for example, the use of an Ordnance Survey map. This map is a model of some piece of terrain that exists in the real world. It may be used descriptively to aid the development of understanding of the nature of that piece of terrain, its geographical features and attributes. It may be used prescriptively to allow us to select a particular route between A and B. Finally, it may be used predictively to allow us to forecast the likely implications of our actions; for example, if I continue on this bearing for this time at this speed I will arrive at C.

However, even between the disciplines of OR and SE there are subtle differences in how these three terms are understood. As Myers et al. (2001) argue, in mature engineering disciplines, such as civil, mechanical, electrical or electronic engineering:

> *[M]odels usually meet the criteria for hard models. (These) models draw on the theories of the natural sciences and engineering to define key attributes and their interrelations, and use an internationally agreed measurement system as the basis of characterizing attributes. Armed with such a model, the engineer can describe the*

process, set standards by prescribing the attributes which the product or process must manifest, and predict the output of a future system from the input and the process.

However, there is little in the mature engineering literature which addresses the methods by which "soft" issues can be addressed and communicated in a rigorous way. There is a clear requirement for methods, tools and notations that allow the consideration of these wider issues, enabling a continuum with the hard processes that must follow in developing tangible, engineered, robust, well-proven products. As the mature engineering disciplines provide no such methods we must look to other areas of systems research for suitable ones.

Though the triad of description, prescription and prediction is central to the utility of modelling in both SE and OR, there is perhaps more in the OR and general modelling literature about these three uses of models. The next section expands on these.

10.5.1   Models used descriptively

Models used in an explanatory or descriptive fashion generally help us to understand something. As Casti (1997) has said:

> *[T]he primary purpose of such a model is not to predict the future behaviour of a system, but rather to provide a framework in which past observations can be understood as part of an overall process. Probably the most famous model of this type is Darwin's Principle of Natural Selection, by which one can explain the appearance and disappearance of the many types of living things that have populated the Earth over the past four billion years or so.*

Such models:

> *[S]erve well to explain what has been observed ... by providing an overarching structure into which we can comfortably fit many known facts. However, when it comes to predicting ... (anything) ... these models remain silent.*

This type of descriptive model is clearly very good for generating insights, for communication and for increasing understanding. These models may even lead to an awareness of causality and dynamics, but they do not tell us how to behave. To a certain extent they can be seen as the first step on the modelling route: the development of insight and understanding in order to allow us to generate the confidence to use models in a prescriptive or predictive sense. They enable the divergent aspect of system understanding and development. As such they are extremely useful in the early stages of problem exploration, where the nature of the problem is not agreed and the nature of the system is not clear.

10.5.2   Models used prescriptively

Prescriptive models prescribe how to behave. More formally, based on some assumptions or observations of the real world a model used in a prescriptive sense will indicate how best to meet specified goals. Hughes (1989) argues that:

> *[A] prescriptive model specifies a course of action. Linear programming, dynamic programming, game theory and decision theory are methodologies that solve problems in ways that tell one what to do.*

It is important to note that this necessarily involves drawing conclusions from the model. Models used prescriptively enable the convergent aspect of system understanding and development. The process of using a model in a prescriptive sense involves learning about the model and extrapolating to the real world.

10.5.3   Models used predictively

Models used in a predictive sense indicate how the world may evolve. Casti (1997) states that:

> *Newton's model for the motion of gravitating bodies is an example of what is called a predictive model. Such a model enables us to predict what a system's behaviour will be like in the future on the basis of the properties of the system's components and their current behaviour.*

Thus, it seems that, as with models used in a prescriptive sense, when models are used predictively it is to discover what the implications of the model are, so as to draw conclusions about the real world. However, this is not really true in isolation: unless the insights gained from the modelling are tested in the real world any insights gained apply only to the model world. Casti goes on to discuss this later. Talking about the solution of a mathematical five-body system, Casti states that the solution "solves only a mathematical version of the real-world problem; what it says about a real five-body problem is anyone's guess." As with prescriptive use this primarily enables the convergent aspect. It seems that there is much overlap between what is meant by predictive and prescriptive use in modelling.

Hence, it seems that models can only be used predictively or prescriptively when the user has a good degree of confidence in the assumptions underlying the model (or theory). The development of these assumptions or theory is accomplished in the initial use of models in a descriptive, explanatory sense. As Hughes (1989) states (with particular relevance to models used in military applications):

[I]t is doubtful that there are predictive models which are entirely distinctive from descriptive or prescriptive models. However, we want models with predictive power. When we are satisfied that a model describes an existing situation or phenomenon adequately, then we want to apply it to process input data and arrive at results in other situations.

This is the nature of simulation in both SE and OR. There is a need to develop models that can help people to address the world that is as yet not known with confidence.

10.6   The status of models in systems engineering

As argued above, this triage of model use does not form a mutually exclusive taxonomy. Rather, for some particular situation a model may be used in a way that is a combination of descriptive, prescriptive and predictive. This may be viewed as the vertices of a triangle as shown in Figure 10.2. This simple visualization enables an investigation of the development of understanding as the SE endeavour proceeds. Initially, the problem is unclear, user requirements are unclear and there is little understanding on which to base firm "hard" engineering models. Such an understanding of problem, stakeholders and requirements comes through iterative development of soft models used in the descriptive sense. This illustrates the notion of divergence as awareness grows through convergence, as we settle on a chosen solution and attempt to understand its implications. As understanding evolves, progress moves from the left-hand vertex toward the right-hand leading edge. In a simplistic sense view (and very much in line with the idea of a simple model being used for descriptive purposes) the SE "journey" goes from the left-hand vertex of the triangle to the leading edge.

The initial stages of the SE endeavour rely on soft models for the description of the problem domain and the world within which it exists. These models

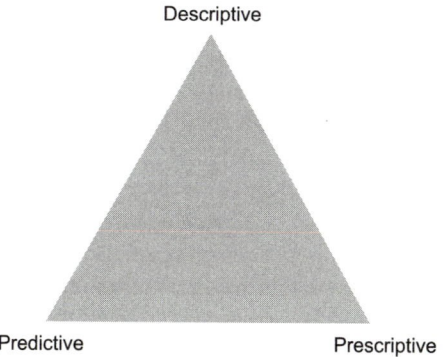

Figure 10.2—Initial status of systems engineering model use.

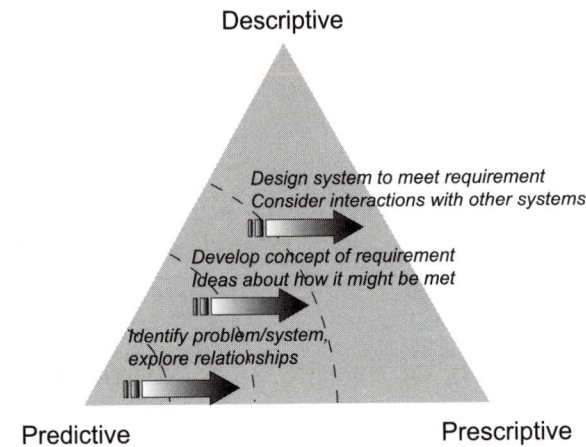

Descriptive

Design system to meet requirement
Consider interactions with other systems

Develop concept of requirement
Ideas about how it might be met

Identify problem/system,
explore relationships

Predictive   Prescriptive

Figure 10.3—Intermediate status of systems engineering model use.

are used as transitional objects that allow the development of agreed problem statements and requirement sets, allowing the development of potential concept solutions. The concept solution models can be used in a progressively prescriptive and predictive sense to analyse how their introduction into the real world problem domain might meet requirements – or not. Evolving understanding is reflected in improved descriptive models in which users have greater confidence and hence their predictive and prescriptive use. This process is illustrated by the annotated triangle in Figure 10.3.

The learning process is iterative and is one in which the development of models leads to the generation of real world understanding, as reflected in Figure 10.4. Descriptive models reflect our assumptions and understanding of some situation and are used prescriptively and predictively based on that understanding. The output of these models will further allow the refinement of our understanding and hence the descriptive models. There is thus an iterative feedback relationship that captures the transition from initial system observance and understanding to the introduction of "solution systems" which users believe will fill the required gap based on their understanding of the system. It is the initial stages of this iterative process which have been conducted informally (if at all) in traditional SE, which needs to be clearly recognized in modern SE.

10.6.1 Validation

Validation is the process of evaluating the consequences of the model against real world observations. This brings out the essential difference between modelling and simulation. If modelling is defined as the development of a representation of some aspect of the real world in some context, then simulation can

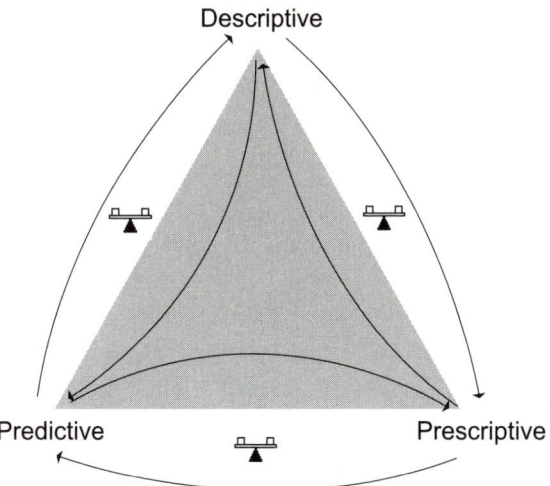

Figure 10.4—Real world understanding from systems engineering model use.

be viewed as the evaluation of the consequences of the model. Thus, at least in time-based models, simulation generally generates behavioural insights from structural information.

In engineering terms this can be construed as the development of initial "high-level" designs and the investigation of their implications through an iterative process of engineering design. This process stops when there is a design that is agreed to meet the requirements of users and is realizable in the real world. That is, the SE endeavour leads from an initial development of understanding through the use of descriptive models, the development of designs and specifications and their assessment, through simulation to the realization of a physical system solution. As part of this endeavour, the key "outputs" that any engineering process requires (such as user requirements documents, system requirements documents, acceptance criteria and detailed design documents) emerge as a consequence of the systemic consideration.

10.7 Conclusions

Much of traditional SE assumes a process for translating clear and unambiguous requirement statements into physical systems. This approach had great success in delivering systems where ambiguity was not present. However, when participants are not clear about the nature of the systems problem or stakeholder requirements there is a need for a broad set of tools to help develop descriptive models that can be confidently used as the basis for the development of prescriptive and predictive models. Several of the methodologies that have been developed in other areas of systems investigation are useful for this. It is only through a comprehensive development of understanding that anyone can be sure that engineering designs (prescriptive models) will suit the appropriate requirements. There needs to be a broad use of these techniques in the early stage of the SE life cycle in order to improve the chances of a system that meets user requirements being delivered. Such a view takes SE far beyond its traditional "hard" boundaries and recognizes the changing nature of modern systems, expectations and environments. In particular, it is essential for SE to develop in this way in order to tackle the increasing complexity, integration and uncertainty of the modern "systemic" world.

References

Collins Dictionary, The (1995) HarperCollins, New York.

ISO 15288 (2001) Systems Engineering – System Life Cycle Processes (Final Committee Draft, ISO/IEC CD 15288 FCD, 22 July). Joint Technical Committee ISO/IEC JTC 1, Information Technology, Subcommittee SC 7, Software and Systems Engineering, Geneva (International Standard).

Myers M., Kaposi A., Britton C. and Kaposi J. (2001) Models for effective analysis of systems: An industrial case study. *Systems Engineering*, **4**(1), 76–85.

Casti J.F. (1997) *Would-be Worlds*. John Wiley & Sons, Chichester, UK.

Hughes W.P. (ed.) (1989) *Military Modelling*, 2nd edn. Military Operations Research Society, Alexandrina, VA.

11 Complementarity in Ministry of Defence OR practice*

Alan P. Robinson, George A. Pickburn and Roger A. Forder
Defence Science and Technology Laboratory (Dstl)

11.1 Introduction

How are hard and soft approaches used in the day-to-day world of OR/MS (Operational Research/Management Science) practice? The obvious answer is, "in many different ways". As an example from the government sector this chapter examines the practice of OR/MS in the UK Ministry of Defence (MoD) and its "supplier" agencies. Its authors are experienced practitioners employed in the Defence Science and Technology Laboratory (Dstl), which is an MoD agency that provides impartial scientific advice to MoD, including OR studies. What follows is their personal view based on their experience and observations. Since the world of defence OR/MS – usually called Operational Analysis (OA) in the MoD – is closed to most people it may be helpful to begin with a brief description of some typical studies. These range from a high-level study through to examples related to equipment acquisition. A final example describes one of the MoD's softer, interpretative methods in action.

11.2 A high-level study

Within the MoD, the terms "high-level operational analysis" or "high-level study" refer to work that is intended to illuminate a policy or planning issue that is broader than, for example, a decision about whether or not to buy a specific type of equipment or to conduct an operation in a specific way. Usually, such work is intended to support resource allocation decisions between a number of different capabilities or different equipment types.

One such study, the Force Projection Study (FPS), was undertaken by Dstl in 2002. The issue examined was the practicability in the medium-term future of undertaking rapid "force projection" – that is, the movement of forces into a theatre of operations in a sufficiently timely manner and at sufficient strength to nip a developing crisis in the bud or at least to forestall its further deterioration. This recognizes that later intervention might well require larger forces and a more protracted campaign to restore the situation.

The essence of the Dstl work was to examine the deployability (i.e., transportability) and operational effectiveness (the ability to achieve military objectives once deployed) of a number of specific "force packages". These latter consisted of Army units and their equipment, ground equipment and supplies to support the operation of RAF fixed wing aircraft and helicopters. Deployability was measured in two ways. First, by the time taken to move the force to theatre with the numbers of aircraft and ships already in the Ministry's forward equipment plan. Second, by the numbers of aircraft and ships that would be needed to meet a target deployment time. Operational effectiveness was measured by the ability of the force to achieve its desired outcome – the latter, depending on the scenario, comprised "winning" a conflict, successfully deterring an enemy or conducting a humanitarian operation.

At face value the preceding description defines a typical "hard" OA study based on well-established models of strategic sealift and airlift operations, combat capability and so on; however, closer inspection reveals significant "soft" and complementary elements. Take, for example, the issue of the scenarios selected for the work. Any attempt to match force requirement to operational need implies some concept of the nature of those operations and, hence, of a scenario. Scenarios are not forecasts of the future, although they must be plausible, nor are they contingency plans, though they might be related to the latter. Rather, they are examples of the type of circumstances in which UK forces might be used. As such the scenarios adopted for any study should adequately explore the range of such circumstances within the boundaries defined by UK defence policy. Clearly, there is a whole raft of soft elements involved in scenario selection, including the use of facilitation and elicitation techniques to tease them out and to populate them with plausible data and assumptions. Importantly, scenario selection must also achieve appropriate buy-in from study stakeholders, in terms of both the number and variety of scenarios selected and the specific details of each. Scenario selection may be supported by quantitative data: in this study, distance from the UK and other accessibility parameters would be particularly relevant. Decisions on how many scenarios to analyse will also be constrained by purely practical issues, such as study time line and affordability.

The issue under examination was the movement of forces into theatre "in a sufficiently timely manner". But just how timely is "sufficient"? The practicalities of rapid force projection are very sensitive to the deployment times desired. Is it possible to reach some objective view as to where the UK should pitch its ambitions in this respect? The impact on a developing crisis of the arrival of a rapidly deployed force is inevitably a variable one, depending on the precise situation and on a variety of military and psychological factors. It is therefore fanciful to seek a precise answer. One approach used to support the Force Projection Study was to review historical instances of where rapid force projection seems to have been effective and to draw some guidance from these. This did provide some useful pointers. But a further complication arises, because in most cases the UK will not be undertaking operations unilaterally, but as part of a coalition. Clearly, then, the UK's force projection timescales should be compatible with those of likely allies, particularly the USA, which will often be the largest coalition contributor. The issue then is: where allies have declared policies on this issue, how far should they be regarded as practical and achievable and – remembering the study is addressing a future time frame – how far aspirational? Hence, although it is probably the most important single parameter in the analysis the desired deployment time is in fact a decidedly soft one. This occurs not only as a result of the inherent uncertainties of the situation but also because of international security politics.

Deployment time is also of course heavily influenced by the nature and size of the forces to be deployed. In this study the alternative force packages were developed by a military panel. Many of these packages were built around the still conceptual, lighter weight land vehicles and systems which are under active consideration within the Ministry for future acquisition. Even with this military guidance, however, fresh issues soon arose about the composition of the force to be transported, which had a major effect on the assessments. A key element in rapid force projection is airportability of equipment. However, even when the fighting elements of the force comprise vehicles and systems that are more or less readily airportable, packages for the tasks envisaged would normally include a few heavy, specialized support vehicles, which at least in their current manifestations are very far from being airportable. How far, therefore, should we regard such vehicles as an essential element for the rapid entry tasks being considered? Or how far is it reasonable to assume that by the dates under consideration their capabilities can be provided in some other way? And if we start to chop away at "inconvenient" parts of the force package, where do we stop?

Helicopters are large, awkward items that can be limiting factors on the airportability of any force of which they are a part. However, for many scenarios it is possible for helicopters to fly under their own power to the theatre of operations ("self-deployment"). Organizing this is not trivial, as it requires suitable staging airfields, possibly in-flight refuelling and some inevitable degradation in immediate serviceability and availability on arrival. The extent to which the analysis should assume helicopter self-deployment was therefore soon identified as a major issue to which there is no single right answer, given the complex operational trade-offs involved.

The Force Projection Study was originally seen as running a number of well-defined cases through existing models and providing "answers" that decision makers could use directly. Enough has been said to demonstrate that in the event the process of analysis was a more complex and iterative one. As models were run and outputs obtained, new issues were exposed and the assumptions and data items that were found to be drivers were not necessarily those anticipated. These insights were considered by the Dstl analysts, customers and stakeholders, judgements made and fresh cases for analysis identified. And even if the answers were not quite so clear-cut as had been hoped the illumination obtained was considerable. The hard analysis therefore constituted only part of a more complex process, a process that was well described by Edward Quade of RAND some 45 years ago:

> *A model introduces a precise structure and terminology that serve primarily as an effective means of communication, enabling participants in the study to exercise their judgement and intuition in a well-defined context and in proper relation to the judgement and intuition of others ... Through feedback from the model, the experts have a chance to revise early judgements and thus arrive at a clearer understanding of the problem and its context.*

11.3   Equipment acquisition studies

Equipment is procured by the MoD for use by the UK Armed Forces. The acquisition is managed by the Defence Procurement Agency (DPA) against a requirement expressed and owned by the Defence Staff in MoD Headquarters. The process of acquisition is defined by a standardized process embodied in the Acquisition Management System (AMS); the process is known as the CADMID cycle, the acronym identifying the individual through-life steps of the process – Concept, Assessment, Demonstration, Manufacture, In-service and Disposal. Figure 11.1 illustrates the cycle. All equipment procured for the Armed Forces follows this process.

Progress through the CADMID cycle is managed by the DPA, which with the Defence Staff ("Customer 1") is required to seek approval of its proposed

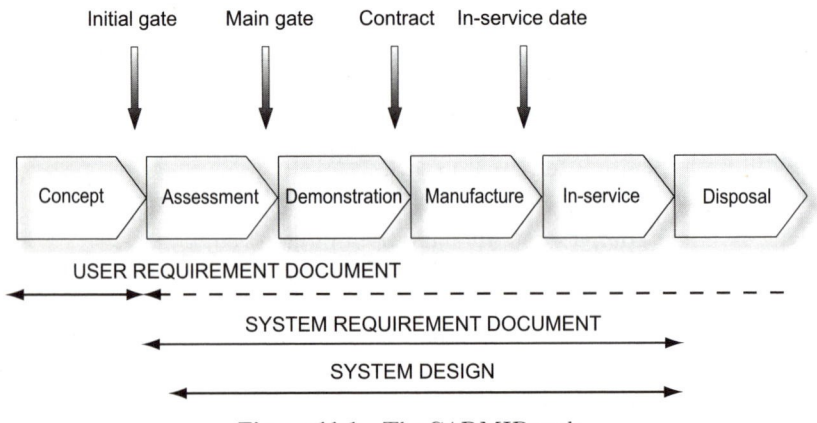

Figure 11.1—The CADMID cycle.

acquisition strategy from defined MoD HQ approving authorities. There are two main steps of approval: Initial Gate which falls between the Concept and Assessment stages, and Main Gate which occurs after Assessment and before Demonstration. At each "gate" the project staffs in DPA will be expected to provide justification of the need for the proposed capability and the scale of investment required to implement it. It will also need to provide evidence of the cost-effectiveness of a range of options for meeting the original requirement. Proof of need is derived from a balance of investment study, while the scale of the procurement and the choice among options for meeting the requirement is derived from more detailed analysis. These aims and modes of investigation are known collectively as equipment acquisition studies.

The next section summarizes three current, typical studies from this class of work: buying a warship, procuring a communications system and providing information systems capability to the logistics chain.

11.3.1 What makes a warship?

How can OR identify the key features of design, construction, operation and maintenance of Royal Navy warships? Recent experience in Dstl in warship procurement illustrates that a mix of OR methods can be helpful.

The requirement for a warship is defined by three things – defence policy (together with its associated planning assumptions), the potential threats to national interests that the warship might play a part in countering and the environment in which it may be called on to operate. Together, these define the roles that we would wish the warship to be able to undertake. Naval doctrine determines how the ship is operated in different roles. How far we can go in meeting the requirement depends of course on affordability and the constraints of the Defence Budget.

The role of a warship is key to determining the elements of capability required on the ship. Almost all warships operate in several different roles at different times, and this implies that warships will require some form of multi-role capability. This in turn leads to the first major problem – what capabilities do warships need, what is the relative importance of these capabilities and do all warships need the same capabilities?

In tackling this problem the MoD has found it desirable to conduct two forms of analysis force mix studies and platform capability studies. The two are closely related: force mix studies address the mixture of forces (e.g., ships, fighter aircraft, etc.) required to provide a capability in the most cost-effective way, while platform capability studies concentrate on what capability is required by a specific platform (a ship in this case) in a given situation.

Force mix studies can be very controversial, with different services bringing differing perspectives to the problem. The key to success is agreeing the study assumptions and boundaries early on and keeping all of the interested parties involved throughout the study process, so that they understand and accept the results. Force mix studies are often conducted using campaign level models; these model a campaign or series of campaigns in order to determine what types of system are needed in what quantities in order to achieve the campaign objectives. For example, a land attack capability could be provided in a number of ways – using land-based aircraft, using carrierborne aircraft, using ship-launched missiles, or using submarine-launched missiles or using a combination of all four. At this level of modelling the individual capabilities of the systems concerned (ships, submarines, aircraft, etc.) are defined in fairly generic terms – in just enough detail to underpin conclusions about the broad shape and size of the force mix.

The models themselves may be stochastic or deterministic. Deterministic models give fixed answers, but may not allow for variations in the likelihood of success due to such events as the weather. Stochastic models allow more statistical variations to be considered, but must be run many times in order to give a statistically valid answer. Both types of model may be used to assess the improvement in campaign level effectiveness due to new systems; it is also possible to run historical campaigns through the models in an attempt to identify what gave the victors the edge in the campaign. Neither type of model is good at assessing the aspects of campaigns which have a strong "subjective" element, such as the effects of improved situational awareness or improved communications systems.

Having established which capabilities are best provided by ships or submarines it is then necessary to decide how many different kinds of ships and submarines are required, what specific capabilities should be provided on each and what systems should be fitted to provide these capabilities. These decisions are informed by the more detailed platform capability studies mentioned above.

One option would be to have a separate ship or submarine type to provide each of the required force capabilities. However, this is generally inefficient, not least because the balance of capabilities required will vary from situation to situation. So, although ships (or, less often, submarines) are usually designed with a primary role and hence primary capability in mind, other, secondary capabilities are provided to allow the platform to undertake a wider range of roles when and where necessary. This allows the operational tasks to be supported with a smaller fleet.

Any given capability can often be provided by several alternative systems or system combinations. Its effectiveness in a variety of scenarios can usually be assessed without too much difficulty using well-established models. The systems can be costed in terms of development, production and support costs. The net result is a long list of options for systems that might be fitted to the ship, with an estimate of the capability that each would provide and the cost that would be incurred. The key question becomes, "Which combination of options gives the best balanced warship (in capability terms) at an affordable price?'' This requires the appropriate consideration of both primary and secondary roles, since a ship capable of undertaking all required tasks and meeting all likely threats in every situation is inevitably unaffordable. At this point, too, a balance needs to be struck with other elements of the ship design, such as the standard of living accommodation provided for the crew and the type of propulsion system to be fitted, which are difficult or impossible to relate directly to operational effectiveness using explicit models.

One method by which all these issues have been brought together and an overall ship configuration agreed is through the use of a decision conference. This takes the form of a meeting in which project stakeholders are presented with a series of options, together with all available information about their effectiveness, cost and other implications. With the help of a facilitator and appropriate software to record and present the judgements made, they can trade off different systems against cost in order to come up with an agreed design. The method has the key advantage that all major stakeholders, at senior level, can be involved in the decision, which usually ensures that they are then committed to the final design. The major problem is that the process by which decisions are made is subjective and cannot easily be repeated. A clear audit trail in the form of comprehensive meeting notes is useful, especially if it becomes apparent that the required capability cannot be provided without a budget increase. The chances of a budget increase are greatly enhanced if the budget holders are involved in the conference process.

11.4   The Falcon communications system

Falcon is an integrated communications system intended for use in the battle-field to enable command and control of forces at higher levels of organization, such as division and corps. A number of industry partners have offered solutions intended to meet the requirements that have been specified by the Defence Staff. The aim of the OA is to determine which offering will be the most cost-effective. To do this, several linked approaches are being used. Battle simulation will be used to assess the direct military utility of the options in combat scenarios. In addition, a range of supplementary methods is in use to assess the ability of the options to meet organizational and doctrinal objectives of the Falcon-equipped forces.

The output measures used to assess the merits of the competing offerings will be, in broad terms:

- Organizational flexibility: the extent to which the communication infra-structure will allow military organizations to reconfigure themselves and reassociate dynamically to generate the agile mission groups needed for future warfare. This will be addressed by a subjective method based on network modelling and multi-criteria methods.

- Support to the development of the doctrine of military manoeuvre: the ability of a large-scale (e.g., national within an international coalition) force component to position and manoeuvre itself while remaining in communication with its allies. This will be derived from studies of the inter-operability of the relevant communications systems in the terrains and geographical settings of foreign policy interest.
- Ability to set and control the pace of operations: this is a crucial indication of the state of the conflict since, once this control is lost, things are likely to deteriorate. This will be derived from survey of the effectiveness and efficiency of different command modes subject to the capacity and topology of the communications networks on offer.
- Completeness of the operational "picture" at different levels of command. This will be derived from an analysis of the capacity and topology of the communications networks on offer.
- Ability to defeat an enemy: seemingly a straightforward measure, but one that needs to be considered at a number of levels. This will be derived from a battle simulation.

This study is one in which the complementarity is a natural and extensive feature of the analysis toolset.

11.5   Defence logistics: "from factory to foxhole"

The MoD In Transit Visibility (ITV) project calls for the procurement of a logistics information system designed to track consignments through the complex and dynamic logistics chain "from factory to foxhole". The aim of the OR work is to identify the likely cost-effectiveness of the options on offer from industry.

Surprising as it may seem the MoD has no end-to-end model of its logistics capability. The OR has therefore included subjective methods to structure the problem and identify the key issues. However, the procurement options were assessed in terms of their performance at the foot of an assessment hierarchy by objective methods based on transaction analysis and network-structuring techniques. In future, Dstl aims to develop its capability to simulate the whole logistics network so that a more balanced approach can be contemplated in similar future assessment scenarios; however, even once such a simulation is in place any study using it will still have significant soft elements.

11.6   The Strategic Assessment Method (SAM)

Within Dstl, "Strategic Analysis" is used to describe the application of scientific methods to assist executive decision makers operating at the policy formulation and strategic-planning level of their organization(s). SAM is one core component of Dstl's strategic analysis capability.

In a defence context, SAM's primary application is to provide early warning of emerging security issues to support conflict prevention and crisis mitigation via the identification of intervention options. SAM has been used recently in a number of areas including support to:

- UK policy on defence diplomacy and conflict prevention;
- MoD policy planning on environmental stresses via a case study set in the Nile Basin to test the method.

Central to the SAM approach is the production of a shared model (a common understanding) of the system under study, covering the important drivers, issues and interactions that shape the security context of the region of interest. Typical drivers covered include demography, economic globalization, science and technology, environmental change, politics and alliances, access to knowledge and perceptions and attitudes. Thus, for example, in the Nile Basin case study the key drivers centred round medium-term issues of adequate access to water resources.

Describing and analysing the interrelationships between different parameters in a security situation can be difficult using the written word because of the complexities of the relationships. But SAM visualization allows a clearer, simpler picture of the problem to be exposed to, and explored with, decision makers. The full SAM process comprises five stages, although the first three can be used alone to support "environmental scanning" if decisions on intervention options are not pressing – indeed, the two case studies were of this type. The process is strongly structured to focus down to the key issues informing senior decision makers while preserving an audit trail back to the data and experts' judgements. The five stages are:

- *Scoping* – identifying the issues, the stakeholder community that the analysis will support and sources of data, expert knowledge and advice.
- *Expert judgement capture* – using advanced and highly efficient structured knowledge elicitation, the aim is to identify and make explicit a set of factors that describe in outline the trends, events, risks and opportunities most relevant to the future state of the system that is the subject of the strategic assessment.
- *Analysis* – the information collected in earlier stages is structured and built into a qualitative model of the system and its interactions. Using visualization tools this model can be reviewed by the contributors and then used to identify the risks, opportunities, key indicators and strategic options.
- *Option preparation* – the decision maker's policy analysts or assessment staff are presented with the results of the previous stages and, with facilitation and support, undertake initial assessment and down-selection.

- *Presentation to decision maker* – this stage could be the principal's usual briefing process but may also be managed as a workshop, with the analysts and model available to drill down, if more detailed explanation of the options is required.

Taken in isolation SAM clearly sits toward the softer end of the spectrum of OR techniques and thus serves as an illustration of the increasing attention to such methods in the MoD. Furthermore, in the context of complementarity it can be used in concert with more traditional methods (e.g., gaming or simulation of SAM intervention options can be undertaken).

11.7 OA in the MoD

So how do studies such as those described get tasked? And how are their findings used to inform decision making in the MoD? To answer these questions it is necessary to provide first a bit of background into the complex organization that is the MoD.

The MoD has two distinct personalities: it is both a department of state and an operating military headquarters. Its key aims are to set policy for the organization and conduct of military personnel, to respond to UK foreign policy requirements for military action and to equip the UK's armed forces. The detailed organization of the MoD is complex. In resourcing terms there are 12 top-level budget holders and a number of agencies (including Dstl) that operate as trading funds. Unsurprisingly, the MoD is in many respects traditional in culture, hierarchic in organization and formal in operating style, not least because of the importance it must attach to issues of political responsibility and public accountability.

At the day-to-day level the MoD addresses issues largely through staff and committee work, with a tacit expectation of broad consensus. To this extent, MoD decision making can be said to be distributed, rather than reflecting the hierarchic nature of its publicly declared organization. This is analogous to the observation by Bagehot (1928) that government proceeds in two modes: the "efficient" and the "dignified".

The MoD is one of the biggest consumers of UK public monies. There is therefore a range of scrutiny and audit mechanisms to which its decisions are subjected. Some operate entirely internally as "red teams", comprised of scientific, technical and finance staff who assess the strengths and weaknesses of the business cases that are required to underpin resource allocation decisions. Externally, the National Audit Office acts as scrutineer in support of the parliamentary committees that oversee audit processes at the political level.

11.7.1   OA organization, tasking and delivery

It is important to realize that there is no overarching policy for the application of OA – each MoD department area is free to develop its own approach in allocating the resources under its command. Thus, all studies are by definition *ad hoc*, though some, especially those addressing higher level issues, such as those related to policy and force structuring, are periodically reworked to take account of changes in the surrounding scenario and foreign policy assumptions and conditions. Furthermore, a number of fora exist to ensure appropriate co-ordination between the study programmes of particular departments and to provide advice and input to specific studies. And, finally, as discussed later the conduct of OA is moderated by a specific set of guidance documents – these carry the authority of the Chief Scientific Adviser who is an external, non-career civil servant scientist, operating at the most senior level of MoD decision making and policy formation.

MoD OA is a large-scale activity involving several hundred staff. The bulk of this is in support of proposals for investment, expenditure and resource allocation. The following topics are addressed:

- policy formulation including force structuring and top-level military planning;
- balance of investment across different military capabilities;
- operational concept development and business process revision;
- logistics and personnel planning;
- expenditure on equipment, both its initial acquisition and through-life support; and
- advice to military front line units.

In broad terms most OA is organized on a customer–supplier basis with Dstl acting as the major – but by no means only – OA supplier. A number of factors affect the way in which OA is used to support MoD decision making.

11.7.2   The extent to which MoD OA is institutionalized

OA within the MoD is institutionalized to a significant extent, in that OA support is mandatory in some areas of decision making and "expected" in many others. This prominence is in part traditional, but it is also because OA is seen as an important component of MoD's overall science and technology base, which of course underpins much of defence business. It also recognizes the inherent difficulty in defence planning, whether in planning for one-off hypothetical contingencies in possibly distant futures or in one-off imminent operations – and thus the need for support to decision makers faced with such challenges.

11.7.3 Impartial or advocacy-based OA?

OA, as used by the MoD, is but one of the inputs used by senior decision makers in formulating a decision; and, although studies will often be formulated with a view to providing "answers", it is even more important that they provide understanding. The collegiate nature of MoD decision making means that this understanding must be provided to all the stakeholders associated with a particular decision: there is no room therefore for advocacy studies.

In order for it to fulfil its role, MoD OA must therefore be:

- objective, with any necessary judgements subjected to open debate and sensitivity analysis;
- quantified wherever practicable, as in many areas of defence numbers really do matter;
- trustworthy, with no undeclared assumptions or unstated simplifications;
- independent of vested interests.

11.7.4 Achieving impartiality and coherence

It is easy to aspire to impartial, coherent OA studies that enable decision makers to do their job of taking appropriate decisions – and, naturally enough, rather harder to deliver against that aim! Nevertheless, much can be – and is – done as outlined briefly below.

The sheer breadth and depth of the MoD OA programme could lead to considerable risk of incoherence; so, a number of coherence management mechanisms have been established to mitigate its consequences. For example, a "Coherent Studies Framework" has been developed by Dstl to assist OA practitioners to establish previous related studies during the study design phase, while OA study "road maps" are prepared to promote shared understanding of study aims and programming between customers and suppliers. Coherence in models and methods is addressed via an MoD Analysis Development Forum which maintains an overarching strategy for the use of modelling and simulation in support of the MoD's OA (as described in more detail later).

Impartiality and coherence can also be challenging to deliver in a customer–supplier relationship, unless appropriate safeguards are in place. This is particularly true as many parts of the MoD assert strongly the sovereignty of each project's management team. This has led to more independence of approach, less tendency to call on "outside" expertise such as OA specialists and on occasions more tendency to "know" the correct answer and expect any study to deliver it.

Partly to mitigate such challenges, the conduct of MoD OA is moderated by a specific set of guidance documents. These address:

- the conduct of cost-effectiveness analysis – issued by the MoD's Chief Scientific Adviser (1995). In the context of procurement-related activity

this type of analysis is used within requirement definition studies and combined operational effectiveness and investment appraisals (COEIAs), although similar principles apply in other areas of OA support;
- the use of subjective and objective methods, as issued by the MoD's Director General of Scrutiny and Analysis (DG(S&A), 2002); and
- model and method verification and validation (DG(S&A), 2002).

Furthermore, the practice and process of OA in MoD revolves around two key documents: the concept of analysis (CoA) written at the start of a study and standardized methods of reporting at its conclusion or at significant interim points. In procurement-related decision making this is via an OA supporting paper (OASP), which is one of the documents used to support decisions by the MoD's Investment Approvals Board. Similar reporting principles, however, apply to OA input in support of other formal MoD decision-making processes.

The CoA is an agreed specification for the conduct of an OA study. It covers the issues to be addressed and the methods to be used. It forms a vehicle for debate, negotiation and agreement of the content and approach of a study with both its direct customer and with a broader raft of stakeholders, including independent scrutineers.

The OASP, on the other hand, is the reporting medium of much OA in the MoD. It is required to address the issues of interest to the stakeholders, specifically in the case of procurement projects, proof of the need to be satisfied, the scale of investment required and the cost-effectiveness of competing options for meeting a requirement. The OASP forms the underpinning to the policy paper or business case prepared to set out the decision to the senior staff who will formally take it.

11.8 Models, methods and strategy in MoD OA

11.8.1 Approaches used in MoD OA

A wide range of analysis and elicitation techniques is employed in MoD practice. There is a long tradition of objective ("hard") techniques, based on event and time-based simulation. Underpinning these, but not always explicitly acknowledged as such, is an amalgam of subjective methods employed in supportive analyses, such as problem elicitation and definition, and in the definition and development of scenarios.

The following list gives an indication of the breadth of the approach in the MoD:

- Simulation, both event and time-stepped.
- Optimization methods, primarily mathematical programming in its various guises.

- Statistical and other mathematical models.
- *Ad hoc* models, often using spreadsheets and databases.
- Collection and analysis of data from current, recent and historical operations. Increasingly, too, experimentation in both "real" (typically via field-based training) and synthetic worlds is used to test hypotheses and derive information for use in models and methods.
- Gaming.
- "Standard" subjective approaches, such as Soft Systems Methodology, cognitive mapping and influence diagrams, etc. These are delivered by MoD OA suppliers through facilitated discussion and debate.
- Tailored versions of subjective approaches, such as Dstl's SAM and techniques of benefits analysis and structuring, drawing on the concept of benefit trees.
- Multi-Criteria Decision Analysis (MCDA) and other structured, judgement-based benefit assessment methods.
- Judgement panels, either to capture military and operational expertise or to establish estimates of equipment performance for conceptual systems, or in other cases where experimental data or detailed engineering assessments are unavailable.
- Interest is now being taken in the techniques and models created and used within the business community. Most of these techniques are non-quantitative in nature and require extensive judgement for their application.

11.8.2   Hard, soft and complementary approaches

"Hard" OA techniques have tended to dominate MoD OA; however, subjective methods have always played a significant, if often tacit, part in the conduct of operational assessments and analysis in the MoD. Their penetration has expanded substantially in recent years as the remit and scope of MoD OA has increased. This increase is in general welcome, but needs careful management and audit to maintain the quality of assessment needed by the MoD.

To ensure this the MoD has recently commissioned from Dstl a statement of guidance on the use of subjective methods (DG(S&A), 2001). Key conclusions from this guidance are as follows:

Much, if not all, of the (extant) guidance relevant to objective methods is pertinent also to subjective approaches. This is to be expected as individual methods form part of a continuous spectrum of techniques. The overriding requirements are to:

- *Strive to maximise objectivity and rigour;*
- *Gauge the validity of the overall approach in terms appropriate to the problem domain.*

Critical issues specific to subjective approaches include:

- *The distortions deriving from un-represented effects of interactions between factors;*
- *The provenance and validity of data has heightened significance because it is derived from judgements;*
- *Auditability through clear separation (of objective and subjective methods, and of methods and data).*

It is important to recognise that there are, in general, subjective phases in otherwise objective approaches, typically in the initial problem structuring and scenario definition phases, and that this guidance is relevant to them.

It is likely that a multi-methodology strategy, implemented in accordance with this guidance, is the right approach for most assessments. This is consistent with the heritage of OR/OA, and most likely to result in well-structured, rigorous, and quantitative analysis, of maximum utility to the decision maker.

11.8.3   MoD OA strategy

The increasingly explicit attention by MoD practitioners to softer, less quantitative methods is mirrored in the strategy adopted by the MoD Analysis Development Forum. In its first formal manifestation in 1997 this was a "Model Strategy" and as such paid primary attention to constructive simulation and the MoD's requirements in this area. More recent iterations of the strategy are designated an *MoD Modelling and Simulation Strategy for OA* (Robinson, 2000). The terminology change is deliberate: the paper pays as much attention to the softer methods of analysis as to more traditional (to MoD) hard, quantified techniques. In doing so the strategy addresses the concept of appropriate rigour in the use of softer methods and considers the general fitness-for-purpose of OA models, methods and studies. Furthermore, the current version of the strategy also pays explicit attention to the role of the analyst in the process in recognition of the old aphorism that "a fool with a tool is still a fool"! This is not, of course, to suggest that the MoD previously ignored the importance of its analysts – rather that increased attention to the full spectrum of OA techniques demands explicit recognition of the different skills necessary to do justice to the various methods available to practitioners. For example, the skills to design, build and use constructive simulation models are not necessarily synonymous with those required to facilitate a decision conference.

11.8.4   Fitness-for-purpose as a key link between hard and soft methods

Explicit attention to the concept of fitness-for-purpose is vital in order for confidence to be placed in the findings of analytical studies. It demands that an appropriate amount of evidence should be available to show that a study and any models or methods it uses provide an appropriate representation of reality in the context of the problem in hand. This incorporates approaches to verification, validation and accreditation (VV&A) that have been practised formally in the MoD and elsewhere in respect of quantified methods (in particular, constructive simulation). Note that the MoD does not utilize a formal accreditation approach to its OA models, partially in recognition that it is only in the context of the study at hand that a decision can be taken on the appropriateness of any particular approach. Importantly, however, fitness-for-purpose does not stop at consideration of the model to be used, but extends consideration to the analytical process as a whole. This recognizes that the models and methods used form a necessary but not sufficient component and, therefore, must be considered alongside the availability of appropriate data and the quality and capabilities of the analysts undertaking the work.

In support of this the MoD pioneered the use of validation logbooks, originally for constructive models, designed to capture the information necessary to demonstrate fitness for a particular purpose (or otherwise!) in a responsive and timely fashion. Such logbooks maintain information on:

- validation state;
- the user roles required and the available user base;
- the state of the data required by the model/method;
- key model/method strengths and weaknesses.

In extending the logbook concept to softer methods and to approaches that are a mix of the quantified and qualitative, MoD best practice and supporting guidance is being extended. The Dstl SAM has been used as the initial exemplar for the MoD's work on extending validation and verification (V&V) to softer methods. SAM was recently reviewed by the Operational Analysis Group of the Defence Science Advisory Council (DSAC), who agreed that SAM provided the MoD with a "sound, insightful, and auditable method of analysing complex strategic situations."

More generally, in extending fitness-for-purpose concepts more widely across "hard" and "soft" methods, particular emphasis is being placed in two areas. First, in extending the logbook concept to softer methods it has been necessary to consider a wider set of user/analyst roles. Interpretative methods, for example, rely strongly on the skills of the facilitator involved. Formally defining and recording the roles and skills required for Dstl's principal softer methods has proven valuable (e.g., in identifying training needs, key skill shortages, succession plans and so on).

Second, there is the need to extend concepts of V&V from their constructive modelling roots. Method verification assessment has been taken to cover whether the expected types of behaviour are seen when executing the method, and whether the expected types of output are produced by the method (akin to checking that a model's behaviour matches the design specification).

In terms of validation, it is necessary first to note that MoD guidance on the former currently assumes a realist approach to validation (Roy, 1993), in that it seeks to compare predictive outputs with historical or real world events. Since some OA methods do not produce such predictive outputs – such as those used as an aid to strategy development, where education and community building are the key outputs – it is not feasible to use the realist approach to validate them. Alternatives to the realist approach are therefore being investigated, including the instrumentalist (in the sense of having utility) and constructivist (adding new insights) approaches to validation. The former approach tests whether the method has utility and adds value for its customer and stakeholders, while the latter tests the method's ability to perform an educative function in illuminating thinking or developing new insights.

Overall, the logbook concept is being successfully extended to enable its application across the raft of models and methods used in support of the MoD's analysis. The use of validation approaches in addition to realist validation, which remains strongly supported wherever it is pertinent, permits all OR approaches to be considered on a similar footing. There remains a need, of course, to ensure that the logbook approach is added value since an overbureaucratic system could overwhelm many of the potential benefits. However, given the MoD's institutional organization and the associated need for clear audit trails, the process has the power to greatly assist in generating confidence in the credibility of the models and methods used by analysts in support of the MoD and, hence, in the studies using those approaches.

11.9 Complementarity in MoD OA

We now move to the overall issue of complementarity. From the outside, MoD OR is frequently perceived to be predominately "hard" in nature in terms of both the processes it adopts and the techniques it utilizes – in part for some of the institutional reasons outlined earlier and in part because the full scope of MoD OA is not always seen externally for obvious security reasons. It should be noted that "hardness", as opposed to "softness", cannot be defined along a single spectrum. Instead, there are a number of aspects to any such categorization.

11.9.1 Complementarity in OA techniques

First, in technique terms the complementarity between "hard" and "soft" has been covered explicitly in the previous sections. A summary is given in Table 11.1 in which a model is any representation of the problem at hand. This could be a constructive simulation, influence diagram, rich picture, linear programme, etc. (e.g., OA using real world or experimental data can rarely

Table 11.1—Dstl view of hard and soft in relation to modelling techniques.

Hard	Soft
Uses real world or experimental data	Uses judgements
Uses quantitative models	Uses qualitative models
Seeks formal optima and "answers"	Seeks exploratory or "what if?" insights
Uses algorithmic models of human responses	Uses human-in-the-loop models

exist without softer input). This may be in terms of the selection and description of the scenarios to be analysed, judgements in such areas as likely enemy reaction, and for data and assumptions about the performance of equipment that may not yet exist, let alone have entered service. Equally, analysis to produce formal optima or "answers" is seldom useful without some insight into the reasons that underpin those findings – this relies on an appropriate mixture of sensitivity analyses and on the use of qualitative as well as quantitative approaches. Finally, the examples have shown how MoD use of appropriate man-in-the-loop models and methods can be particularly valuable.

11.9.2   Complementarity in MoD OA processes

What, then, of the process issues? Certainly, it is true to say that MoD OA practitioners now formally undertake more activity on the right-hand side of Table 11.2 than even a few years ago. Decision conference-based methods provide just one example of where MoD analysts now get involved directly in such work. Equally, analysts get more heavily involved in problem formulation than used to be the case. In part, this is due to changes in the world environment compared with the relative stability of the Cold War. This means, in turn, increased attention to understanding the issues that require analysis, whether

Table 11.2—Dstl view of hard and soft in relation to the OA process.

Hard	Soft
Analysts asked to tackle problems	Analysts used to tackle "messes"
Stakeholders involved in problem structuring and model formulation but formal methods not used	Formal methods used to involve stakeholders in problem structuring and model formulation
Analysts not directly involved in decision-making events	Analysts facilitate decision-making events

in response to possible enemy interactions or to government policy considerations. The latter increasingly have wider security implications and are not constrained solely to defence issues.

11.9.3 Complementarity between OA and staff work

A final interesting perspective on complementarity is provided by considering the interaction between OA and the standard, institutional staffwork process. Seen from a non-analytical viewpoint (left-hand side of Figure 11.2) the MoD's decision making is an iterative process, in which:

- an issue is identified and defined;
- staff work is undertaken to illuminate the issue and offer options for decision maker consideration;
- there is debate on the options at hand; and, finally
- a decision is reached – or a redefinition of the issue occurs and a further iteration undertaken!

In essence, addition of an OA element to this process provides an "analytical supercharger" as illustrated on the right-hand side of Figure 11.2. This overall process can be seen, now from an analytical stance, as one of problem structuring and issue elicitation – making sense of the "mess" – as well as analysis of the particular problem. From such a perspective the MoD approach to OA has an important role in turning messes into problems, but it may on occasions start by having to do the reverse! This may be necessary so that a new

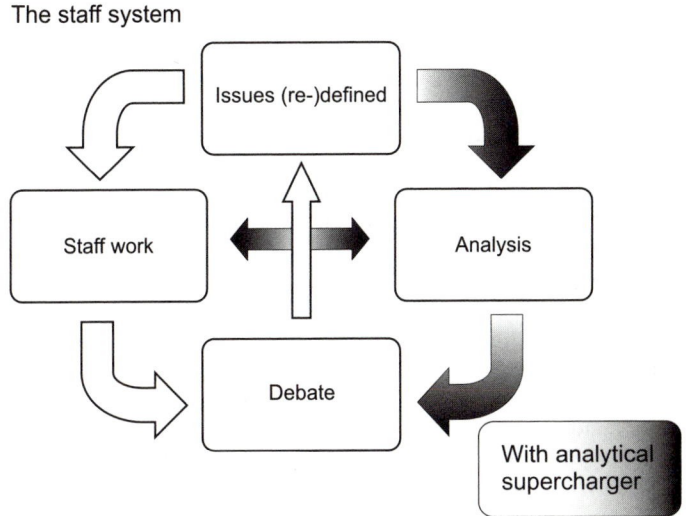

Figure 11.2—Complementarity between OA and staff work.

understanding of the "real" problem can be derived. Furthermore, the OA process is linked intimately with the MoD bureaucratic machine as a whole.

It might also be added that the right-hand side of the diagram collapses to that on the left, given that MoD OA is institutionalized and, thus, inherently built into the iterative cycle on the left-hand side. Nevertheless, the complete diagram is preferred – at least by analysts – as it explicitly recognizes some of the roles and interactions of MoD OA. Furthermore, it also demonstrates that complementarity in the MoD's analysis has always been present, albeit more explicitly now than hitherto.

11.10   Final thoughts

In sum, this chapter has demonstrated that the MoD operates across the whole of the space defined by the above tables, with the right-hand "soft" aspects receiving increasingly explicit attention. The MoD is a complex and demanding political operating environment for OA which demands a flexible and responsive approach by practitioners across a wide range of applications. The result is that every study of necessity employs a mix of models and methods that must form a complementary and coherent whole capable of withstanding expert professional scrutiny by scientist, military and policy staffs. Even when the MoD's OA process or specific studies appear "hard", scratching the surface of either individual studies or of the total system reveals significant complementarity. This is exemplified in the example studies cited, each of which illustrates both the "broad church" of techniques and the strategy of complementarity of approaches to be found in MoD OA practice.

References

Bagehot W. (1928) *The English Constitution*. Oxford University Press, Oxford, UK.

Chief Scientific Adviser (October 1995) *Guidelines for Operational Analysis Studies in Support of EAC Submissions*. Ministry of Defence, London.

DG(S&A) (May 2001) *Guidance on the Use of Subjective Methods in Operational Analysis*. Director General (Scrutiny and Analysis), Ministry of Defence, London.

DG(S&A)(December 2002) *Guidelines for the Verification and Validation of Operational Analysis Modelling Capabilities*. Director General (Scrutiny and Analysis), Ministry of Defence, London.

Robinson A. (2000) *The MoD Modelling and Simulation Strategy for Analysis*, Internal publication. Ministry of Defence, London.

Roy B. (1993) Decision science or decision aid science? *European Journal of Operational Research*, **6**(2), 184–203.

12 Bringing it all together

Michael Pidd
Lancaster University

12.1 A personal reprise

The preceding chapters all address, in different ways, how hard and soft approaches can be combined. Reading them it is clear that there is both agreement and dissent, and, as the editor of the book, I regard this as healthy. The agreement shows that the contributors have enough in common to communicate with one another. The dissent shows that this is a lively area of debate and practice in which both researchers and practitioners are still learning. The rest of this opening section attempts to summarize the contributions of the earlier chapters to provide a basis for a synthesis of ideas from which others may progress. Needless to say, the various authors may feel that I have misunderstood their ideas, for which I can only apologize.

It ought to be easiest for me to summarize Chapter 1, since I am its author. It discusses the systems modelling approaches that I think lie at the core of Operational Research and Management Science (OR/MS). Most OR/MS texts take for granted that mathematics lies at the core of the models and techniques that they describe. However, in the UK at least, it is widely recognized that other approaches, collectively labelled as soft OR, are also based on rational and external representations that prove extremely useful. The chapter's discussion of modelling is against a backdrop that considers the type of problems and issues to which both hard and soft approaches are applied. Its core argument is that once people attempt to tackle wicked problems (Rittel and Weber, 1973), then soft approaches come into their own. This does not mean that hard models have no value in such a situation, but they simply run out of steam. Are these soft approaches only an extension of hard modelling or are they based on radically different assumptions, which means they cannot be used together with them? To start toward an answer and to lead the reader into the rest of the book, Chapter 1 ends with a brief discussion of paradigm incommensurability.

In Chapter 2, Michael Lyons introduces some of the main ideas and issues in the field of complexity which are currently very popular. Many of these ideas come from the general systems principles articulated by writers, such as

Ackoff, 1971; Ashby, 1956; Beer, 1972, 1979; and von Bertalanffy, 1950, who identified aspects such as emergence, variety and cybernetic control. Complexity theorists range from those who regard it as a mathematical endeavour to others who are more interested in the light that its insights may shed on human behaviour. As an organizationally based practitioner, Lyons is interested in the insights that can be brought to bear when trying to encourage organizational change. In this, he regards organizations as complex adaptive systems that cannot be fully specified. He points out that complex, systemic problems are impossible to solve in a once-and-for-all sense, because when we make changes there are usually unintended consequences and these may even make the final state worse than the first (i.e., these are wicked problems: Rittel and Webber, 1973). Instead, he suggests that model-based approaches can help people to understand some of the likely consequences of organizational change. However, this will only be useful if people recognize that both hard and soft approaches are needed and that both are limited in predictive power. There is still no guarantee that such changes will be successful, but useful progress is much more likely.

Peter Checkland and Sue Holwell contributed Chapter 3, based on Checkland's own development of Soft Systems Methodology (SSM). The original exploration and description of SSM (Checkland, 1981) included a careful exploration of some of its philosophical underpinnings, a theme that continues in Chapter 3. They ask if it is possible to make a precise distinction between hard and soft and, if so, what is it and what follows from this? In addressing these issues, they point out that SSM and other soft approaches are learning or enquiring systems and not a set of methods to be slavishly followed. Understanding and appreciation of the assumptions of SSM and other soft approaches is, they argue, much more important than learning to follow a methodical series of stages when conducting a study. This leads them to the view that the terms "soft" and "hard" really refer to radically different perspectives. The hard perspective being based on a usually un-discussed functionalism that takes the world for granted and that works well in the natural sciences. However, the management of an organization involves social phenomena that must be explored using approaches based on other assumptions. The soft perspective is based on a view that people socially construct their worlds using descriptions that stem from their presuppositional world views. Since all problem solving and design must involve some form of social construction, if only to conceive of alternative solutions or designs, this leads to a view that all practical OR/MS should involve some explicit consideration of those world views. In Checkland and Holwell's terms this means that any complementarity between hard and soft must be asymmetric (i.e., hard frameworks and approaches can be accommodated within a soft framework, but not vice versa). This view is captured in Figure 12.1.

In Chapter 4, Ruth Kowalczyk summarizes an investigation into aspects of the performance of intensive care units (ICUs) and high-dependency care

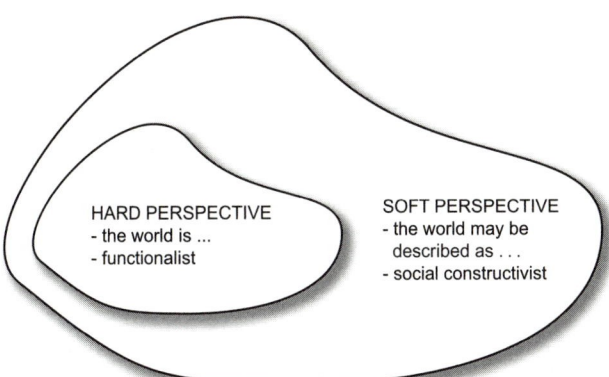

Figure 12.1—Soft encloses hard.

(HDC) in the UK's National Health Service. She does this to tease out some principles about how qualitative and quantitative approaches may be combined in evaluation research. Though the qualitative:quantitative distinction is not identical with a hard:soft distinction, the principles that she describes are helpful in considering how complementarity may be achieved in practice. In her research a quantitative study examined trends and developed comparative performance measures at a national level. This macro-level analysis was supplemented by a qualitative, micro-level study of a single ICU. To bridge the gulf between the two, she advocates an approach based on critical realism (Mingers, 2000), depicted in Figure 4.1. This shows a realist ontology that leads to an evaluation framework, within which both qualitative and quantitative approaches are used. Both the quantitative and qualitative approaches produced useful insights and their combination highlights the link between societal structures, such as professional groups, and the observable outcomes of ICUs and HDUs. Thus, the work discussed in Chapter 4 involves neither soft encompassing hard (as in Figure 12.1) nor in hard encompassing soft. Instead, there is a useful synergy between the two.

George Paterson's contribution forms Chapter 5 and is firmly based on his experience in analytical work for Shell, latterly in Shell International. He points out that most OR/MS work is delivered by consultancy groups, which may be internal to an organization or part of an external consultancy company. He points out that clients, who need assistance of some form or another, are not always sure where to turn when faced with several sources of consultancy help. Hence, they tend to operate with a series of labels that identify the skills and competences available to them. However, few business problems come neatly labelled as hard or soft and many involve a combination of the two. It is also true, he argues, that both hard and soft approaches involve the use of models, which form the core expertise of OR/MS workers. The problem that faces many OR/MS consultancies is that their expertise is

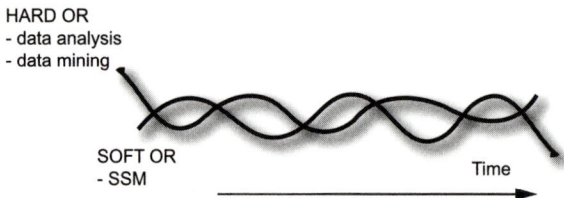

HARD OR
- data analysis
- data mining

SOFT OR
- SSM

Time

Figure 12.2—Hard and soft intertwined.

seen by many clients as based firmly in the domain of hard analysis. This leads to a situation in which the successful, deliberate and complementary use of hard and soft approaches is very rare, since clients often perceive soft investigations as based on people and process skills – which they wrongly do not expect from OR/MS consultants.

In Chapter 6, Joyce Brown and Ceri Cooper summarize an extensive study of the operation of the UK's personal taxation system, carried out by a team drawn jointly from the Inland Revenue's own staff, Lancaster University and consultants skilled in the use of SSM. As with Kowalczyk's research into intensive and high-dependency care, the study involved a combination of quantitative and qualitative work. Interestingly, the start of the quantitative work, which was based on extensive multivariate data analysis and data mining, preceded the qualitative work. The latter was based on SSM which, as the study progressed, began to form the methodological basis for the entire programme of work. The two approaches were highly complementary and, as the work progressed, fed off one another in parallel as one produced insights that were helpful in the other stream of work. Thus, the two threads became interwoven as work went on, as depicted in Figure 12.2. This interweaving is important since its shows that quantitative (hard) approaches can be of value in problem structuring and that soft approaches offer more than early and formal problem structuring (i.e., hard approaches can precede the successful use of soft methodologies as well as the more common occurrence of soft before hard).

System dynamics approaches were first developed in the 1960s (Forrester, 1961) and have seen a resurgence of interest in the last decade, due in part to the availability of better and friendly software. This software encourages the use of system dynamics in a visual interactive mode that helps people to understand the dynamic behaviour of the systems in which they work. In Chapter 7, John Morecroft uses a system dynamics study conducted for the BBC World Service to illustrate how models can become transitional objects that help to modify people's thinking and their understanding. A model embodies someone's view of something, in this case the operations of World Service. Initially, it may be very simple since people's understanding may be rudimentary at the start of an investigation. What then can happen with careful process management is a two-way process, neatly captured in Figure 7.2, in which a model becomes a shared, tangible representation that affects people's thinking as they start to understand it. As they start to understand they see the deficiencies in the model and set about refining it. Hence, model development and shifts in people's thinking become intertwined as the project proceeds. That is, a properly managed modelling process can enable people to develop shared understanding – a theme touched on by Lyons in Chapter 2 and by Eden and Ackermann in Chapters 8 and 9. Doing this requires a complementary set of skills – what Paterson in Chapter 5 called analysis and people process skills.

Colin Eden, Fran Ackermann and colleagues at Strathclyde University are well known for their work in using cognitive mapping to help people to think through difficult issues. Applications include organizational strategy development (Eden and Ackermann, 1998) and litigation over disruption and delay in large projects (Ackermann et al., 1997). Cognitive mapping and the SODA (Strategy, Options, Development and Analysis) methodology would be included in any list of soft OR approaches. Chapters 8 and 9 need to be taken together since they address some of the very practical issues to be faced when attempting soft OR – cognitive mapping in this case. They stress the importance of client management and of understanding the perspective of the client(s) in a fast-changing world in which deadlines loom and priorities shift. These considerations have led them to develop approaches, often based on Visual Interactive Modelling (see Pidd, 2003, chap. 9) used in a flexible and contingent way. The idea is to provide decision and process support to managers as and when they need it, rather than in some way or place determined by an analyst. It could certainly be argued that the case that they make applies as much to the use of hard approaches as it does to soft. Indeed, as they comment in Chapter 9 what matters to the client is not whether hard or soft approaches are used; rather that appropriate methods and approaches are used.

Chapters 10 and 11 take us into an application domain that probably employs more OR/MS analysts than any other – defence. Perhaps the scale of OR/MS operations in the defence sector should not be surprising, given that recognizable OR first appeared in the UK military during World War II. In Chapter 10, Sean Price and Philip John, from the UK's Royal Military College, Cranfield University, discuss how defence systems analysis has changed in the last decade and how yet more change is still needed. They contrast traditional defence systems engineering, with its emphasis on the design and delivery of military hardware, with its modern counterpart that takes a much broader view. In doing so they compare and contrast OR/MS with systems engineering, implying that the hard : soft debate in OR/MS has its counterpart in the traditional : modern debate in defence systems engineering. In both domains the issue of complementarity and how best to achieve it loom large.

Chapter 11 is very much a team effort from Alan Robinson, George Pickburn and Roger Forder, all very experienced analysts from the UK's Defence Science and Technology Labs (DSTL). Much Operational Analysis (OA), as OR/MS is known in the UK defence world, is institutionalized (i.e., its use is mandatory in many areas of defence, especially in large-scale procurement of equipment). It is also used as a matter of choice in support of military operations. With over 50 years of work behind it, UK defence OA is in an enviable position of close co-operation with its clients. The hard: soft debate is heard within defence OA, though this is most often seen in a distinction drawn between objective and subjective analyses, the former based on hard, rigorously tested data. As in the Inland Revenue (see Chapter 6) it is essential that any methods used are available for external audit and scrutiny, for public money is involved and scrupulous fairness is important. Hence, DSTL has developed its own approaches, such as the Strategic Assessment Method (SAM), to ensure that soft methods are applied as rigorously as hard approaches. Complementarity occurs in several ways, most notably in the techniques used and in the processes used to support decision makers, and is practically rather than theoretically based.

12.2 So, what can we learn?

12.2.1 A different view of complexity

As discussed in the Preface this book stems from the work of the Interdisciplinary Research Network on Complementarity in Systems Modelling (INCISM) funded by the UK's Engineering and Physical Sciences Research Council (EPSRC). The network was one of several that were established to look at the potential for future research into system theory. Behind this was a concern that man-made systems were growing larger and more complex and that designing and managing these was proving increasingly difficult. The call for proposals that resulted in INCISM was concerned with complex systems of the type discussed by Lyons in Chapter 2. There are many definitions of complexity and most common sense ones seem to equate the notion to that of complication (i.e., a complex system is one that is large, with many interacting elements and many ways of interacting with its environment).

By contrast the *IEEE Standard Computer Dictionary* (IEEE, 1990) defines complexity as "the degree to which a system or component has a design or implementation that is difficult to understand and verify." A comment ascribed to Rosen and Mikulecky (Mikulecky, 2003) is that "complexity is the property of a real world system that is manifest in the inability of any one formalism being adequate to capture all its properties." These add to the notion of complication the idea that complexity relates to the perception and experience of an observer or participant, rather than leaving it wholly as an objective property of the system. In the terms introduced by Lyons in Chapter 2 such systems cannot be fully specified and their behaviour cannot be completely forecast. Notice, though, that there is no mention of human intent in the above definitions, which seem intended to apply to systems that may be composed wholly of non-human elements – such as communication networks and fish stocks. Such systems are often modelled using agent-based simulations in which many independent agents develop seemingly complex and emergent behaviour by following relatively simple rules that govern their interactions.

The chapters of this book reflect the interests of INCISM participants who wished to develop ideas related to the modelling of systems that involve human beings (i.e., of human organizations). Checkland (1981) developed the concept of "human activity system" to describe notional purposive systems that express some purposeful human activity (i.e., they include human action and intent). As Checkland and Holwell point out in Chapter 3, human activity systems are not intended as descriptions of any actual activity to be found in the real world. Instead, they are useful constructs that can act as ideal types to allow debate about system change and improvement (i.e., human activity systems are simplifications that allow us to develop some understanding of activity and actions within complex organizations). Such simplification is inevitable and, as discussed later, is probably desirable when trying to understand and model complex systems.

At various points in this book, different authors have referred to the idea of wicked problems, as suggested over 30 years ago by Rittel and Webber (1973). Their original work was concerned with the planning of cities and other areas in which people would live and work. Wicked problems are systems of problems in which complete resolution is unlikely, mainly due to clashes between the value systems of stakeholders. Living in a world in which people have different value systems, analysts and designers must find some way to enable people to collaborate so as to make progress, rather than to argue and disagree.

According to Conklin and Weill (n.d.):

A wicked problem meets the following criteria:

- *The problem is an evolving set of interlocking issues and constraints. Indeed, there is no definitive statement of the problem. You don't understand the problem until you have developed a solution.*
- *There are many stakeholders – people who care about or have something at stake in how the problem is resolved. This makes the problem solving process fundamentally social. Getting the right answer is not as important as having stakeholders accept whatever solution emerges.*
- *The constraints on the solution, such as limited resources and political ramifications, change over time. The constraints change, ultimately, because we live in a rapidly changing world. Operationally, they change because many are generated*

> *by the stakeholders, who come and go, change their minds, fail to communicate, or otherwise change the rules by which the problem must be solved.*

- *Since there is no definitive Problem, there is no definitive Solution. The problem-solving process ends when you run out of time, money, energy, or some other resource, not when some perfect solution emerges.*

The work discussed in this book is targeted at people who are trying to make progress with such wicked problems. These are not just complex in the sense used by complexity theorists, but are complex because of the features listed above by Conklin and Weill (n.d.). There is no magic formula that may be used to tackle these, but it seems that external representations or models are a great help in doing so. Models are always imperfect representations, but, as pointed out by Morecroft in Chapter 7 and Lyons in Chapter 2, they can serve as devices to enable people to learn about the likely consequences of possible action.

12.2.2   Combining hard and soft approaches

Given the difference of views expressed by the authors of the various chapters of this book, is there anything useful to be said about the theory and practice of systems modelling? Not surprisingly, I think there is and will try to draw out some lessons. Perhaps, the first and most obvious is that practitioners are by and large unfazed by the complementary use of hard and soft methods. In the terms used by Eden and Ackermann in Chapter 9, practitioners are, like their clients, much more concerned with whether methods and tools are appropriate than whether they are hard and soft. Their aim is to do something useful on a limited budget and with looming deadlines. Thus, for George Paterson in Chapter 5 the main concern is not whether hard and soft methods may be used together. Rather he is concerned that OR/MS groups position themselves so that clients can make use of their expertise in both hard and soft areas. For DSTL's operational analysis group, writing in Chapter 11, the main concern is to ensure that soft approaches, as they construe them, are as rigorous and open to external audit as the hard approaches. In the Inland Revenue study summarized by Joyce Brown and Ceri Cooper in Chapter 6 the important issue was how to gain maximum synergy from using hard and soft approaches in parallel. It seems that, in practice, the aim is appropriate use of appropriate methods to tackle a given set of issues that may evolve through time.

However, this does not justify the arbitrary combination of hard and soft methods. The Inland Revenue study certainly paid great attention to methodological issues, which is perhaps not surprising as Peter Checkland was a member of the project team. It is clear, too, that any combination of soft approaches used in DSTL is carefully planned and considered because it must not wilt under the glare of external scrutiny. These two cases are a very small sample, but they show that there is benefit to be gained from the careful consideration of how to link hard and soft approaches. Are there any principles that can serve as guides?

It seems to depend on how the terms "hard" and "soft" are interpreted. Checkland and Holwell, writing in Chapter 3, interpret the issue of hard and soft complementarity in terms of perspectives that relate to underlying assumptions about what we can know (ontology) and how we know this (epistemology). To greatly simplify their argument, a soft perspective assumes that we can know more than a hard one, and the idea behind soft approaches like SSM and cognitive mapping is to provide ways to access this extra insight. Thus, in their terms, once an analyst starts to use methods designed to access this extra knowledge, she has stepped beyond a hard realm and into a soft one (i.e., the soft encloses the hard – Figure 12.1). Their plea is that such a step should be made in a carefully considered way since a little extra knowledge can be a dangerous thing. Soft approaches require appropriate tools and people need to be trained in their use.

This emphasis is clear in the Inland Revenue study of Chapter 6 and the DSTL approaches described in Chapter 11. Checkland himself acted as mentor during the Inland Revenue study, helping the team to develop an approach suited to the situation and based firmly on the principles of SSM. DSTL OA staff, too, recognize that the extra insights and knowledge gained from their various soft approaches must be carefully handled with appropriate tools by properly trained staff. Using soft approaches is no more a matter of simple common sense than is the correct application of integer programming. Used inappropriately, any method, whether hard or soft, can lead people to draw the wrong conclusions. Thus, in Chapters 8 and 9, Colin Eden and Fran Ackermann discuss the practical considerations of using cognitive mapping approaches to access, interpret and use this extra knowledge. Doing so requires procedural rationality and procedural justice. Like Checkland and Holwell, Eden and Ackermann see the soft approaches enclosing the hard.

What does this mean in practice? Perhaps the first lesson is that shifting from hard to soft, if done, needs to be carefully planned and managed. There are several reasons for this. The first is very practical – the client for whatever study is in progress may be unwilling to accept that the systems modellers whom they have engaged for some technical work have the capabilities to carry high-quality soft work. This is an extension of the point made by Paterson in Chapter 5. Why should they engage analysts to do work for which they are not equipped? This brings us to the second lesson: competence in using soft approaches cannot be picked up by reading a chapter in a book, important though that is. As Eden and Ackermann point out, there are skills to be practised and practicalities that must be attended to. The third lesson is that it is harder than many people think to shift one intellectual universe to another. Perhaps a way forward is to accept that to carry out properly complementary work requires several people – some skilled and practised in hard modelling and others attuned to softer perspectives. If the two can respect one another's insights, there is hope for successful complementarity.

12.2.3 On systems modelling

Developing useful models of complex systems, especially those that involve human action and intent, is difficult. It is also in one sense unsatisfactory. As argued by many people, myself included (Pidd, 2003), any model is a simplification – and therein lies its power. It is a mistake to assume that a high-fidelity model (i.e., one that models everything in as much detail as possible) is always the best way to proceed. Systems models, as argued in Chapter 1, are built for a wide range of reasons and applications. Some are intended to replace human action and decision making, and these do need requisite variety (i.e., their behaviour must be able to mimic that of the real world in every way that is considered important). Others are used to help people develop understanding, as exemplified by John Morecroft's discussion of the BBC World Service in Chapter 7. Here the initial model was as simple as possible and was sequentially enhanced as the analysts and their clients learned more about the systems being modelled. Its fidelity was never high, and it included concepts such as "regional political stability" (see Figure 7.8) which are appealing and intuitive, but rather hard to pin down. Nevertheless, it was of great value in helping the managers of World Service to think through the options available to them and may even have helped them to create new ones.

It is also worth noting that there is a difference between soft and hard perspectives, as defined by Checkland and Holwell in Chapter 3, and soft and hard skills. It is hard to disagree with Checkland and Holwell's assertion that, for perspectives, complementarity is asymmetric. Soft dominates hard. However, when considering the skills needed for successful systems modelling, the water gets much murkier. It is certainly possible to be a successful mathematical modeller and to have no obvious soft skills. As an analogy this may also be true of some surgery, where a highly skilled surgeon may have a very poor bedside manner and yet may still do excellent technical work – as long as he can rely on others to engage with the patients. However, in today's tightly resourced organizations that contain very little slack, it is surely obvious that soft skills are needed alongside hard ones. How else can problem structuring proceed? How else can a client be engaged with implementation?

What of the other aspects of the hard : soft divide discussed in Chapter 1? It is hard to see how anyone could disagree with the notions of validity that span hard and soft. It is also clear that most models will contain data that are uncertain, estimated and, often, subjective. Perhaps the divide is not as great as some imagine? The bumblebee flies, but we just don't fully understand how.

References

Ackermann F., Eden C. and Williams T. (1997) Modeling for litigation: Mixing qualitative and quantitative approaches. *Interfaces*, **27**, 48–65.

Ackoff R.L. (1971) Towards a system of systems concepts. *Management Science*, **17**(11), 661–71.

Ashby W.R. (1956) *Introduction to Cybernetics*. Chapman & Hall, London.

Beer S. (1972) *Brain of the Firm*. Allen Lane/The Penguin Press, London.

Beer S. (1979) *The Heart of Enterprise*. John Wiley & Sons, Chichester, UK.

Checkland P.B. (1981) *Systems Thinking, Systems Practice*. John Wiley & Sons, Chichester, UK.

Conklin J. and Weill B. (n.d.) Wicked problems: Naming the pain in organizations. Available at http://www.touchstone.com/tr/wp/wicked.html

Eden C. and Ackermann F. (1998) *Making Strategy: The Journey of Strategic Management*. Sage Publications, London.

Forrester J.W. (1961) *Industrial Dynamics*. MIT Press, Cambridge, MA.

IEEE (1990) *IEEE Standard Computer Dictionary*, A compilation of IEEE Standard Computer glossaries. Institute of Electrical and Electronics Engineers, New York.

Mikulecky D. (2003) The world is complex: How to distinguish complexity from complication. http://www.people.vcu.edu/-mikuleck/

Mingers J. (2000) Contribution of critical realism as an underpinning philosophy for OR/MS and systems. *Journal of the Operational Research Society*, **51**(11), 1256–70.

Pidd M. (2003) *Tools for Thinking: Modelling in Management Science*, 2nd edn. John Wiley & Sons, Chichester, UK.

Rittel H.W.J. and Webber M.M. (1973) Dilemmas in a general theory of planning. *Policy Science*, **4**, 155–69.

Von Bertalanffy L. (1950) An outline of general systems theory. *British Journal of Philosophical Science*, **1**, 139–64.

Index